Artificial Intelligence, Simulation and Society

Series Editor

Petra Ahrweiler, TISSS Lab, Institute of Sociology, Johannes Gutenberg University, Mainz, Germany

This book series brings into its fold key and emerging topics on the interactions between growing artificial intelligence technologies and their social impacts. It addresses various aspects of the relationship between AI, simulation, and society and provides insights into their intersections and stimulates discussions on the opportunities and challenges they present. The series is multi- and transdisciplinary in scope, and dynamic. It invites academic contributed volumes and monographs, but also more popular work suitable for lay readership, and innovatively includes some science fiction to initiate readers into the scope and aims of this novel series.

The specific themes and topics covered under the series are:

- **The ethical and societal implications of AI**: The series delves into the ethical considerations and societal impacts of AI technologies. It explores topics such as privacy, bias, job displacement, and the role of AI in shaping social structures from a social science point of view (sociological, political, economic, cultural, legal).
- **Simulation and modeling of social systems**: The series explores how simulation techniques are used to model and understand complex social systems and create artificial societies in silico. It covers topics such as social network analysis, agent-based modelling (ABM), and the simulation of collective behaviour.
- **AI and social simulation**: The series explores how AI technologies are used in social simulation, for example, modelling intelligent agents in agent architectures of ABM, or calibrating and validating models using intelligent data mining and analysis techniques.
- **AI and simulation in social philosophy**: It looks at how AI and simulation are depicted in social philosophy, for example, the role of AI and simulation in socio-technical evolution, the position of AI and simulation in Western rationalism, philosophical counter-designs of current developments, ontological and epistemological limitations and barriers of AI and simulation.
- **AI, simulation and society in fiction**: The series also innovatively examines the portrayal of AI and simulation in and as fiction, demonstrating how these themes reflect societal fears, aspirations, and ethical dilemmas. The series contains both original fiction and second-order analyses.
- **AI and simulation in entertainment**: It covers simulation techniques, combined with AI, that are used to create virtual worlds and characters that mimic human behaviour. Such simulations are used, for example, in video games, virtual reality experiences, and entertainment applications.
- **AI and simulation in various disciplines**: The series discusses the applications of AI and simulations that are/will be transforming various disciplines and domains such as healthcare (e.g. in medical diagnosis, drug discovery, and patient care), work (e.g. automation, Industry 4.0, workforce dynamics), or education (e.g. virtual reality, personalised learning systems, intelligent tutoring systems). It discusses the potential benefits and challenges of integrating these technologies into the conventional space.
- **AI, simulation, and policy**: The series analyses how AI and simulation techniques can inform the policy cycles. It discusses the use of predictive modelling, analysis of what-if scenarios, and decision support systems in shaping policies in various policy domains such as public policy, technology policy or environmental policy.

Petra Ahrweiler · Nigel Gilbert

Editors

Participatory Modelling and Simulation to Improve AI-based Public Social Services

Scientific Advice for Policy and Practice

 Springer

Editors
Petra Ahrweiler
TISSS Lab, Institute for Sociology
Johannes Gutenberg University,
Mainz, Germany

Nigel Gilbert
Department of Sociology
University of Surrey
Guildford, Surrey, UK

ISSN 3004-9822   ISSN 3004-9830 (electronic)
Artificial Intelligence, Simulation and Society
ISBN 978-3-032-15282-4   ISBN 978-3-032-15283-1 (eBook)
https://doi.org/10.1007/978-3-032-15283-1

This work was supported by German Volkswagen Stiftung.

This Springer imprint is published by the registered company Springer Nature Switzerland AG
The registered company address is: Gewerbestrasse 11, 6330 Cham, Switzerland

If disposing of this product, please recycle the paper.

Preface

This book, *Participatory Modelling and Simulation to Improve AI-based Public Social Services—Scientific Advice for Policy and Practice*, is the second volume presenting results from interdisciplinary research conducted across the globe. The research originates from the international project *Artificial Intelligence for Assessment* (AI FORA), in which social scientists collaborated with computer scientists to examine systems of Artificial Intelligence (AI) that are now being (or are planned to be) used to distinguish beneficiaries from non-beneficiaries in welfare provision decisions—a process known as *social assessment*. The project employed participatory methods involving stakeholders from policy, industry, law, and other domains, including civil society and, in particular, vulnerable groups. These groups were included through AI FORA's "Safe Spaces" initiative, hosted at Benedictine monasteries.

Because criteria for social assessment vary significantly across cultures, AI FORA conducted nine empirical case studies to enable international comparison. These studies collected data on social assessment practices and AI use in welfare systems in Spain, Estonia, Germany, Iran, India, Nigeria, Ukraine, China, and the USA. Led by the project's social science partners, the results were published in the first volume, *Participatory Artificial Intelligence in Public Social Services—From Bias to Fairness in Assessing Beneficiaries* (2025), as part of the same series.

This second volume, authored by case study partners and led by the project's computer scientists, is structured into three sections that together illustrate the AI FORA approach and its transformative potential for designing AI systems in public social services. Each section corresponds to a distinct phase of the project's trajectory—from developing models that make decision processes explicit, to engaging policymakers in shaping AI adoption, and finally, to looking ahead toward future research directions and applications.

The first section presents the *agent-based models (ABM)* developed within AI FORA to represent welfare decision-making systems across diverse national contexts. These models formalize how applicants, social workers, and institutions interact under existing rules and constraints, exposing bottlenecks, inefficiencies, and fairness trade-offs often hidden in practice. By providing computational testbeds for exploring alternative rules and policies, ABM serves as a powerful tool for participatory reflection and the collective design of AI-based decision-support systems that are context-sensitive and socially legitimate.

The second section demonstrates how modelling results were *translated into policy dialogue*, ensuring that scientific insights could inform real-world decision-making. Through dedicated workshops and stakeholder engagements, policymakers, practitioners, and experts discussed simulation findings on fairness, efficiency, data quality, and the role of AI in welfare provision. These contributions illustrate how participatory dissemination formats can build trust, foster interdisciplinary collaboration, and support the development of governance frameworks that align AI adoption with public values and societal needs.

The final section explores *future directions* for participatory AI research and practice, drawing on lessons learned in AI FORA to envision new methodologies and applications. The chapters present a vision for ethically robust, human-centric AI supported by participatory modelling and simulation; propose approaches to anticipate and mitigate systemic biases across institutions; consider how the AI FORA methodology could be adapted to new domains such as climate crisis management; and examine how immersive technologies can enhance collaborative creativity in AI design. Collectively, these contributions chart a path forward for the evolution of participatory AI frameworks, demonstrating how they can help shape more inclusive, transparent, and adaptive AI systems for the public good.

The two scientific volumes are accompanied by literary fiction designed to introduce non-scientific audiences to the research themes. The introductory novel, *Angels and Other Cows—A Celestial Adventure into AI Worlds, the Social Good, and Unknown Connections*, published in Springer's *Artificial Intelligence, Simulation and Society* series in 2024, is already available. A concluding fantasy novel, completing this AI FORA series, is expected in 2027.

One of the leads of AI FORA's Safe Spaces, M. Maire Hickey OSB from Kylemore Abbey in Ireland, sadly did not live to see the publication of this second scientific volume; the project team mourns her passing in 2025. The editors extend their deepest gratitude for the many constructive—and at times challenging—discussions with the outstanding academic colleagues, project partners, and reviewers who helped shape the research presented in this book. Among others, we thank: Martha Bicket, Ebin Deni Raj, Mahesh Sasikumar, Ashly Ann Jo, Maris Männiste, Triin Vihalemm, Albert Sabater Coll, Beatriz Lopez, Roger del Campepadros, Hassan Bashiri, Erik Johnston, Jesús Siqueiros Garcia, Martin Neumann, Elisabeth Späth, Blanca Luque Capellas, David Wurster, Elisabeth André, Ruben Schlagowski, Sumathi Srinivasalu, Tome Sandevski, George Kampis, Zsolt Juranyi, Massimo Rusconi, and Dario Brockschmidt.

Acknowledgements

All research presented in this volume was funded by the German Volkswagen Stiftung under grant agreement number 98 560. Participatory workshops were partly funded by the IPP Interdisciplinary Public Policy programme of Johannes Gutenberg University Mainz, Germany (JGU). The editors also gratefully acknowledge additional funding for open access publication from Volkswagen Stiftung and JGU.

Mainz, Germany Petra Ahrweiler
Guildford, UK Nigel Gilbert
March 2026

Contents

Contributors

Petra Ahrweiler TISSS Lab, Institute of Sociology, Johannes Gutenberg University, Mainz, Germany

Elisabeth André Chair for Human-centered Artificial Intelligence, University of Augsburg, Augsburg, Germany

Hassan Bashiri Department of Computer Science, Hamedan University of Technology, Hamedan, Iran

Beatriz López University of Girona, Girona, Spain

Martha Bicket Centre for Research in Social Simulation, Department of Sociology, University of Surrey, University Campus, Guildford, UK

Roger Campdepadrós University of Girona, Girona, Spain

Isaac de Palau University of Girona, Girona, Spain

Izabel Sabino De Sousa School for The Future of Innovation in Society, Arizona State University, Tempe, USA

Nigel Gilbert CRESS, Department of Sociology, University of Surrey, Guildford, UK

Ashly Ann Jo Indian Institute of Information Technology Kottayam, Valavoor, India

Erik W. Johnston School for The Future of Innovation in Society, Arizona State University, Tempe, USA

Blanca Luque Capellas TISSS Lab, Institute of Sociology, Johannes Gutenberg University, Mainz, Germany

Beatriz López University of Girona, Girona, Spain

Reeham R. Mohammed Jimmy and Rosalynn Carter School of Public Policy, Georgia Institute of Technology, Atlanta, GA, USA

Maris Männiste Lecturer in Critical Data Studies, Institute of Social Studies, University of Tartu, Tartu, Estonia

Martin Neumann Brandenburg University of Technology, Cottbus, Germany

Sergi Payarol University of Girona, Girona, Spain

Ebin Deni Raj Department of Computer Science and Engineering, Indian Institute of Information Technology Kottayam, Kottayam, India

Albert Sabater University of Girona, Girona, Spain

Mahesh Sasikumar Department of Computer Science and Engineering, Indian Institute of Information Technology Kottayam, Kottayam, India

Ruben Schlagowski Chair for Human-centered Artificial Intelligence, University of Augsburg, Augsburg, Germany

Elisabeth Späth TISSS Lab, Institute of Sociology, Johannes Gutenberg University, Mainz, Germany

Sumathi Srinivasalu University of Madras, Chennai, India

Avo Trumm Researcher of Information Management and Analysis, Institute of Social Studies, University of Tartu, Tartu, Estonia

Triin Vihalemm Professor of Communication Research, Institute of Social Studies, University of Tartu, Tartu, Estonia

David Wurster TISSS Lab, Institute of Sociology, Johannes Gutenberg University, Mainz, Germany

Chapter 1
Participatory Artificial Intelligence in Public Social Services: Modelling for Policy and Practice

Petra Ahrweiler⬤ and Nigel Gilbert⬤

Abstract This introductory chapter sets the context, purpose, and structure of this, the second volume in the AI FORA series. It begins by outlining the opportunities and controversies surrounding the use of Artificial Intelligence (AI) in welfare systems worldwide. The chapter positions the book as a continuation of *Participatory Artificial Intelligence in Public Social Services: From Bias to Fairness in Assessing Beneficiaries* (Springer, 2025), the first AI FORA volume, which provided empirical insights into how welfare assessments are currently made and highlighted fairness, legitimacy, and bias challenges in AI-supported decision-making. Building on this foundation, Volume II introduces a participatory, model-based approach to designing future AI systems for public services. The AI FORA research strategy is presented as an iterative process that combines agent-based modelling (ABM), serious games, synthetic data generation, and policy workshops. This strategy creates a safe innovation space where stakeholders can make decision processes explicit, explore alternative rulesets, and collaboratively prototype AI systems aligned with societal values. The chapter discusses three key roles of modelling in this process—representing current welfare practices, enabling experimentation with new rules, and bridging human deliberation and machine learning to build transparent AI prototypes. It explains why ABM is uniquely suited for capturing the complexity and heterogeneity of real-world welfare systems and supporting democratic innovation cycles. The chapter concludes by outlining the book's structure, showing how subsequent chapters document AI FORA's approach across multiple national contexts, connecting computational modelling to policy practice, and setting future directions for participatory, trustworthy AI in public services.

P. Ahrweiler (✉)
TISSS Lab, Institute of Sociology, Johannes Gutenberg University, Mainz, Germany
e-mail: petra.ahrweiler@uni-mainz.de

N. Gilbert
CRESS, Department of Sociology, University of Surrey, Guildford, UK
e-mail: n.gilbert@surrey.ac.uk

P. Ahrweiler and N. Gilbert (eds.), *Participatory Modelling and Simulation to Improve AI-based Public Social Services*, Artificial Intelligence, Simulation and Society,
https://doi.org/10.1007/978-3-032-15283-1_1

Artificial Intelligence (AI) is rapidly transforming public administrations worldwide, promising to make social service delivery faster, more consistent, and data-driven. Governments increasingly turn to algorithmic decision-support systems to determine eligibility for welfare benefits, allocate scarce resources, and prioritise applicants. Yet, the deployment of AI in welfare systems has been fraught with controversy. Automated systems have been criticised for entrenching historical biases, producing opaque and seemingly arbitrary decisions, and undermining public trust in state institutions. In some cases, poorly designed algorithms have caused real harm, leading to wrongful benefit denials, stigmatisation, and legal disputes.

These challenges highlight a fundamental tension: AI does not operate in a social vacuum. Welfare systems are not only technical infrastructures but also expressions of societal values, reflecting contested views of fairness, deservingness, and solidarity. Simply "digitising" existing rules or importing algorithmic models from other contexts risks ignoring the institutional complexity and moral underpinnings of welfare decision-making. The result can be a mismatch between what the technology delivers and what society considers just or legitimate.

This book is the second volume in the AI FORA series, following the publication of *Participatory Artificial Intelligence in Public Social Services: From Bias to Fairness in Assessing Beneficiaries* (Springer, 2025). While Volume I focused on the empirical foundation of AI FORA—investigating how algorithmic decision-making currently shapes welfare services across diverse national settings—this second volume builds on those findings by developing and applying computational modelling methods for policy and practice. Together, the two volumes form a comprehensive account of AI FORA's research agenda, moving from empirical understanding to participatory, model-based design of future AI systems for public services.

This book presents an alternative vision for designing AI in public social services—one grounded in participation, transparency, and iterative experimentation. Drawing on the AI FORA project, it introduces a modelling strategy that creates a safe space for innovation, where diverse stakeholders can explore how welfare assessments are currently made, debate what "better" decision rules might look like, and test the potential role of AI before any real-world implementation. The approach combines agent-based simulation, serious games, and policy dialogue to bridge the gap between technical feasibility, societal values, and institutional realities.

By documenting this process and its outcomes across multiple countries, this volume aims to demonstrate that AI for public services can be co-created rather than imposed. It argues that future welfare technologies must be context-sensitive, value-driven, and democratically governed, not merely efficient or data-rich. The chapters that follow offer both practical lessons and conceptual insights, showing how participatory modelling can help shape a more trustworthy and socially responsive future for AI in welfare provision.

The AI FORA Research Strategy: A Participatory Approach to Designing "Better AI"

The AI FORA research strategy described in this volume builds directly on the empirical insights published in Volume I (Ahrweiler 2025). While the first book documented the realities of welfare decision-making and surfaced key challenges of fairness, legitimacy, and bias in existing AI use, the current book translates those findings into a participatory modelling framework for designing socially desirable AI systems. Readers are encouraged to consult the first volume for detailed qualitative and quantitative analyses of current welfare assessments and AI adoption, which provide the empirical foundation for the modelling and policy approaches described here.

The AI FORA research strategy allows governments and communities to prototype socially desirable AI systems before they are deployed. At its core, the AI FORA strategy combines agent-based simulation, serious games, and machine learning prototyping in an iterative, participatory process (cf. Figure 1.1; already published in Ahrweiler et al. 2024). This approach provides a safe testbed for exploring how AI could—and should—make decisions in welfare systems, ensuring that such systems are responsive to the societies they serve.

The strategy consists of seven steps:

1. Mapping the existing system.

The process begins by analysing how public social services are currently assessed and allocated in a specific national or regional context. This step combines policy analysis, technical investigation, and participatory system mapping workshops. The

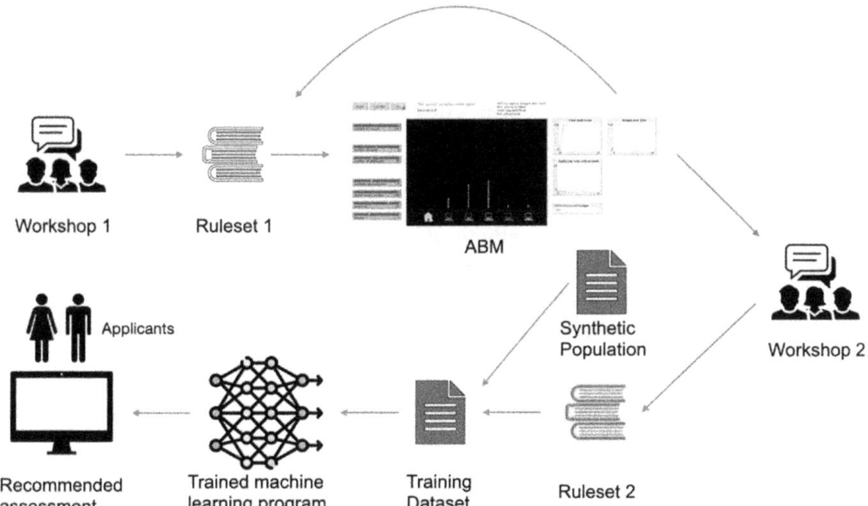

Fig. 1.1 The AI FORA research strategy (Ahrweiler et al. 2024)

resulting conceptual model identifies actors, decision rules, institutional routines, and points of potential bias. It provides the foundation for formal modelling and stakeholder engagement.

2. Building an initial agent-based model (ABM).

An ABM is then developed to computationally simulate the current social assessment process. Agents represent applicants and social workers, interacting under the existing decision rules and resource constraints. This baseline model ("Ruleset 1") reveals systemic behaviours, such as bottlenecks, inequities, or unintended exclusions, and serves as a transparent artefact for stakeholder discussion.

3. Stakeholder engagement through gamification.

To ensure that diverse societal perspectives inform AI design, AI FORA uses serious games. Participatory workshops immerse social workers, policymakers, NGOs, and other stakeholders in simulated assessment scenarios based on real-life applicant narratives. Participants deliberate on fairness, eligibility criteria, and trade-offs, collaboratively proposing improved decision rules. This process generates a revised "better ruleset" (Ruleset 2) that captures local value judgments and practical expertise.

4. Iterative refinement between games and models.

The ABM and serious games form a feedback loop: proposed rules are tested in the model, systemic outcomes are analysed, and stakeholders review results to refine their proposals. This iterative process makes hidden biases and unintended effects visible, fostering collective learning and co-design of fairer assessment practices.

5. Scaling up with synthetic populations.

To evaluate how new rulesets would affect entire populations, AI FORA generates synthetic datasets that statistically mirror real demographic data while preserving privacy. Running both current and improved rulesets on these datasets allows assessment of distributional impacts, such as who receives services under different decision regimes.

6. Prototyping AI decision-support tools.

The improved rulesets and synthetic data are used to train a machine learning model that replicates stakeholder-agreed decision logic, rather than historical biases. This results in a prototype AI tool capable of advising social workers or policymakers on eligibility decisions. Unlike black-box systems, this approach ensures that AI recommendations are transparent, traceable, and socially validated.

7. Validation and policy insights.

Finally, stakeholders review the prototype AI's outputs, providing qualitative and quantitative feedback on fairness, legitimacy, and practical feasibility. Policymakers can then use these insights to guide real-world AI system development, avoiding costly mistakes and building public trust in technology-assisted social services.

Through this high-level research strategy, AI FORA demonstrates that responsible AI design in public services requires participatory, context-aware, and testable innovation pathways. By integrating social science, computational modelling, and stakeholder expertise, this approach bridges the gap between technological potential, societal values, and policy needs, offering a blueprint for "better AI" in welfare provision worldwide.

The Role of Modelling in the AI FORA Research Strategy

AI in public social services often operates as a "black box", relying on historical data and opaque algorithms to decide who receives welfare benefits or support. The AI FORA strategy takes a fundamentally different approach: as depicted in Fig. 1.1, it uses a combination of empirical research and computational modelling as the backbone of a participatory strategy to design socially desirable, context-aware AI systems before they are deployed.

The results of the empirical research components have been published in Ahrweiler (2025). Data from empirical research in AI FORA's case studies inform the modelling steps. Modelling plays three crucial roles in this process: representing, exploring, and prototyping decision-making systems for welfare provision.

Representing the status quo The first step in AI FORA's modelling concept is to translate existing welfare assessment practices into a formal, computational model. Using agent-based modelling, the project builds simulations of how applicants and social workers interact under current decision rules and resource constraints. This "baseline model" reveals the hidden dynamics of eligibility determination: who waits in queues, how scarce resources are allocated, where bias and inefficiency may arise. By making implicit decision routines explicit, modelling creates a transparent artefact that stakeholders can interrogate, critique, and improve.

Exploring alternatives Modelling then becomes a testbed for innovation. During participatory workshops and serious games, stakeholders propose changes to assessment rules to better reflect local fairness norms or practical experience. These revised rules are fed into the ABM, which simulates their systemic effects. Stakeholders can see, for example, how new rules alter who receives services, whether certain vulnerable groups benefit or lose out, and what unintended bottlenecks might emerge. This iterative loop between human deliberation and computational simulation allows participants to explore "what if" scenarios safely, without risking harm to real people or systems.

Prototyping future AI systems Finally, modelling provides the bridge to algorithmic implementation. Once an improved ruleset has been developed and validated in simulations, it is combined with synthetic population data to assess its effects at scale. The resulting dataset can then be used to train a machine learning model that replicates the stakeholder-agreed decision logic. This prototyped AI system is not a black box trained on biased historical data, but a transparent, collectively designed tool aligned with societal values. Policymakers and practitioners can review, test, and refine this prototype before considering real-world deployment.

Through these three functions, modelling acts as the engine of responsible innovation in AI FORA. It translates complex social processes into an analysable form, provides a safe experimentation space for exploring alternatives, and bridges the gap between human values and machine learning. Far from being a purely technical exercise, modelling becomes a socially embedded practice, enabling dialogue between stakeholders, technology developers, and policymakers on what "better AI" for welfare systems should look like.

The Role of ABM in the Modelling Concept

Agent-Based Modelling (ABM) is the cornerstone of AI FORA's modelling concept to designing "better AI" for public social services because it uniquely supports the representation, exploration, and co-design of complex, value-laden decision processes in ways that other modelling techniques cannot. Unlike system dynamics or purely statistical models, which often rely on aggregate variables or historical correlations, ABM explicitly models individual actors and their interactions within welfare systems. Applicants, social workers, administrators, and institutional rules are represented as autonomous agents with their own attributes, decision logics, and constraints. This micro-level granularity makes it possible to capture the heterogeneity of cases, discretionary judgments, and localised variations in policy implementation that characterise real-world social assessments.

As a result, ABM can reveal emergent dynamics—such as unintended inequities or bottlenecks—that remain invisible in top-down, equation-based models. ABM also provides flexibility in representing institutional complexity and uncertainty. Welfare systems are not governed by fixed formulas; they involve multiple decision-makers operating under changing legal frameworks, incomplete information, and shifting societal values. ABM allows the incorporation of formal rules, tacit norms, stochastic events, and bounded rationality, producing simulations that more closely mirror real decision-making environments. This is particularly important for designing AI systems that are not only technically accurate but also socially legitimate and context-specific.

Beyond descriptive power, ABM offers a safe experimentation and co-design platform. Stakeholders can propose new rules for allocating welfare resources, which are then implemented in the model to explore "what-if" scenarios and anticipate systemic effects. Unlike purely analytical or optimisation-based models that yield prescriptive solutions detached from social context, ABM supports interactive, deliberative experimentation, where participants can test ideas, learn from feedback, and collectively refine decision criteria. This makes it a natural fit for participatory workshops and serious games, where diverse perspectives on fairness, efficiency, and eligibility can be translated into computational logic and immediately visualised for discussion.

Other approaches often struggle to connect local decision rules with system-wide consequences, making ABM particularly valuable for anticipating unintended effects of AI-supported welfare assessments. ABM bridges the gap between micro-level decision processes and macro-level policy outcomes. Simulating individual interactions across synthetic populations allows exploration of distributional impacts and equity trade-offs before real-world implementation.

Finally, ABM creates a transparent, testable foundation for developing prototype AI decision-support tools. Because rules are explicit, traceable, and iteratively refined through stakeholder input, the resulting models provide a blueprint for AI systems that are explainable, auditable, and aligned with societal values. This contrasts with many machine learning approaches that depend on historical data and produce opaque decision boundaries, risking the reproduction of past biases.

In sum, ABM was chosen for AI FORA's modelling concept because it

- Represents heterogeneous actors and decision-making processes more faithfully than aggregate or equation-based models.
- Captures emergent effects of complex institutional interactions.
- Supports participatory co-design and transparent experimentation with alternative rulesets.
- Links individual-level decisions to population-level policy outcomes.
- Provides an auditable foundation for trustworthy AI development.

These qualities make ABM uniquely suited for responsible innovation in public services, enabling governments and stakeholders to prototype AI systems that are socially grounded before deployment.

Gamification and Simulation: A Participatory Innovation Loop

AI FORA's modelling concept leverages a powerful combination of gamification and simulation to involve stakeholders directly in shaping AI-based welfare systems. This approach is increasingly referred to as GAM (Games + Agent-Based Models) in the literature (Szczepanska et al. 2022). The approach has gained prominence in participatory modelling and decision support because it can bridge qualitative, experiential knowledge and quantitative system analysis in the exploration of social complexity. Games provide immersive, rule-based environments where participants—such as service users, frontline workers, and policymakers—can experience real-life dilemmas around eligibility, prioritisation, and fairness.

They allow stakeholders to externalise tacit knowledge, test assumptions, and negotiate competing values in a safe, shared space. This aligns with findings in the GAM literature that role-playing games and serious games enhance stakeholder engagement, foster social learning, and help capture context-specific decision rules that might otherwise remain hidden or implicit.

Agent-based models complement this by enabling systematic experimentation and scaling up of game insights. Decisions and rules proposed during gameplay are encoded into simulations to test their broader consequences under varying conditions. This supports counterfactual "what-if" analyses, exploration of unintended effects, and observation of emergent dynamics that are difficult to foresee during qualitative deliberation alone. According to Szczepanska et al. (2022), combining games and ABMs is particularly valuable because both approaches can integrate qualitative and quantitative data, mirror complex multi-actor systems, and provide feedback loops between real-world decision-making and virtual experimentation.

AI FORA extends the GAM approach in two key ways:

1. It embeds games and simulations in an iterative policy co-design cycle, where stakeholders repeatedly propose, test, and refine alternative decision logics.
2. It explicitly connects GAM outputs to the design of AI decision-support tools, transforming participatory insights into traceable, implementable algorithmic rules.

This dynamic interaction between gaming and simulation goes beyond information elicitation or model validation: it creates a participatory innovation loop where diverse perspectives are translated into formalised models, tested for systemic impact, and transformed into actionable policy and AI design options. By linking human reasoning and computational experimentation, AI FORA contributes to advancing the state of the art in GAM, demonstrating how serious games and ABMs can jointly support transparent, trustworthy, and value-sensitive AI systems for public services. By embedding games and simulations in an iterative, policy-oriented co-design process and explicitly linking their outcomes to the development of AI decision-support tools, AI FORA advances the emerging GAM methodology. It demonstrates how combining games and ABMs can move beyond stakeholder engagement or model validation, providing a structured pathway from participatory deliberation to algorithmic implementation in complex public service contexts.

Policies for "Better AI": Translating Modelling Insights into Policy Dialogue

The final stage of the AI FORA research strategy consists of policy workshops designed to bring the results of participatory modelling into direct conversation with policymakers, administrators, and other decision-makers. These workshops act as a bridge between simulation-based exploration and real-world governance, ensuring that the insights gained from gaming, stakeholder deliberation, and agent-based modelling inform actual welfare system reforms and future AI implementations.

Purpose and format Policy workshops are used to present model outcomes. Results from simulations comparing the baseline (status quo) ruleset with improved, stakeholder-designed alternatives are shared in an accessible, non-technical format.

Visualisations illustrate impacts on fairness, resource distribution, and efficiency at both individual and population levels. To foster dialogue on trade-offs, policymakers are invited to reflect on tensions exposed by the modelling process (e.g., efficiency vs. equity, prioritising certain vulnerable groups) and discuss their policy relevance. Workshop discussions evaluate which rule changes are not only desirable but also legally, institutionally, and politically implementable in the specific welfare context. In addition, the feasibility of translating improved decision rules into AI-based tools (e.g., decision-support algorithms) is discussed, including governance requirements, safeguards, and accountability mechanisms.

Role in the overall research strategy This step ensures that AI FORA's participatory approach does not end in a technical prototype but feeds directly into institutional decision-making. The policy workshops:

- Validate whether co-designed rulesets are actionable and sustainable in real administrative settings.
- Provide policymakers with a risk-free environment to discuss potential reforms informed by transparent simulations.
- Build trust and legitimacy by demonstrating that AI systems can be designed collaboratively, respecting societal values and avoiding opaque, top-down technological impositions.

Building on this research strategy, the chapters in this volume document how AI FORA translated these ideas into practice across different countries and institutional settings. The book follows the trajectory of the research strategy itself: from developing agent-based models that make welfare decision processes explicit, through engaging policymakers to turn modelling insights into actionable reforms, to reflecting on lessons learned and outlining future research pathways. The following sections guide readers through this journey, illustrating how participatory modelling can support the design of more trustworthy and socially grounded AI systems for public services.

Structure of the Book

This volume documents the outcomes of the modelling and policy work of AI FORA and the collaboration of researchers, practitioners, and policymakers exploring how participatory modelling can lead to more trustworthy and socially responsive AI systems in public social services. It is organised into three main sections, each reflecting a critical stage of the policy modelling process: building agent-based models, embedding modelling in policy practice, and setting future research directions. By building on Volume I and expanding its findings into computational modelling and participatory innovation, this second book completes the AI FORA research agenda: from uncovering the current state of algorithmic decision-making in welfare systems to collaboratively designing future AI tools that reflect shared values of fairness and care.

Part 1: Agent-Based Models for Social Services Assessment

The first section of the book introduces the ABM developed within AI FORA to represent existing social assessment systems and explore potential improvements.

These contributions demonstrate how ABM can make welfare decision-making processes visible, testable, and open to participatory redesign across diverse national contexts. Each chapter illustrates how ABM formalises complex decision routines, captures the dynamic interactions between applicants, frontline workers, and institutional constraints, and reveals systemic dynamics of fairness, legitimacy, and resource allocation. Readers will see how ABM:

- Translate real-world policies and tacit decision rules into computational models.
- Reveal trade-offs between efficiency, fairness, and resource distribution that are often hidden in practice.
- Support participatory redesign by enabling stakeholders to explore "what-if" scenarios and co-create improved rulesets.

Many of these models are combined with gamification workshops, allowing stakeholders to express values, debate alternative decision rules, and observe their consequences in simulated environments. Together, the chapters in this section demonstrate ABM's versatility as a participatory tool, providing transparent, testable representations of welfare systems and laying the foundation for AI solutions that are context-sensitive, ethically grounded, and responsive to local norms and institutional settings.

Chapters:

In *"Agent-Based Modelling for Context-Aware AI Systems: Reflections from AI FORA"*, Martha Bicket reflects on the development and application of agent-based models within AI FORA, drawing on case studies from Spain, Estonia, and Germany. The chapter explores how ABM can make welfare decision processes visible and debatable, support stakeholder engagement through serious games, and highlight both the potential and limitations of participatory modelling for shaping AI systems that are aligned with local values and contexts.

In *"Modelling Together for AI-based Social Services"*, Albert Sabater, Beatriz López, Sergi Payarol, and Isaac de Palau examine how ABM and gamification workshops can support participatory design of AI tools in Catalonia's social services, which they empirically investigated in Sabater et al. (2025). Using the Self-Sufficiency Matrix (SSM-Cat) case study, the chapter highlights how collaborative modelling exposes biases, variability in decision-making, and structural challenges, proposing a hybrid approach to create context-sensitive, equitable, and stakeholder-driven AI governance frameworks.

In *"Using Agent-Based Modelling to explore possible implications of AI use in the asylum procedure in Germany"*, Elisabeth Späth, Martha Bicket, Martin Neumann, David Wurster, and Blanca Luque Capellas present an interpretive ABM of the German asylum system, which was empirically analysed by Späth (2025). The chapter explores how modelling can make visible the interplay between bureaucratic legitimacy, refugee agency, and administrative decision processes, providing a tool to reflect on potential pathways for AI integration while highlighting power asymmetries, fairness concerns, and institutional constraints.

In *"Gamifying Fairness: Exploring Algorithmic Decision-Making in Estonia's Welfare System"*, Maris Männiste, Triin Vihalemm, and Avo Trumm use a serious game approach, accompanied by an agent-based model, to investigate perceptions of fairness in unemployment services supported by algorithmic assessments.

The chapter, following empirical investigations of the Estonian welfare system in Vihalemm et al. (2025), highlights how participatory gaming workshops can reveal challenges in standardising fairness, the importance of human judgment in AI-assisted decisions, and opportunities for designing more adaptive and context-sensitive welfare algorithms.

In *"Targeted Subsidies Plan: An Agent-Based Modeling Approach"*, Hassan Bashiri presents a simulation study of Iran's Targeted Subsidies Plan (TSP), which he empirically investigated in Bashiri (2025). The chapter is about modelling household dynamics and subsidy distribution to assess policy effectiveness in reducing income inequality. The chapter demonstrates how agent-based modelling can provide insights into welfare policy design, revealing both the benefits and limitations of targeted cash transfers under real-world constraints such as inflation, sanctions, and data accuracy challenges.

In *"Agent-Based Modelling of the Indian Public Distribution System in AI FORA"*, Ashly Ann Jo, Ebin Deni Raj, and Sumathi Srinivasalu present a simulation of India's Public Distribution System (PDS), a large-scale welfare programme ensuring food security for millions, which was empirically analysed by Srinivasalu et al. (2025). The chapter illustrates how agent-based modelling can capture corruption risks, logistical inefficiencies, and governance dynamics, providing a testbed for evaluating fairness, transparency, and accountability in complex welfare delivery systems and informing responsible AI-based policy interventions.

Part 2: Policy Modelling for Policy Practice

The second section focuses on how AI FORA translated modelling insights into policy-relevant knowledge and dialogue, connecting complex simulation results with real-world governance. Through a series of policy workshops and stakeholder engagements, the chapters demonstrate how participatory dissemination formats can bridge the gap between scientific evidence, public administration, and policymaking, ensuring that AI-based welfare systems are not only technically robust but also socially and institutionally grounded.

This section illustrates how

- Simulation findings can be communicated to policymakers in accessible formats, making complex dynamics understandable and actionable.

- Trade-offs between fairness, efficiency, legality, and data quality can be deliberated collectively, fostering informed decision-making.
- Institutional and political challenges of embedding participatory-designed rules in welfare practice can be surfaced and addressed, strengthening implementation pathways.

By turning modelling into a boundary object (Bowker and Star 1999) between science and policy, these contributions show how participatory approaches can build trust, legitimacy, and shared responsibility in shaping AI-supported social services. They highlight that effective policy modelling requires more than technical outputs - it depends on context sensitivity, stakeholder involvement, and interdisciplinary collaboration to create equitable and accountable AI governance frameworks for the future.

Chapters:

In *"Policy Learnings and Policy Change for AI-based Social Services"*, Albert Sabater, Beatriz López, and Roger Campdepadrós draw on multi-stakeholder policy workshops in Spain to examine how context-specific, participatory processes can guide AI development in welfare services. The chapter identifies key lessons for policy change, emphasising the need to address demographic and local variations, ensure continuous auditing and transparency, and institutionalise participatory oversight to prevent AI-driven inequities.

In *"Policy Perspectives on AI Use for Asylum-Related Assessment Processes in Germany"*, Elisabeth Späth, David Wurster, Blanca Luque Capellas and Petra Ahrweiler report on a policy workshop that engaged policymakers, NGOs, and practitioners to discuss findings from AI FORA's German case study on asylum decision-making. The chapter highlights how participatory dissemination workshops, using insights from agent-based modelling, foster dialogue on fairness, efficiency, and data quality, opening pathways for more inclusive, evidence-informed approaches to future AI use in asylum systems.

In *"Bridging Data and Policy: Disseminating Scientific Insights in Estonia's AI-Driven Welfare Governance"*, Avo Trumm, Maris Männiste, and Triin Vihalemm describe a policy workshop that brought together data experts, policymakers, and public administrators to discuss findings from AI FORA's Estonian case study on algorithmic decision-making in welfare services. The chapter emphasises how dissemination activities can surface data quality and ethical challenges, foster dialogue on human-centric AI design, and inform future policy frameworks for responsible and participatory use of AI in social protection systems.

In *"Translating Evidence to Practice—A Trojan Horse Approach"*, David Wurster, Blanca Luque Capellas, Izabel Sabino De Sousa, and Erik W. Johnston explore how participatory policy modelling workshops can bridge the gap between scientific evidence and decision-making. The chapter highlights how engaging policymakers directly in model-building fosters shared discovery, builds trust, and increases the likelihood that complex modelling insights inform real-world governance, particularly in social policy domains.

Part 3: Looking to the Future

The final section of this volume looks ahead, outlining future research and development pathways for participatory, value-sensitive AI in public services and beyond. Building on lessons learned from AI FORA, the chapters in this section chart a vision for AI systems that are not only technically capable but also ethically robust, transparent, and human-centric. They propose methodological innovations that further integrate qualitative deliberation, gamification, and computational modelling, enabling richer stakeholder engagement and more nuanced system design. This section also explores governance frameworks for participatory AI development outside welfare domains, addressing challenges of accountability, legitimacy, and long-term sustainability. It considers how participatory approaches can be scaled across cultural contexts, adapted to emerging forms of AI such as generative models and large language systems, and extended to new high-stakes areas like climate crisis management. Other contributions investigate how immersive technologies, including augmented and virtual reality, can enhance collaborative creativity and stakeholder engagement, opening fresh possibilities for participatory AI design.

Together, these chapters outline a forward-looking research agenda for responsible AI development as an ongoing, collaborative process—one that bridges technical innovation, societal values, and institutional responsibility to shape more just, trustworthy, and adaptable AI systems for the public good.

Chapters:

In *"Better AI for Public Good: Participatory Modelling and Simulation in Social Services"*, Mahesh Sasikumar, Ashly Ann Jo, and Ebin Deni Raj outline a forward-looking vision for ethically robust AI in welfare systems, grounded in participatory modelling and simulation practices. The chapter introduces a conceptual framework for "Better AI", discusses advanced modelling approaches such as Inverse Generative Social Science, and reflects on future research directions for designing AI systems that are human-centric, transparent, and aligned with public values.

In *"How Participatory Modeling Can Enable Collective Bias Mitigation when AI is Used Across Systems and Institutions"*, Erik W. Johnston and Reeham R. Mohammed explore how participatory modelling can act as a proactive mechanism to detect, contain, and mitigate systemic bias in AI used by public institutions. Drawing on case studies from civic infrastructures and systems of care, the chapter introduces a biomimetic "immune system" analogy for continuous bias monitoring and advocates for participatory governance structures that embed equity and collective responsibility throughout the AI lifecycle.

In *"Transferring the AI FORA approach to another domain: Participatory AI for climate"*, Petra Ahrweiler and Blanca Luque Capellas explore how AI FORA's participatory methodology—combining serious games, sociological analysis, and agent-based modelling—can be adapted to the field of climate crisis mitigation. The chapter demonstrates how structured, stakeholder-driven design processes can support the development of AI systems that are ethically grounded, context-aware, and socially legitimate in high-stakes environmental decision-making.

In *"Collaborative Creativity in Extended Realities Findings from Co-Creative Design Sessions in Augmented and Virtual Reality"*, Ruben Schlagowski and Elisabeth André investigate how immersive XR technologies can support group creativity and participatory design processes for AI systems. Based on co-creative workshops with public sector stakeholders, the chapter identifies opportunities and challenges of AR and VR for collaborative ideation, highlighting their potential to enrich participatory modelling and explainable AI design for future public service applications.

By combining these three perspectives—modelling, policy practice, and future pathways—this volume provides both a detailed record of the AI FORA project and a conceptual framework for participatory AI governance. It shows how computational modelling, grounded in stakeholder input and connected to policy realities, can chart a more transparent, legitimate, and context-sensitive future for AI in public social services.

This introduction has outlined the motivation, approach, and structure of this volume. Modelling and policy work in AI FORA demonstrate that AI does not have to be an opaque, top-down imposition on welfare systems.

Through participatory modelling and simulation, it is possible to make decision processes visible, test alternatives collectively, and co-design AI tools that reflect shared values of fairness and care. The chapters that follow showcase this vision in action, offering models, policy insights, and future-oriented perspectives. Together, they argue for a paradigm shift: from algorithmic decision-making as an automated extension of the status quo to AI as a collaborative, democratic tool for shaping more just and trustworthy systems. The book is concluded with a programmatic chapter on Participatory Artificial Intelligence as the preferred future way of inclusive technology development.

Acknowledgement Research presented in this chapter has been funded by the German VolkswagenStiftung under grant agreement number 98 560.

References

Ahrweiler, P. (2025). Participatory artificial intelligence in public social services. From bias to fairness in assessing beneficiaries. In *Springer Series Artificial Intelligence, Simulation and Society*. Springer. https://doi.org/10.1007/978-3-031-71678-2

Ahrweiler, P., Gilbert, N., Bicket, M., Sabater Coll, A., Luque Capellas, B., Wurster, D., Siqueiros, J., & Späth, E. (2024). Gamification and simulation for innovation. In C. Elsenbroich & H. Verhagen (Eds.), *Advances in social simulation. IT conference proceedings in complexity* (pp. 121–136). Springer. https://doi.org/10.1007/978-3-031-57785-7_11

Bashiri, H. (2025). Social assessment for the targeted subsidies plan as a social service provision in Iran: AI application in the targeted subsidies plan. In P. Ahrweiler (Ed.), *Participatory artificial intelligence in public social services. Artificial intelligence, simulation and society*. Springer. https://doi.org/10.1007/978-3-031-71678-2_7

Bowker, G. C., & Star, S. L. (1999). *Sorting things out: Classification and its consequences*. MIT Press.

Sabater, A., López, B., Campdepadrós, R., & Sánchez, C. (2025). Participatory action research for AI in social services: An example of local practices from Catalonia. In P. Ahrweiler (Ed.), *Participatory artificial intelligence in public social services. Artificial intelligence, simulation and society*. Springer. https://doi.org/10.1007/978-3-031-71678-2_4

Späth, E. (2025). AI use in the asylum procedure in Germany: Exploring perspectives with refugees and supporters on assessment criteria and beyond. In P. Ahrweiler (Ed.), *Participatory artificial intelligence in public social services. Artificial intelligence, simulation and society*. Springer. https://doi.org/10.1007/978-3-031-71678-2_6

Srinivasalu, S., et al. (2025). Social assessment and cultural resistance: The public distribution system in Tamil Nadu, India. In P. Ahrweiler (Ed.), *Participatory artificial intelligence in public social services. Artificial intelligence, simulation and society*. Springer. https://doi.org/10.1007/978-3-031-71678-2_8

Szczepanska, T., Antosz, P., Berndt, J. O., Borit, M., Chattoe-Brown, E., Mehryar, S., et al. (2022). GAM on! Six ways to explore social complexity by combining games and agent-based models. *International Journal of Social Research Methodology, 25*(4), 541–555. https://doi.org/10.1080/13645579.2022.2050119

Vihalemm, T., Männiste, M., Trumm, A., & Solvak, M. (2025). Specialists and algorithms: Implementation of AI in the delivery of unemployment Services in Estonia. In P. Ahrweiler (Ed.), *Participatory artificial intelligence in public social services. Artificial intelligence, simulation and society*. Springer. https://doi.org/10.1007/978-3-031-71678-2_5

Part I
Agent-based Models for Social Services Assessment

Chapter 2
Agent-Based Modelling for Context-Aware AI Systems: Reflections from AI FORA

Martha Bicket

Abstract This chapter reflects on the role of agent-based modelling (ABM) in the AI FORA project, which sought to explore how Artificial Intelligence (AI) for social welfare assessment decisions might be made more context-sensitive and better aligned with societal values. We discuss the development of bespoke ABMs for three case studies—Spain, Estonia, and Germany—and how they were used to support participatory workshops and serious games in pursuit of 'better AI'. By simulating decision-making rules and their effects, the models helped to surface dynamics that are not always visible in practice. They also helped to inform the design of serious games by enabling rules and parameters to be refined in advance. The three case studies differed in their aims, scope and access to stakeholders, which shaped both the resulting models and insights generated. Our experiences highlight the importance of early and sustained stakeholder engagement, with careful mapping and relationship-building to help ensure that models reflect real-world knowledge and that resulting participatory games yield meaningful insights. Together, the case studies establish a prototype for an approach to tailoring and improving AI systems that is grounded in stakeholder engagement and responsive to the ethical, political, and cultural dimensions of social assessment and public service provision.

Introduction

There is growing interest in the use of Artificial Intelligence (AI) to support or automate decisions about access to and allocation of public services or state benefits. From unemployment entitlements to social assistance and public childcare allocations, AI is increasingly being seen as a means of enhancing the efficiency and objectivity of welfare systems. At the same time, this trend raises concerns about fairness, transparency, accountability, and the legitimacy of resulting decisions.

M. Bicket (✉)
University of Surrey, Guildford, UK

© The Author(s) 2026

P. Ahrweiler and N. Gilbert (eds.), *Participatory Modelling and Simulation to Improve AI-based Public Social Services*, Artificial Intelligence, Simulation and Society,
https://doi.org/10.1007/978-3-032-15283-1_2

The AI FORA project sought to address these challenges by exploring how public sector AI systems might be designed and adapted to be better aligned with societal values and more responsive to the cultural contexts in which they are deployed.

This chapter reflects on the use of agent-based modelling (ABM) in the AI FORA project. The aim of this work was to build ABMs for each of the country case studies and use these to support participatory workshops with serious games in which stakeholders collaboratively explored improvements to the underlying assessment algorithms. The chapter begins with a short introduction to agent-based modelling. It then draws on our experience of three of the project's case studies in particular–Spain, Germany, and Estonia–and offers some reflections on the value and limitations of ABMs in this context.

Agent-Based Modelling and Serious Games

An ABM is a computational model that simulates the actions and interactions of agents. It is built from the following basic conceptual elements: agents, an environment, social structure, interactions and time (Dilaver and Gilbert 2023). The agents are the decision-making units in the model—these might represent individuals, households, organisations or even countries. Agents are autonomous and heterogeneous, and can interact with each other as well as with their surroundings. The environment is the space in which the agents operate, often pictured as a grid, where each patch may also have its own characteristics. Social structure and interactions define how agents behave and respond to one another or to their environment. Finally, time advances in steps (or 'ticks'), allowing us to observe how patterns and outcomes emerge as agents act and interact over many cycles.

Complex, system-wide dynamics can arise from these straightforward, local rules. ABMs can help us explore and interrogate complex systems (such as social systems) and their dynamics by representing them from the bottom up. In AI FORA, ABMs were used to create simplified representations of social assessment processes; they were built to mirror aspects of real-world social welfare decision-making, such as how eligibility is assessed and how resources are allocated. These ABMs were then used to support the design of serious games that could be played with stakeholders.

Serious games, on the other hand, are often defined as the use of games for educational purposes, with education considered in its broadest sense to include exploration and problem solving (Ritterfeld et al. 2009). They have been used for a range of applications, including for data collection, communication, decision-making, and to deepen stakeholder engagement (Bakhanova et al. 2020; Szczepanska et al. 2022). AI FORA used serious games to enable stakeholders to reflect on what 'better AI' might mean in practice.

The AI FORA Rationale and Approach

Real-world public decision-making systems—including those involving AI—are shaped by local social, institutional, and political contexts. Existing social assessment processes may be opaque or poorly documented and may rely on subjective value judgements. To enable meaningful participation in the development of automated and AI-driven social assessment systems, stakeholders need tools that can help them visualise and explore how these processes currently operate and what different versions of them might look like. A key part of the AI FORA project explored how ABMs and serious games might be used to this end to deliver 'better' AI for social assessment.

We built tailor-made ABMs for a selection of case studies in different countries and used these to support the design and delivery of 'serious games' to be played with stakeholders in participatory workshops.

Each ABM captured a simplified version of the social assessment decision-making context, including key agents, their characteristics, the environment in which they interact and the rules governing their interactions as well as the assessment algorithm. These models were not designed to predict real-world outcomes, but rather to act as scaffolding for stakeholder engagement—providing a shared, flexible artefact through which different perspectives could be articulated and discussed. Each ABM was developed in close collaboration with its country case study partners and supported the design of bespoke serious games to be played with stakeholders to test and adapt alternative assessment rules.

The design of the ABM and follow-on activities took the following shape:

1. The first step was to hold a virtual 'case study mapping' workshop to collect information about and map out a simplified representation of the case study's social welfare provision decision-making process. This was attended by the country case study partner, the team responsible for the design of the ABM from the Centre for Research in Social Simulation (CRESS) at University of Surrey, and colleagues from the consortium lead coordinator Johannes Gutenberg University (JGU). This was not a formal system mapping exercise in the methodological sense, but rather a practical flowcharting activity intended to elicit key inputs, actors, steps, and decision points in the current assessment process. We used the online tool PRSM (prsm.uk) to collaboratively build a flowchart of these key elements during the workshop. Case study partners were asked to identify the main agency responsible for making social assessments, to elaborate on how these assessments are currently made, and suggest relevant agent attributes that might feature in the ABM. This workshop aimed to generate three core outputs: a flowchart of the existing social welfare decision-making process; a provisional ruleset describing current assessment practice(s); and a list of key agent attributes relevant to the process.

2. The information gathered in this initial case study mapping workshop was used to draft a preliminary ABM/game specification outline, capturing the main actors,

the rules governing their interactions, and the parameters of the environment. The specification was refined with feedback from partners.

3. A first draft of the ABM was then developed using NetLogo and refined with partner input.
4. The ABM was used to inform the design of a serious game.
5. The serious game was played by stakeholders, who proposed and voted on changes to the assessment ruleset.
6. In one case (Spain), as a demonstration of how the ruleset could be used within an AI-based assessment system, a neural network which could be used to assess applicants was trained using data generated from this improved ruleset (see Ahrweiler et al. 2024).

Case Studies

This chapter reflects on three of the case studies undertaken within AI FORA: Spain, Germany, and Estonia. These are briefly introduced below. Each case is described in detail in its own chapter elsewhere in this book. Each of the three case studies varied not only in topic and cultural context but also in terms of scope, level of access to stakeholders, availability of background information, and the order in which (and degree to which) the ABM development and related activities were carried out.

Spain: The 'Complex Needs' Game/ABM

This case study focused on social service workers tasked with allocating limited resources to applicants with multiple, complex needs. The assessment process was based on a tool called the SSM-CAT2 used in Catalonia. The ABM component of this case study (#1–4 in the process list above) ran from October 2022 to April 2023, with the serious game stakeholder workshop taking place in May 2023.

Estonia: Career Counselling Support

This case study was loosely based on the career counselling support for job-seekers available through the Estonian Unemployment Insurance Fund (EUIF). The initial mapping workshop was carried out in March 2023, followed by an intensive period of game development from March to September 2024, culminating in a serious game stakeholder workshop which took place in October 2024. The final ABM was completed in November 2024.

Germany: The Asylum Application Process

This case study modelled the asylum application process in Germany, based on insights from desktop research, interviews and focus groups, with particular attention to the agency of applicants and the perceived legitimacy of the system. The initial mapping workshop was carried out in May 2023, followed by a period of iterative ABM development between February and December 2024. The case study drew on a rich dataset of process information collected by the local partner and explored both the various stages of the application process and the avenues for appeals.

Reflections on the Case Studies and Modelling Process

The Spanish ABM process was tightly integrated with the serious game design and stakeholder engagement. The model proved useful both as a means of validating the logic of the assessment process and as a tool for testing potential game dynamics before the stakeholder workshop. Several refinements emerged through the iterative ABM design process, such as distributing budgets unevenly across agents to reflect municipal-level variation, and separating the concepts of 'need' and 'critical need' to capture and reflect the consequences of not receiving support. The Spanish case was the only one in which the full AI FORA strategy was carried out, using a synthetic population and the stakeholder-refined ruleset to train a neural network to explore the impacts of social assessment decisions for distributing services in the real-world context.

The Estonian case study took a more lightweight approach, both in terms of modelling complexity and stakeholder involvement. Although the case study wanted to explore the EUIF's OTT algorithm, which provides an assessment of the level of career counselling support needed, details about this real-world algorithm were sparse. Additionally, due to limited access to stakeholders in the field, the serious game was played instead with university students. This meant that the game and its accompanying ABM functioned more as a prototype of the participatory process for adapting an automated assessment algorithm, but its value for informing actual practice was limited.

The German case study presented a different modelling challenge. From the outset, the scope of the case study was particularly broad. In ABM design meetings with the case study partner, we spoke at length about how to manage the scope of the ABM but there wasn't a clear part of the system that was seen to be more or less important for the case study's main research objectives. One area of interest in the case study was the tension between the applicant's agency in the asylum-seeking process and the perceived legitimacy of the bureaucratic process. Initially, the ABM was limited to the application stages but later it was extended to include the appeals process too, treating the number of appeals as an indicator of the system's legitimacy from the applicant's perspective. The broad scope meant that there were many assumptions that we had to make during the ABM building process. The case study partner had collected a wealth of information about the asylum process (before, during and after the asylum application process) and so we incorporated a lot of this knowledge as accurately as feasible (e.g. the number of 'Hardship Commission' recommendations that get adopted, improving the asylum status of the applicant). However, the wide scope meant that there were also many variables and interactions we had to simplify or use our own judgement to define. Consequently, at best, the value of the model lies in being a tool for exploring the general types of issues and contributing factors that one might encounter in such a system rather than giving detailed insights into the dynamics of the system itself. Also, as the model grew bigger, it took longer to implement any further changes to its design due to the number and interconnectedness of the different elements. Unlike the Spanish and Estonian case studies, the German case study ABM was not used to design or run a serious game with stakeholders.

Despite these variations, some cross-cutting lessons can be drawn from these case studies. One clear success was the way the ABMs and serious games helped make assessment processes visible and debatable. By simulating decision-making rules and their effects, the models helped reveal both overt and hidden dynamics— such as how budget constraints, agent biases, or differing definitions of 'need' can shape outcomes in ways that may be difficult to observe in practice. The serious games played in the Spanish and Estonian case studies supported stakeholders in identifying features of the system they wanted to change and in exploring some of the implications of those changes through gameplay.

The interactive, iterative relationship between the models and the serious games also proved valuable. The ABMs were used not just to simulate the existing system but also to test how the proposed game would play out—allowing for adjustments to rules, parameters, and agent attributes in advance of the workshop. In return, the games provided a space for stakeholders to propose and debate changes, which could then be translated back into the model for further exploration or—in the case of Spain—the development of a neural network.

However, not all aspects of the process went smoothly. One of the more significant challenges was the dependence on stakeholder access and involvement. Where partners had built stronger relationships with relevant actors, as in Spain, the insights from the participatory elements were more directly relevant and valuable. Where this access was limited, as in Estonia, the ABM and gameplay remained more hypothetical and distant from real-world practice. Future participatory processes aimed at adapting AI assessment processes and tailoring them to local notions of fairness, for example, would be better supported by a more detailed stakeholder mapping exercise and engagement strategy. Early engagement, including stakeholder mapping and relationship-building, is critical to ensure that the models reflect real-world knowledge and that the games are meaningful.

Another limitation was the variation across case studies in terms of how closely they adhered to the full overarching AI FORA strategy. Although the initial project strategy envisioned a coherent sequence from mapping workshop to ABM to serious game to machine learning, only the Spanish case study completed all steps (and in this order). In the German and Estonian cases, a range of practical barriers such as stakeholder availability prevented the models from being developed and used to their full potential. This in turn limited the opportunity for comparative insights and reduced the coherence of the overall methodological framework.

Conclusions

This work in AI FORA helped to establish a prototype for an approach to tailoring and improving AI systems that is grounded in stakeholder engagement and responsive to the ethical, political, and cultural dimensions of social assessment and public service provision. Through the development and use of ABMs, we contributed to the design and delivery of participatory stakeholder workshops for policymakers, public service administrators, and members of the public in a range of case studies, including in Spain, Estonia, and Germany. Spain and Estonia used serious games to explore stakeholder priorities and ways to improve social assessment processes in the different case study contexts.

The project demonstrated that it is possible to use participatory ABMs to open up conversations about the values embedded in public service AI and to co-create more desirable alternatives. These conversations are essential if AI is to serve the public in ways that are not only efficient but also fair, transparent and just—and perceived as such.

Acknowledgments Research presented in this chapter has been funded by the German VolkswagenStiftung under grant agreement number 98 560.

References

Ahrweiler, P., Gilbert, N., Juranyi, Z., Bicket, M., Sabater, A., Kampis, G., Capellas, B. L., & Wurster, D. (2024). Using ABM and serious games to create "better AI". In *2024 annual modelling and simulation conference (ANNSIM)* (pp. 1–16). https://doi.org/10.23919/ANNSIM 61499.2024.10732031

Bakhanova, E., Garcia, J. A., Raffe, W. L., & Voinov, A.. (2020). Targeting social learning and engagement: What serious games and gamification can offer to participatory modeling. *Environmental Modelling and Software, 134*, 104846. https://doi.org/10.1016/j.envsoft.2020. 104846

Dilaver, O., & Gilbert, N. (2023). Unpacking a black box: A conceptual anatomy framework for agent-based social simulation models. *Journal of Artificial Societies and Social Simulation, 26*(1), 4. https://doi.org/10.18564/jasss.4998

Ritterfeld, U., Cody, M., & Vorderer, P. (Eds.). (2009). *Serious games: Mechanisms and effects* (1st ed.). Routledge. https://doi.org/10.4324/9780203891650

Szczepanska, T., et al. (2022). GAM on! Six ways to explore social complexity by combining games and agent-based models. *International Journal of Social Research Methodology, 25*(4), 541–555. https://doi.org/10.1080/13645579.2022.2050119

Chapter 3
Modelling Together for AI-Based Social Services

Albert Sabater, Beatriz López, Sergi Payarol, and Isaac de Palau

Abstract This chapter examines the integration of algorithmic technologies in social service provision in Spain through a case study of Catalonia's Self-Sufficiency Matrix (SSM-Cat), an evidence-based assessment tool adapted for social service governance that allows measuring a person's ability to be self-sufficient, that is, to carry out daily activities independently. Based on this case study, the chapter reflects that while the adoption of artificial intelligence (AI) in public services grows, significant gaps persist in equity-oriented frameworks and participatory design methodologies. In addition, we demonstrate how Agent-Based Modelling (ABM) and gamification workshops can bridge these gaps by facilitating co-creation between policymakers, social workers, and vulnerable communities. Further, the ABM simulations are helpful because they reveal critical inconsistencies in how practitioners interpret standardized tools, thus highlighting the need for shared decision-making protocols to tackle such problems. Based on our research, we identify three systemic challenges: (1) inadequate science-policy interfaces for translating technical AI concepts into governance; (2) insufficient mechanisms for incorporating frontline practitioner knowledge into algorithmic design; and (3) inherent biases in administrative data that risk reinforcing structural inequalities. Through our case study and its extension, we propose a hybrid approach combining techniques such as clustering analysis, participatory ABM, and deliberative forums to create context-sensitive AI systems. Our findings reveal the importance of advancing towards a more transparent, stakeholder-driven AI governance approach that prioritizes participatory methodologies. The

A. Sabater (✉) · B. López · S. Payarol · I. de Palau
University of Girona, Girona, Spain
e-mail: albert.sabater@udg.edu

B. López
e-mail: beatriz.lopez@udg.edu

S. Payarol
e-mail: sergi.payarol@ajgirona.cat

I. de Palau
e-mail: isaac.palau@ajgirona.cat

P. Ahrweiler and N. Gilbert (eds.), *Participatory Modelling and Simulation to Improve AI-based Public Social Services*, Artificial Intelligence, Simulation and Society,
https://doi.org/10.1007/978-3-032-15283-1_3

chapter concludes with policy recommendations for embedding dynamic evaluation frameworks, institutionalizing co-design processes, and promoting interpretive cultures around algorithmic tools as essential steps to ensure AI technologies serve as tools for seeking equity rather than exclusion in welfare provision.

Introduction

Although research shows that innovation has been part of public sector modernization agendas over the past two decades or so, including for the local level of government (Criado et al. 2025), evidence-based AI applications that involve participative modelling methods for the provision of social services are still scarce or a peripheral concern (Sabater et al. 2025). This is despite the gradual implementation of AI-based software in the public sector and its use in the social service provision. Although there are potential threats and challenges posed by AI technologies that require developing and implementing appropriate policies and institutional mechanisms that connect scientific and expert knowledge with policymaking, current pressures to use AI dismisses too often a key question: what problem exactly are we trying to solve by using an AI system in social services? In order to answer this question, the path forward should be clearer: meaningful AI integration in social services requires not just better tools, but a deeper commitment to inclusivity, accountability, and systematic foresight through interactive and participatory formats.

However, the science-policy interfaces encounter multiple interrelated challenges that significantly influence which technologies and how AI systems might both inform and shape social service delivery systems at different levels. A prime example is the growing use of chatbots such as ChatGPT in public services. Its current deployment takes place at the same time there is a lack of a consistent and equity-oriented frameworks concerning these AI systems in the provision of social services. Although the consequences are still unfolding, it has become clear that comprehensive methodologies that involve the continual assessment and recalibration of AI systems are needed to ensure that technology remains a tool for enhancing social good rather than exacerbating existing social divides.

In this short chapter, we first provide an example of contextualized, value-sensitive, responsive, and dynamic AI system that can be co-designed from existing systems to prototype better AI for advising social workers. The example is focused on the use of an agent-based model (ABM) and a complex needs social assessment used by local authorities in the region of Catalunya (Spain) known as the SSM-Cat. Second, we review one of the key problems of real implementation, namely the shortage of professionals who can translate between AI research and social policy. As we highlight later on, bridging this gap demands not only better tools but also participatory frameworks. Third, we stress the importance of addressing bias and modelling together to build trust among both service providers and recipients, and to move away from the automated reinforcement of existing inequities. Finally, we provide some future directions based on our AI FORA case study and its extension at the City Council of Girona through the Pigall project.[1]

Complex Needs and ABM

The primary objective of this case study was to investigate the perceptions, attitudes, and acceptance of AI-based social assessment technologies among policymakers and administrative agencies at the local level in Catalonia, a Spanish region at the forefront of adopting digital technologies for public sector innovation. Given the disproportionate representation of vulnerable groups among social service users, particular attention was devoted to examining the implications of AI systems for these populations.

Since assessing poverty, social exclusion, and vulnerability requires comprehensive data and access to diverse information sources, this study employed a digital assessment tool designed to assist social service professionals in diagnosing and identifying complex cases, while also guiding intervention strategies and the individualized follow-up. This tool, known as the Self-Sufficiency Matrix has been experimentally used by municipal authorities in Catalonia (SSM-Cat). Originally developed in the Netherlands (Lauriks et al. 2014) and the United States (Richmond et al. 2015), the SSM-Cat was subsequently adapted and validated by the Department of Work, Social Affairs, and Families of the Generalitat de Catalunya, in collaboration with Municipal Associations, the College of Social Work, and the College of Educators and Social Educators.

Traditional methods of assessing social provision for complex needs often rely on subjective evaluations by social service professionals, thus introducing variability in decision-making. In contrast, the SSM-Cat was implemented, in part, to mitigate such discretion by quantifying an individual's level of self-sufficiency across 13 distinct dimensions. By employing this assessment process, the tool streamlined the social worker's role, enabling a more structured, consistent and efficient evaluation of complex social needs.

The adoption of the SSM-Cat at the municipal level pursued two primary objectives. First, it aimed to enhance transparency in social service decision-making processes. Second, it provided a standardized and comparable instrument for monitoring the distribution of social services across municipalities, thereby promoting greater consistency and equity in service allocation (see Fig. 3.1).

Using this framework, a participatory modelling strategy was devised, as illustrated in Fig. 3.2, to facilitate the transition from existing to desired social assessment systems. The process started with a workshop and gamification to map the extant system into a flowchart. This informed an initial ruleset (Ruleset1) and the development of an Agent-Based Model (ABM), which simulated the current System and

---

[1] https://exteriors.gencat.cat/ca/ambits-dactuacio/afers_exteriors/ue/fons_europeus/detalls/noticia/20230313_ia-girona.

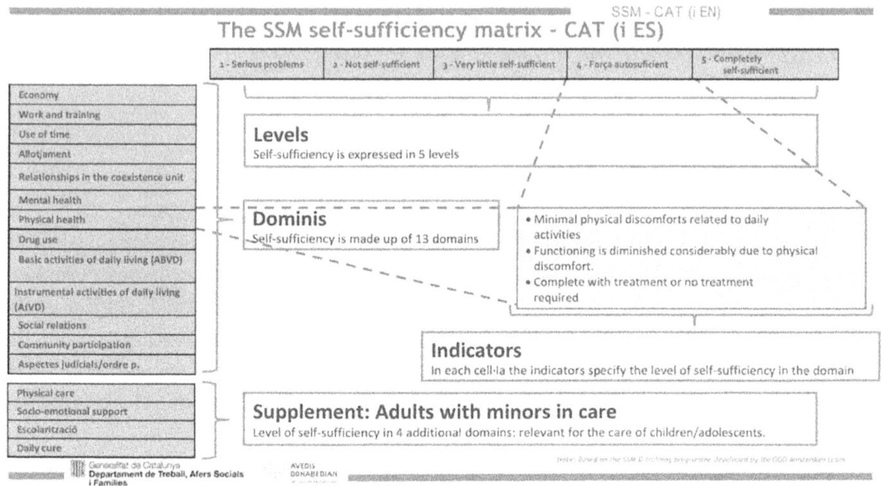

Fig. 3.1 The Self-Sufficiency Matrix (SSM)

Fig. 3.2 The ABM process

exemplar agent attributes. Following the use, refinement and validation of Ruleset 1 through gamification, the ABM's logic was translated into another serious game for stakeholder engagement. In a subsequent gamification workshop, stakeholders collaboratively adapted the game's rules. From the records of this gameplay, an improved assessment criterion (Ruleset2) was accomplished.

Within this context, the gamification and the ABM were employed to examine the perceptions, attitudes, and acceptance of AI-based social assessment technologies among local policymakers and administrative agencies. Crucially, the ABM ensured that the rulesets were logically coherent and complete, thus serving as a structured foundation for algorithmic refinement, as such rulesets often fail to account for informal practices, which may be perceived as inadequate or yield unintended systemic outcomes. Consequently, any ruleset requires stakeholder engagement, particularly by incorporating the insights and experiential knowledge of social workers or clerks who employ, define, and interpret rulesets like the Self-Sufficiency Matrix or SSM-Cat used in the gamification and ABM.

Therefore, the gamification workshop was designed to examine social workers' decision-making behaviours within policy implementation using the SSM-Cat. Participants were tasked with allocating limited social service resources among applicants, many of whom presented multifaceted and complex needs. The clerks' objective was to distribute resources in a manner that maximized aggregate applicant well-being. As previously mentioned, the model was adapted from the SSM-Cat to identify individuals with complex care needs across 13 dimensions. However, for operational simplicity, the simulation focused only on six key applicant attributes: 1) household income; 2) accommodation status; 3) employment and training; 4) mental health; 5) physical health; and 6) number of dependents.

Each attribute was scored on a scale of 1 (low self-sufficiency) to 5 (high self-sufficiency), yielding a composite need score between 6 and 30 per applicant. At the start of each round, applicants demonstrating self-sufficiency (defined as scoring ≤ 2 across all six well-being dimensions) remained at home. All other applicants were randomly distributed among available clerks for evaluation. Clerks assessed applicants using an algorithmic decision-making process based on a predefined ruleset and the applicants' attribute profiles.

At the end of each round, the social service budget was distributed to successful applicants in order of severity: the highest-scoring applicant was allocated an amount equal to their overall need score, then the next highest, and so on until the budget for that round was used up. Applicants' need scores were then updated:

- If the applicant received support: one need category improves (score decreases by 1).
- If the applicant did not receive support: one need category worsens (score increases by 1), as well as all categories with a score ≥ 4.
- Additionally, there was a 10% chance that one attribute worsens by 1 and a 10% chance that one improved by 1.
- If there were any critically needy applicants (overall need score $\geq$ threshold) at the end of the round, this impacted the upcoming round's available budget, but did not improve applicants' need scores. The run ended if there was no budget left at the beginning of a round to allocate to applicants.

After the gamification, the ABM simulated a number of rounds (100) from applicants (20) who were either at home or queuing at a social service desk. The number of desks corresponded to the user-defined number of clerks (5). The model was developed using NetLogo (see Fig. 3.3 for the interface representation after ten simulation rounds).

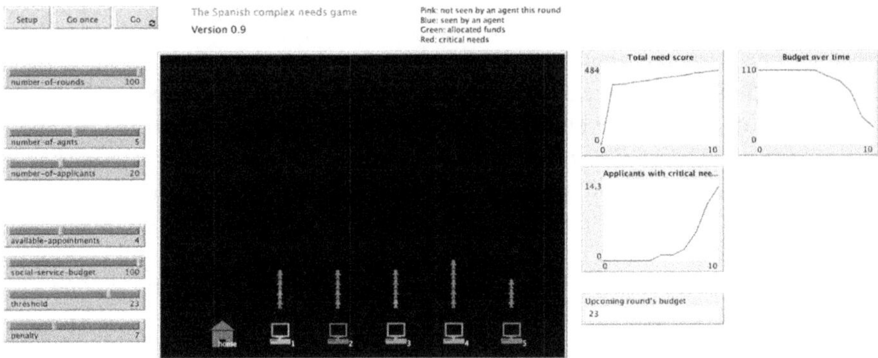

Fig. 3.3 Spanish case study ABM

Each simulation round represented 1 day in the agents' activity cycle (home, desk, office meeting, home), with round completion occurring when all agents returned to the home state. For the attributes of household income and number of dependents, applicants were comparatively ranked within their cohort, receiving need scores between 1 and 5 based on their relative position in the distribution.

Through participation in the gamification, clerks (agents) were expected to cultivate a shared interpretive culture regarding fairness as they progressively aligned their evaluations of applicant profiles using the Self-Sufficiency Matrix (SSM-Cat). This objective was aligned with the tool's primary purpose: to systematically identify complex social care needs following specialized training. A critical finding emerged from stakeholder deliberations: certain assessment criteria routinely employed by social workers were absent from the SSM-Cat framework. This prompted debate over whether these criteria should be formally incorporated into the tool to reflect current practice or whether prevailing practices should instead adapt to the existing matrix.

To illustrate this process, we show an example of improvements from the initial ruleset (ruleset 1) to the improved assessment criterion (ruleset 2) after one round of playing (see Fig. 3.4). While the use of ruleset 1 shows a system where most applicants' situations deteriorated, the use of ruleset 2 after the first gamification and simulation clearly demonstrates a highly effective intervention where the vast majority of applicants saw their need scores improve, thus indicating a highly efficient allocation strategy. In other words, while the process may depict a system under significant strain, if the allocation process or ruleset is not appropriate and the budget is insufficient, it prevents the overall situation from degrading even more. In contrast, if the ruleset becomes a highly successful round of intervention, the system is able to provide support to the vast majority of applicants, leading to a net improvement in the community's overall well-being.

Notably, what clerks and other stakeholders demonstrated by playing and interacting with the simulation was an acute awareness of biases and discriminatory practices in social service allocation within their context and actively sought to mitigate such risks. It is also worth mentioning that despite this shared commitment to equity, initial rounds of the simulation revealed substantial divergence in decision-making outcomes, even when evaluating identical applicant profiles. This variability underscored significant discrepancies in how individual social workers interpreted the SSM-Cat's criteria. In response, stakeholders concurred on the necessity of developing a unified interpretive culture across agencies regarding the application of the SSM-Cat. They further acknowledged that structured training incorporating profile-based case studies and narrative exercises, as modelled in the simulation, could facilitate this goal. These observations suggest that collaborative decision-making processes, characterized by deliberative discussion and knowledge exchange, may foster consensus on evaluation standards and promote more consistent implementation of the assessment tool.

	Ruleset 1		Ruleset 2	
	Scores round 1	Scores round 2	Scores round 1	Scores round 2
Applicant 1	3	4	3	2
Applicant 2	2	3	4	3
Applicant 3	1	2	3	2
Applicant 4	3	2	3	2
Applicant 5	2	3	3	2
Applicant 6	4	3	2	1
Applicant 7	2	3	3	2
Applicant 8	2	3	3	2
Applicant 9	1	2	2	1
Applicant 10	2	1	2	1
Applicant 11	4	3	3	2
Applicant 12	3	4	4	3
…	…	…	…	…

Fig. 3.4 Example of improvements from Ruleset 1 to Ruleset 2

Dissemination and Primary Concerns

Although this project has been primarily focused on some social services in Catalonia, it is reasonable to believe that the main and the specific concerns extend beyond our case study. Within this context, we can state that a primary concern is the pressing need to build specialized translation capacity within the so-called science-policy interface. Effective dissemination of AI research findings to policymakers requires a cadre of professionals equally fluent in complex technical concepts such as algorithmic bias, predictive modelling, and ethics in AI, and the nuanced realities of policy formulation and implementation. Currently, Spain's advisory systems suffer from a shortage of these crucial "knowledge brokers" who can interpret and contextualize technical research for political decision-makers while simultaneously communicating policy constraints back to researchers. This gap becomes especially critical when advising on sensitive AI applications in welfare provision, healthcare diagnostics, or educational assessment systems, where technical choices have profound societal consequences (Birhane 2021). The absence of such translation expertise risks creating either oversimplified policy responses to complex AI challenges or technically sound but politically unfeasible recommendations.

Equally important is the challenge of creating participatory evidence systems that move beyond traditional technocratic models of scientific advice. For AI applications in social services, effective policymaking must incorporate not just technical expertise but also public values, ethical considerations, and local community knowledge. Current advisory models frequently exclude these vital perspectives, potentially resulting in AI systems that, while technically proficient, fail to account for ground-level realities or community-specific needs. Developing new interface structures that systematically blend rigorous technical evidence with community expertise through deliberative forums, citizen assemblies, and participatory design processes could help bridge this gap. Such approaches used in the AI FORA project would be particularly valuable for AI applications affecting vulnerable populations, where the risk of algorithmic harm is greatest and the need for inclusive policymaking is most acute. Underpinning all these challenges is a key issue for both data governance and evidence-based AI policymaking.

The AI FORA project has also made clear that effective regulation and implementation of AI in social services requires access to comprehensive, high-quality administrative data while respecting privacy concerns and ethical boundaries. Despite progress in these areas, significant gaps remain in data accessibility, standardization, and sharing frameworks. Researchers and policymakers alike face obstacles in accessing key datasets needed to properly evaluate AI systems' performance or assess their social impacts. Addressing these limitations through improved data governance structures with appropriate privacy safeguards and ethical oversight would clearly help the quality of AI research and strengthen the evidence base for policy decisions. This becomes particularly crucial for monitoring AI systems already deployed in social services, where continuous evaluation and adjustment are essential to prevent unintended consequences. A practical example of this for the project was also the use of the PIO Model from the Observatory for Ethics in Artificial Intelligence of Catalonia, an assessment tool based on Principles, Indicators and Observables (see www.oeiac.cat) that aims to facilitates compliance with current rules and regulations on risks associated with AI through a comprehensive verification process.

Moreover, it is also worth noting that these structural and procedural challenges exist within a broader cultural context that requires transformation. While some institutions have shown growing appreciation for scientific input in recent years, many policymakers still approach AI through either overly optimistic or excessively cautious lenses, thus viewing it either as a technological panacea or an unmanageable risk rather than as a complex tool that requires nuanced, evidence-based governance. This dichotomous thinking can lead to either uncritical adoption of AI systems or blanket prohibitions that stifle potential benefits. Strengthening the role of scientific advice in this domain could provide a crucial counterbalance, grounding policy debates in empirical assessments of AI's actual social impacts rather than speculative extremes.

Addressing Bias and Modelling Together

The work undertaken in our case study using an interacting cycle of agent-based modelling and serious games points to an approach by which the technology can be specified in a stakeholder-driven way, so that it is more transparent and discursive about bias and discrimination. In addition, it includes values such as the social justice concept of the society in which it will be used and is responsive to the needs of vulnerable groups.

However, it is well documented that AI technology not only may provide biased information but also may inadvertently reinforce existing cultural, social, and economic inequalities (Eubanks 2018). Thus, if an AI system is trained on data that reflects unequal access to resources or opportunities, it may further entrench these disparities by providing advantages to dominant groups. This problem is especially important when used in the context of social assessment. "It's the data, stupid!" is an often-cited phrase indicating that, though data is the problem, data is data and cannot be changed.

Therefore, one of the critical issues with the use of AI is to analyse sensitive administrative data that presents both significant potential and notable challenges for improving social services targeting vulnerable populations. While local administrative datasets contain invaluable insights for shaping effective policies, their analysis often suffers from systemic biases that can distort findings and lead to flawed decision-making (Zajko 2022).

Data Reliability and ABM

Throughout this project, we have seen two particularly persistent issues undermine the reliability of data: inconsistent recording practices over time and inherent statistical biases in representation. These inconsistencies create substantial barriers to accurate analysis, as definitions of key metrics like service use or vulnerability status frequently change across reporting periods. For instance, what qualifies as "housing insecure" or generally "at-risk" in 1 year may be measured differently in the next, thus making comparisons difficult. Simultaneously, statistical biases emerge when certain demographic groups or geographic areas appear disproportionately in the data, either due to uneven service accessibility or reporting discrepancies. These representation gaps can cause AI systems to develop skewed understandings of community needs and (potentially) exacerbate existing inequities in service provision.

Beyond mere communication of the importance of these issues, addressing these challenges requires moving beyond purely technical solutions to embrace a more holistic approach. For this purpose, we have actively engaged with a range of stakeholders, mostly frontline social workers and policy officials, in order to identify and mitigate potential biases. Social workers have been of particular importance to contribute practical knowledge about how data collection realities differ from official protocols, while policy officials and social workers alike provide essential perspectives on how administrative categories actually reflect lived experiences. Furthermore, the importance of local context has been fundamental to develop a collaborative methodology that may help create better AI tools that are both technically sound and contextually appropriate for specific communities. This contextual sensitivity becomes particularly critical when working with vulnerable populations, where standardized approaches often overlook crucial nuances affecting service accessibility and effectiveness. Hence, the integration of AI with stakeholder expertise represents a significant shift from traditional practices in social service delivery. Rather than positioning technology as a standalone solution, the AI FORA approach has helped to gain a better understanding not only of the presence of biases in administrative records and to generate more reliable insights into community needs and program effectiveness, but also on the system limitations and decision-making processes as they remain crucial for building trust among both service providers and recipients.

As we have seen earlier, an important way to take this forward is by incorporating policy modelling techniques, particularly agent-based modelling (ABM), which has emerged as a critical interface between scientific research and policymaking, especially in complex domains such as AI governance for social services. At its core, policy modelling functions as a powerful translation mechanism that converts abstract theoretical concepts and empirical findings into tangible, policy-relevant scenarios. Since these models can illustrate phenomena that would otherwise remain theoretical -showing, for instance, how algorithmic bias might systematically disadvantage certain demographic groups in welfare eligibility or how the introduction of predictive tools in child protective services could alter caseworker decision-making patterns over time—it is particularly valuable in overcoming the cognitive barriers that often prevent policymakers from fully engaging with technical research.

However, it also needs to be said that the effective use of policy modelling for dissemination requires careful attention to several critical factors. First, model transparency is paramount as policymakers must understand the key assumptions and limitations underlying simulations to avoid misplaced confidence in model outputs. There is a particular risk of creating new "black boxes" when sophisticated models are presented as oracular systems rather than as tools for evidence-based policies. Second, continuous validation against real-world data is equally important, especially for modelling and improving AI systems that may evolve in unexpected ways post-deployment. Needless to say that the most effective policy modelling initiatives incorporate mechanisms for ongoing refinement as new empirical evidence emerges.

Clustering Analysis

In addition to ABM, we have also seen in our project that integrating clustering analysis can further enhance the robustness and granularity of policy models. Clustering analysis, a method used to group data points with similar characteristics, can help identify patterns and segments within administrative datasets that might not be immediately apparent. For example, in the context of welfare eligibility, clustering analysis has helped us reveal distinct groups within the population that are affected differently by algorithmic decisions, which also serves policymakers to gain a better understanding of how biases manifest and propagate within specific subgroups. Further, this type of analysis can be used in conjunction with ABM to refine the parameters and assumptions of the models. For instance, if we consider the implementation of predictive tools for housing vulnerability services, clustering analysis can help identify different types of caseworker decision-making patterns based on historical data on applicants' profiles, and these clusters can then be used to create diverse agent profiles in an ABM simulation, each representing a distinct decision-making style. By incorporating these techniques, it is possible to analyse an "interpretation culture" on fairness issues as agents may or may not agree in judging applicants' profiles. In addition, the combination of clustering analysis and ABM can facilitate the identification of emergent behaviours and systemic risks that might not be evident through traditional analytical methods. In other words, this integrated approach can provide further understanding of the potential impacts of policy changes, thus allowing policymakers to anticipate and mitigate unintended consequences more effectively.

Future Directions

The findings from this study highlight the necessity for policymakers to develop nuanced approaches to AI adoption in social services that move beyond technical capabilities to address systemic and ethical dimensions. First and foremost, there must be more rigorous mechanisms to distinguish evidence-based AI applications from speculative claims, particularly given the pervasive hype surrounding algorithmic solutions in public sector contexts. Our work with the SSM-Cat tool and Agent-Based Modelling (ABM) simulations demonstrates that meaningful evaluation requires both quantitative validation and qualitative insights from frontline practitioners. This dual approach helps surface hidden assumptions in algorithmic systems while ensuring they align with the complex realities of social service provision, where vulnerable populations often bear disproportionate risks from untested technologies.

Building on these insights, we believe that future research must prioritize the development of comprehensive evaluation frameworks that assess AI systems through interdisciplinary lenses. Such frameworks should integrate technical metrics like clustering analysis for bias detection with sociotechnical considerations drawn from stakeholder participation. The significant variability in how social workers interpreted identical applicant profiles in our simulations, despite using the same assessment tool, reveals the critical need for standardized yet adaptable implementation protocols. These protocols should be co-designed with diverse stakeholders to account for contextual factors that pure algorithmic approaches might miss, particularly in what Eubanks (2018) conceptualizes as low-rights environments, where marginalized groups have limited recourse against technological harms.

Further, the ABM approach employed in this study offers distinct methodological advantages for examining these complex socio-technical dynamics. By simulating interactions between heterogeneous actors (social workers, applicants, and algorithmic systems) within an institutional environment, ABM captures emergent phenomena that traditional evaluation methods overlook. Our model's capacity to reveal inter-practitioner variability in SSM-Cat interpretation, despite identical training protocols, also demonstrates how ABM surfaces latent inconsistencies in policy implementation. Furthermore, since the model can replicate real-world uncertainties, it is particularly useful to provide policymakers with a robust sandbox for stress-testing allocation algorithms before deployment. As such, the approach represents a significant advance over static risk-assessment frameworks, thus enabling dynamic analysis of how micro-level decisions aggregate into systemic patterns of resource distribution.

The ABM methodology also provides a unique platform for participatory policy refinement through its inherent modularity and transparency. Unlike black-box AI systems, using programs such as NetLogo for implementation allowed stakeholders to visually track how rule modifications can have a particular effect through the simulated ecosystem. This aligns with scholarly consensus that computational social science methods must maintain interpretability in public sector contexts, particularly when the evaluation of a simulation is guided by the expectations, anticipations and experience of the community that uses it (Ahrweiler and Gilbert 2005). In this sense, the gamification workshops' success in providing the conditions for deliberation about fairness criteria suggests that ABM continues to have potential not only for the construction process (i.e. as a consensus-building tool) but also to apply evaluation methods typically used for everyday simulations to scientific simulation and vice versa. Although it remains to be seen whether or not future applications could integrate machine learning to analyse emergent cluster patterns in decision-making behaviours, it is becoming increasingly apparent that identifying implicit bias warrants intervention. Although current automated decision-making (ADM) systems can, in principle, be laid bare for all to see, the sheer complexity of these systems based on deep learning models prevents straightforward monitoring (Dowding and Taylor 2024). Therefore, hybrid methodologies that position ABM not merely as an evaluative tool, but as a more transformative approach to advance transparency and explainability in algorithmic governance are crucial if we believe that a significant problem of trust in ADM systems should be addressed at the level of stakeholders and institutions.

Ultimately, the AI FORA research advocates for a paradigm shift in how AI systems are developed for social services, positioning co-creation as central rather than ancillary to the process. The participatory methods piloted in this study, including ABM simulations and gamification workshops, point towards more inclusive governance models. In addition, our experience with the Pigall project as an extension of the AI FORA project confirms that qualitative insights from social workers are essential for pre-empting ethical pitfalls, while ABM provides a structured environment to prototype and validate solutions. By combining statistical techniques with deliberative stakeholder engagement, we can develop AI tools that are both technically robust and socially accountable, thus transforming algorithmic decision-making from a tool of potential exclusion to one of empowerment in an era of growing public-sector automation.

We have seen that our system's core complexity lies in its mandate to serve individuals and families with multifaceted vulnerabilities, often dealing with intersecting issues like poverty, migration, unemployment, mental health, and disability. Thus, frontline social workers operate within this fragmented structure, tasked with assessing complex, real-life situations and allocating limited resources according to regional laws and local protocols. The challenge is to balance standardized rights-based entitlements with the need for personalized, holistic support in a context of chronic underfunding and administrative complexity. Indeed, this has also made evident that the Spanish system is a critical case study for understanding how technology may impact a decentralized, yet universally aimed, safety net. In conclusion, our case study reinforces the potential benefits of using the AI FORA process across a complex local social services system that requires the connected, person-focused work that also defines effective local social services.

Acknowledgement Research presented in this chapter has been funded by the German VolkswagenStiftung under grant agreement number 98 560.

References

Ahrweiler, P., & Gilbert, N. (2005). Caffè Nero: The evaluation of social simulation. *Journal of Artificial Societies and Social Simulation, 8*(4), 14. https://www.jasss.org/8/4/14.html

Birhane, A. 2021. Algorithmic injustice: A relational ethics approach. *Patterns, 2*(2). https://doi.org/10.1016/j.patter.2021.100205

Criado, J. I., Alcaide-Muñoz, L., & Liarte, I. (2025). Two decades of public sector innovation: Building an analytical framework from a systematic literature review of types, strategies, conditions, and results. *Public Management Review, 27*(3), 623–652. https://doi.org/10.1080/14719037.2023.2254310

Dowding, K., & Taylor, B. R. (2024). Algorithmic decision-making, agency costs, and institution-based trust. *Philosophy & Technology, 37*(2), 68. https://doi.org/10.1007/s13347-024-00757-5

Eubanks, V. (2018). *Automating inequality: How high-tech tools profile, police, and punish the poor*. Picador, St. Martin's Press.

Lauriks, S., de Wit, M. A. S., Buster, M. C. A., Fassaert, T. J. L., van Wifferen, R., & Klazinga, N. S. (2014). The use of the Dutch self-sufficiency matrix (SSM-D) to inform allocation decisions to public mental health care for homeless people. *Community Mental Health Journal, 50*, 870–878. https://doi.org/10.1007/s10597-014-9707-x

Richmond, M., Pampel, F., Zarcula, F., Howey, V., & McChesney, B. (2015). Reliability of the Colorado family support assessment: A self-sufficiency matrix for families. *Research on Social Work Practice, 27*(6), 695–703. https://doi.org/10.1177/1049731515596072

Sabater Coll, A., López, B., Campdepadrós, R., & Sánchez, C. (2025). Participatory action research for AI in social services: An example of local practice in Spain. In P. Ahrweiler (Ed.), *Participatory artificial intelligence in public social services. Artificial intelligence, simulation and society*. Springer. https://doi.org/10.1007/978-3-031-71678-2_4

Zajko, M. (2022). Artificial intelligence, algorithms, and social inequality: Sociological contributions to contemporary debates. *Sociology Compass, 16*(3), e12962. https://doi.org/10.1111/soc4.12962

Chapter 4
Using Agent-Based Modelling to Explore Possible Implications of AI Use in the Asylum Procedure in Germany

Elisabeth Späth, Martha Bicket, Martin Neumann, David Wurster, and Blanca Luque Capellas

Abstract The Agent-Based Model (ABM) described in this chapter simulates a simplified model of the asylum procedure in Germany, capturing registration, hearing, decision, and court appeal. Its primary aim is to visualize the complexity of the asylum process and highlight how artificial intelligence (AI) applications must be understood within their operational context. The model serves both as a heuristic tool for understanding decision-making and an instrument to examine potential barriers and trade-offs in using AI technologies, and what they might imply for those affected by the technology, i.e. refugees and street-level bureaucrats. The research aims will be approached with a parameter sensitivity analysis, exploring links between decisions by the Federal Office for Migration and Refugees (German acronym: BAMF) and appeal outcomes, as well as narrative scenarios that illustrate possible refugee pathways. These examples are contextualized with stakeholder perspectives exploring possible implications of AI use. The findings indicate that AI-based technologies are likely to make decision-making processes more opaque, undermining refugees' agency, and lead to dispersed accountability, especially if the structural problems as

E. Späth (✉) · D. Wurster · B. Luque Capellas
TISSS Lab, Institute of Sociology, Johannes Gutenberg University, Mainz, Germany
e-mail: espaeth@uni-mainz.de

D. Wurster
e-mail: dwurster@uni-mainz.de

B. Luque Capellas
e-mail: bluqueca@uni-mainz.de

M. Bicket
Centre for Research in Social Simulation, Department of Sociology, University of Surrey, University Campus, Guildford, UK
e-mail: m.bicket@surrey.ac.uk

M. Neumann
Brandenburg University of Technology, Cottbus, Germany
e-mail: neumama1@b-tu.de

P. Ahrweiler and N. Gilbert (eds.), *Participatory Modelling and Simulation to Improve AI-based Public Social Services*, Artificial Intelligence, Simulation and Society,
https://doi.org/10.1007/978-3-032-15283-1_4

well as risks of AI use remain neglected. The chapter concludes that early stakeholder engagement, technology assessment, and governance are crucial.

Introduction

In the context of migration, Agent-Based Modelling (ABM) has primarily focused on the analysis and prediction of "migration flows", often in relation to conflicts and climate change (Hinsch and Bijak 2022; Klabunde and Willekens 2016). A small but growing number of studies have addressed bureaucratic processes—particularly those involved in asylum procedures (e.g., Boshuijzen-van Burken et al. 2020). In Germany and other countries within and beyond Europe, the current asylum system is often referred to as an "asylum lottery" (Marshall 2025; Riedel and Schneider 2017), characterized by a *kafkaesque bureaucracy* (Eule et al. 2020) due to opaque and prolonged decision-making processes. Promising greater efficiency and objectivity, various types of artificial intelligence (AI)-based technologies are being increasingly incorporated into asylum-related decision-making by European governments (Ozkul 2023); recent political calls in Germany have advocated for "more AI and more judges" to accelerate asylum decision-making (Zeit Online 2025). The Federal Office for Migration and Refugees (German acronym: BAMF)—the authority responsible for asylum procedures in Germany—has been using an AI-based technology, "Dialect Identification Assistant System" (DIAS), since 2017 to determine asylum seekers' countries of origin. This has been criticized for various, significant reasons: next to inaccuracy problems, since relying mainly on dialects to determine a person's country of origin is unreliable (Lulamae 2022; Ozkul 2023), as language cannot be strictly defined by national borders, and evolves throughout a person's life course as well as socialization. While each of those AI-based technologies requires specific ethical, legal, and practical considerations, as the case of DIAS has shown (e.g. Ozkul 2025; Palmiotto 2024; van der Kist 2025), AI applications generally need to be understood in the context in which they are operationalized, in terms of the processes involved in decision-making and the factors that co-determine decision-making outcomes.

This chapter introduces an ABM designed to explore these complexities, examining implications of AI-based technologies through the lens of stakeholder perspectives. The ABM models the dynamics between state decision-making and refugees as they navigate the asylum process (e.g., registration, hearing, decision), as well as related post-decision processes (e.g., court appeals) within the German context: While administrative staff face high workloads and policy flux, refugees are often confronted with opaque procedures, experiencing the administration as a "black box". This can lead to perceptions of unfair treatment, unjust outcomes, and increased likelihood of court appeals. The purpose of the model is to "untangle" the asylum procedure and identify key points that are critical to assessment and outcomes. The hypothesis underpinning this approach is that the use of AI, if applied to current institutional practices, may increase the opaqueness of decision-making and lead to more dispersed accountability. As such, the model serves as a heuristic tool for exploring the implications of AI-based technologies in asylum systems.

The ABM's output is analysed via a two-part methodology. On the one hand, to understand the macro-level of asylum decision-making, a parameter sensitivity analysis was conducted examining the impact of parameters on the simulation results, to explore the relation between the workload of BAMF and the number of (un)successful court appeals. However, a sensitivity analysis only allows a static analysis that does not enable for dissecting the causal pathway from the start to the end condition of a simulation (León-Medina 2017). This can be achieved by following selected agents and providing a narrative description of the rules executed for these agents during the simulation (micro-level perspective). This approach could help to develop an understanding of individual behaviour and motivation vis-à-vis individual (institutional) decision-making illustrated with synthetically constructed narratives (based on empirical as well as fictional data). Thereby, "insider" and "outsider" perspectives (cf. Clegg et al. 2016) of asylum bureaucracy could be understood in an illustrative way.[1]

The overarching purpose of the ABM is to provide a tool, on the one hand, to visualize the different factors involved. In a tested and calibrated form, ABMs can support decision-makers to gain a better understanding of the complexity of the policy domain (Gilbert et al. 2018). On the other hand, in relation to possible AI use, this ABM could offer a framework to anticipate system interactions, outcomes, and explore trade-offs, understanding the relationship between individual behaviour at the microlevel and system behaviour at the macro-level (Ahrweiler 2017).[2]

Description of the Model

Simulations, such as ABMs, typically rest on a simplification of a complex social system. In these simulations, heterogeneous agents (individuals or organizations), differ in their behaviours, and decision-making processes. This diversity enables ABMs to simulate complex systems by reflecting real-world variation and interactions. Importantly, the main value of this lies much more in being a tool for exploring the types of issues and contributing factors that one might encounter in such a system than being accurate or representative (Hinsch and Bijak 2022). The following ABM is a (very) simplified model of the asylum procedure in Germany. The ABM's design derived from desktop and empirical research (conducted in 2022 and 2023), to inform the processes as well as "parameters" co-determining decision-making outcomes.

---

[1] This distinction draws upon the analysis by Clegg et al. (2016): "Weber's focus is concentrated on the mechanics and working of bureaucracy from the insider point of view of the ideal typical bureaucrat; Kafka looks at the bureaucratic subject from the experience of the outsider, from the perspective of the subject; his interest is in the phenomenology of power rather than issues of governance." (p. 160)

[2] While there was no direct validation of the ABM with participants taking part in the research, a simplified representation of the model was presented and evaluated by policymakers.

Although many more parameters could have been chosen, especially more "non-human actors" (Latour 2005), such as protocols and regulations (see Andreetta and Borrelli 2024), a limit was necessary to design and operationalize the model. Furthermore, it was a deliberate decision not to include a parameter on the AI-based technology (e.g. DIAS) itself, especially because there was a lack of information on its use in the different stages (registration and hearing) and to what extent this influences the final decision.[3]

The main sources for designing the ABM (as well as the narratives in Sect. Narratives: Understanding Critical Junctures in Decision-Making (Micro-Perspective) and Exploring Implications of AI Use with Stakeholders.) were qualitative interviews with refugees and participatory modelling sessions (Quimby and Beresford 2022) with nine "experts". Experts are here defined as professionals working in organizations, such as welfare organizations and refugee councils, who provide support and counselling to migrants and refugees (e.g. legal advice; counselling and information on supporting organizations and infrastructures). In four small focus groups, in a gamification setting, the experts were asked to imagine the path from registration at the BAMF branch until a major (bureaucratic) milestone, such as being economically independent or even naturalization (the final stage/goals were defined by experts themselves). The expert groups were randomly assigned one of two *fictional* refugee profiles. Creating a gamification setting to inform the ABM was based on the idea of involving experts to "co-construct an abstract representation of a real-world system" and gaining an insider and local knowledge to widen the understanding" (cf. Type 1, Game → ABM, Szczepanska et al. 2022), i.e. of the asylum system in Germany. The gamification approach centred around thinking about scenarios regarding barriers ("what can go wrong") and opportunities, for instance, ways how to come to terms with these barriers.

While the complete ABM (see Fig. 4.1) also captures processes after the asylum procedure (e.g. having a job/no job/good job; hardship commission; cf. Station "post-decision"), the following description (including results and discussion, respectively) will only focus on the asylum application procedure: registration, hearing, decision and court appeal.

Agents

Each applicant is initialized with a range of attributes[4] that impact their progression through the asylum and appeals processes:

---

[3] Based on an inquiry by Ozkul (2025), the BAMF stated that "there were no statistics on this matter" (ibid.).

[4] As stated before, more parameters, i.e. attributes could have been chosen. The following attributes ascribed to the agents can be considered as "dominant" in the empirical data as well as in the literature, among other studies: "federal state receiving the application" (Riedel and Schneider 2017); "administrator/organisational bias" (Affolter 2021; Dahlvik 2018; Gundacker et al. 2025; Schittenhelm and Schneider 2017); "health/vulnerability status" (e.g. Boettcher and Neuner 2022;

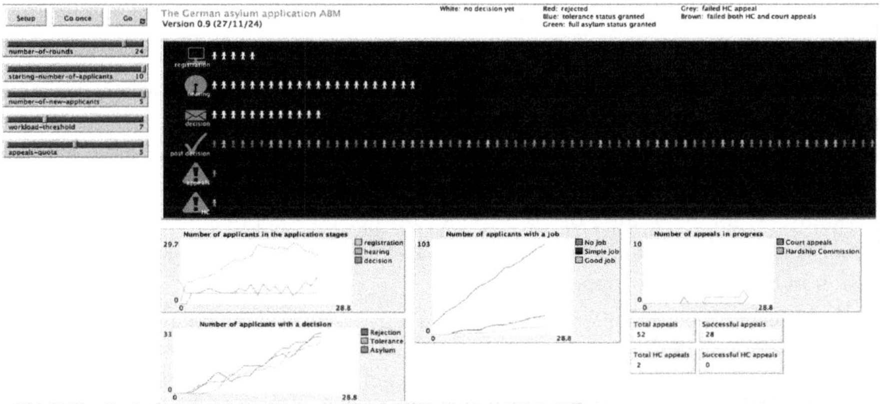

Fig. 4.1 German asylum application procedure; Applicants are colour coded (white: "no decision yet"; green: "asylum"; blue: "tolerance"; red: "rejected")

- **Country of origin:** Applicants from certain countries have a higher chance of receiving asylum status than others. ["lower priority country of origin"; "higher priority country of origin"].
- **Documents:** Applicants may have full, partial, or no documentary evidence of their identity and education. ["all"; "some"; "none"].
- **Interpreter:** Deemed "good" if there is a positive match between the applicant and interpreter's genders, ethnicities and spoken languages. This determines the effectiveness of communication during the hearing stage, which increases an applicant's chances of progressing to the next stage of the application process. ["good"; "bad"; "none"].
- **Supporter:** The support of a lawyer, volunteer or migration counsellor from a welfare organization. Having a supporter improves an applicant's chances of a positive, i.e. fair decision outcome. ["yes"; "no"].
- **Health status:** May influence an applicant's vulnerability and support needs. ["0= high vulnerability"; "5 = low vulnerability"].
- **Federal state (bias):** The federal state where the application is received and processed. [8 federal states with "high bias"; 8 federal states with "low bias"].
- **Administrator (bias):** The administrator is (here) the person who is responsible for the decision. The outcome of the decision is co-determined by the organizational bias/culture (represented by the federal state bias) as well as the administrative workload (if it is higher than a defined workload threshold) ["high bias"; "low bias"].
- **Status decision (outcome):** "waiting", "asylum", "tolerance", "rejection".
- **Number of years in Germany**: 0–3 years.

Bradby et al. 2015; Mulcaire et al. 2024; Schock et al. 2015); role of social and human capital co-impacting other attributes, such as supporting infrastructures (Kosyakova and Brücker 2020)

Environment and Interactions over Time

Applicants are positioned at one of four "stations": registration, hearing, decision, and court appeal.

Registration: A given number of applicants begin at the registration station, which marks the beginning of their pathway through the asylum application procedure in Germany. At the beginning of each round, further new applicants enter the system here. Each applicant at the registration station automatically progresses to the hearing station in the following round.

Hearing: Applicants are randomly assigned an interpreter for the hearing stage at initialization: good, bad or none. If the interpreter is "good", indicating a positive match between the applicant and interpreter's genders, ethnicities and spoken languages, then there is a 90% chance that the applicant will proceed to the decision station for the following round. If the interpreter is "bad", indicating a less successful match, then the chance of progressing to the next station in the next round is only 30%. If the applicant was not assigned an interpreter, then they only have a 10% chance of progressing to the next station in the next round. Applicants who are not successful remain at the hearing station and will have another chance to progress in each successive round.

Decision: Applicants at the decision station wait for the opportunity to have their application assessed by an administrator who will award them one of three statuses: rejection, tolerance status or full asylum status. Applicants may have to wait multiple rounds to be seen.

Applicants are more likely to be seen and receive full asylum status if they have complete documents (proof of identity and education, etc.), a supporter such as a lawyer, voluntary worker or counsellor from a welfare organization, and are from a high priority country of origin. Applicants are less likely to be seen or receive asylum status if there are missing documents or if their federal state's caseload (the number of applicants in that state in the registration, hearing or decision stages) is high. Depending on the status awarded, the applicant will receive permission to work or right to remain in Germany accordingly (see Table 4.1).

Court appeal: Applicants file an appeal if they want their application to be reconsidered by the courts. They may do so because they feel that they have experienced discrimination, or that their case has been treated unfairly or poorly (e.g. administrative errors).

Table 4.1 Interrelation between status and refugees' right-to-remain and -work

Status awarded	Work permission	Right to remain
Rejection	No	No
Tolerance	No	Yes (but may be subject to change)
Asylum	Yes	Yes

Eligibility

Applicants who have received full refugee status do not appeal their status. For everyone else, if the applicant's administrator had a workload higher than a given threshold then there is a 70% chance that the applicant will file an appeal. This is based on the assumption that the higher the workload, the greater the chance that an administrative error may have taken place. Similarly, if there was a high level of organizational bias then there is another 30% chance that the applicant will file an appeal.

Success Criteria

The same criteria above are applied again to decide which applicants are successful in their appeal. Those who had an administrator with a high workload have a 70% chance of being successful in their appeal, and those who had a high level of organizational bias, co-influenced by the federal state bias, have a further 30% chance.

Only a certain number of appeals can be heard by the courts each round. Appeals are processed until the appeals quota is reached for that round. Other applicants remain at the station to have their appeal heard at the next available opportunity in the following rounds.

If applicants are successful in their appeal, then their status improves to the next best decision outcome only (rejection is changed to tolerance; tolerance is changed to full asylum status).

Methodology, Results and Discussion

Parameter Sensitivity Analysis: Understanding the Link between BAMF'S Workload and Number of (Successful) Appeals (Macro-Perspective)

As analysed by Bogumil and Kuhlmann (2022), there is a correlation between workforce, the number of asylum applications being processed, and the quality of decisions made by the BAMF, which in turn impact the volume and success rate of appeals. To "trace" this correlation in the ABM and to understand the macro-level context of asylum procedure decision-making, a parameter sensitivity analysis, a standard tool for understanding the dynamics and emergent patterns of agent-based simulation, has been conducted. Parameter sensitivity analysis consists of a systematic variation of key parameters of a model and a subsequent analysis of the corresponding variation in the simulation results. This enables an investigation of the impact of the parameter values on the model output and dynamics. A key question is whether the model dynamics is highly sensitive to the values of the parameter which is varied (i.e. whether it has a high causal influence) or whether the dynamics is quite robust with regard to this parameter (Borgonovo et al. 2022). Here, a parameter sensitivity analysis was conducted to explore the sensitivity of appeal outcomes in relation to the "workload threshold" of the BAMF, as the courts represent a pivotal role (cf. Thränhardt 2023). This threshold indicates the threshold at which the administration is overwhelmed by the workload, i.e. a high workload threshold represents a well-equipped administration, whereas a low workload threshold stands for an administration that will be rather overwhelmed. The workload threshold was varied between 5, 10, 15, and 20, while all other parameters were held constant. The static analysis reflects aggregated patterns with 1000 simulation runs per parameter constellation.

The results of the sensitivity analysis show that the overall number of appeals remains consistently high at around 2/3 of all applicants until the workload threshold reaches 20, its highest level, i.e. indicating a "better-equipped administration" (see Fig. 4.2). However, even more significant than the *quantity*, i.e. number of staff, is the *quality* of the decision, which is displayed by the relation between all appeals and successful appeals (see Table 4.2): while more than half of all appeals are successful when the workload threshold ranges from 5 to 15, the number of successful appeals is halved at the highest workload threshold level. The proportion of successful appeals serves as an indicator of the asylum system's legitimacy from the perspective of the (bureaucratic) system itself: an appeal is successful when the court detects a mistake in the original decision-making process. Conversely, when the workload threshold is 20, the proportion of successful appeals drops significantly (by more than 5%) as fewer errors occur when the administration is not over-stretched.

Whereas this sensitivity analysis provides insights into how the number and success rate of appeals shift with changes in the workload threshold and can thereby

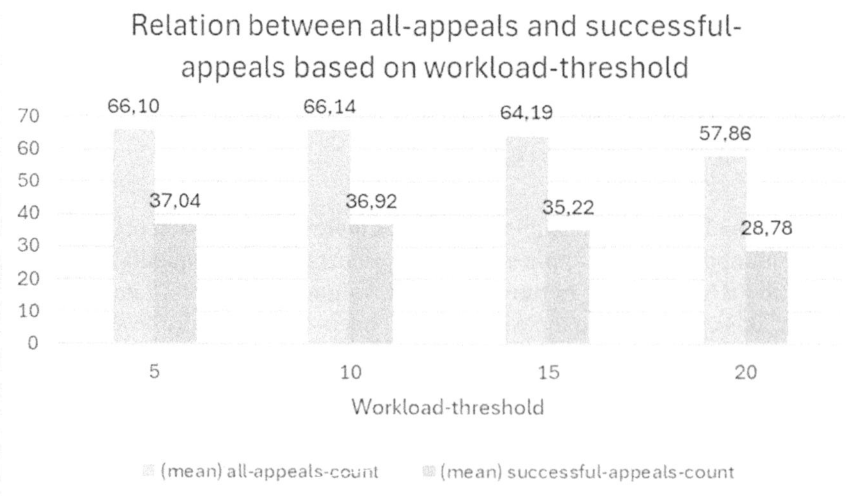

Fig. 4.2 Parameter sensitivity analysis based on parameter "workload-threshold"

Table 4.2 Impact of parameter "workload-threshold" on number of (successful) appeals

Workload-threshold	Quotient all-appeals/successful-appeals	Decrease
5	56.04%	
10	55.82%	0.22%
15	54.86%	0.95%
20	49.74%	5.12%

only give an *indication* on the relation between appeals and successful appeals (at least in *this* analysis), the following narratives give some insights into possible*causal pathways*, i.e. the motivations behind or reasons for certain behaviours. This can be achieved by following selected agents through the simulation run (Squazzoni 2008).

Narratives: Understanding Critical Junctures in Decision-Making (Micro-Perspective) and Exploring Implications of AI Use with Stakeholders

To exemplify the experiences of refugees as they navigate their way through the asylum system, two agents (from 135 agents in 25 simulation rounds) were selected. These agents were mainly selected, on the one hand, to display a longer timespan via narratives (as these agents "enter" rather at the beginning of the simulation run), and on the other hand, because these agents file an appeal so that these scenarios could thereby be discussed in relation to possible AI implications. Their way is illustrated by Tables 4.3 and 4.4, followed by a narrative explaining the parameters that had an impact on the model's output ("critical junctures"), i. e. an agent's pathway. These narratives were synthetically constructed by combining the history of the agent with qualitative data from interviews (with refugees) and participatory modelling sessions, and interpreted via *fictional narratives* (Neumann and Lotzmann 2017), including *fictional refugee names.* The selection of individual pathways represents a form of selective, theoretical sampling (Corbin and Strauss 2008) from the simulation outputs to cover a spectrum of *possible pathways* a refugee can take through the asylum system. In contrast to traditional approaches to the analysis of simulation outputs, which focus on aggregated patterns at the macro level at the final stage of a simulation, the analysis of narratives delves into the micro level of the possible *causal pathway of agents* within the simulation run. A narrative-based approach is valuable because multiple perspectives can be considered simultaneously. In doing so, it offers insights into bureaucratic processes, forms of legitimization, and perceptions of relevant stakeholders. The following narratives will then be set into the context of exploring possible implications of AI use with stakeholders.

Table 4.3 Pathway Agent 7 (rejection)

round	country-of-origin	documents	supporter	health-status	interpreter	federal-state	workload-treshold	administrator-bias	years-in-germany	status-decision-outcome	right-to-stay	appealed
3	higher priority	some	no	3	good	11	7	low	0,250	rejection	no	0
4	higher priority	some	no	3	good	11	7	low	0,333	rejection	no	0
5	higher priority	some	no	0	good	11	7	low	0,417	rejection	no	yes
6	higher priority	some	no	0	good	11	7	low	0,500	rejection	no	yes
7	higher priority	some	no	0	good	11	7	low	0,583	rejection	no	yes
8	higher priority	some	no	0	good	11	7	low	0,667	rejection	no	yes
9	higher priority	some	no	0	good	11	7	low	0,750	rejection	no	yes
10	higher priority	some	no	0	good	11	7	low	0,833	rejection	no	yes

Table 4.4 Pathway Agent 12 (rejection -> tolerance)

round	country-of-origin	documents	supporter	health-status	interpreter	federal-state	workload-treshold	administrator-bias	years-in-germany	status-decision-outcome	right-to-stay	appealed
1	lower priority	some	yes	2	good	1	7	high	0,845	waiting	pending	0
2	lower priority	some	yes	2	good	1	7	high	0,928	waiting	pending	0
3	lower priority	some	yes	2	good	1	7	high	1,012	waiting	pending	0
4	lower priority	some	yes	2	good	1	7	high	1,095	rejection	no	0
5	lower priority	some	yes	2	good	1	7	high	1,178	rejection	no	0
6	lower priority	some	yes	2	good	1	7	high	1,262	rejection	no	0
7	lower priority	some	yes	2	good	1	7	high	1,345	rejection	no	0
8	lower priority	some	yes	5	good	1	7	high	1,428	tolerance	yes	yes
9	lower priority	some	yes	5	good	1	7	high	1,512	tolerance	yes	yes
10	lower priority	some	yes	5	good	1	7	high	1,595	tolerance	yes	yes

Narrative of Agent 7: Nadim B. From Syria (Status Decision Outcome: Rejection)

Nadim B. comes from Syria (for the purposes of the model, a country of origin with "higher priority" status) but has only some of his documents. During his flight, Nadim met someone who tells him it is better to say to have lost some documents. *"(…) unfortunately, they are being given bad advice, (…) by others, word of mouth advice (Supporter/Refugee from Afghanistan, Interview, R1)"; "(…) somebody told them that's better to say you don't have any papers, and then you have like a long time because they have to find out who you are"* (Expert 1, Participatory modelling, Group 1). After some waiting time, Nadim receives a rejection because his identity cannot be clarified. He becomes desperate and, after some time, he reaches out to a lawyer who helps him file an appeal (see box 1). However, the appeal is not successful, and Nadim's (mental and physical) health begin to deteriorate (see box 2). *"But my lawyer did and I waited again, after two months, a letter came back again, (…) I'm stressed all the time (…), and I can't sleep properly because I'm so sad (…). I've left my family, my town's broken too and that's all behind me, that's broken too, what should I do?"* (Refugee from Syria, Interview, R2).

Having only "some" documents, it could have been the case that the DIAS might be used to identify Nadim's country of origin, possibly leading to rejection. As already highlighted in the literature (see Ozkul 2025), one expert mentioned that it is not possible to apply an "objective standard" in determining the identity of someone based on their language or dialect spoken:

If the person is rejected (…) because there is doubt about this, then it is essential to appeal against this decision, because there is no objective standard for determining this, mainly based on dialects or something like that. Because Syria alone is a multi-ethnic state, there are a thousand different dialects. And they also like to speak their own languages when in doubt. It's not that simple. (…) In any case, I would always appeal against such a decision by artificial intelligence (…) because it cannot be that the impression a program has in legal proceedings carries more weight than the statement of the person concerned. I would find that quite disreputable if that were the case (Expert 8, Participatory modelling, Group 2).

Research participants in the focus groups and participatory modelling sessions emphasized the crucial importance of having an independent asylum procedure counselling beforehand, providing refugees with adequate support and guidance concerning all information relevant to the asylum procedure, thereby also addressing what was labelled as "misleading information". Additionally, the relationship between lengthy procedures, lack of perspective and their consequences for both health and the motivation to continue, partly due to limited options and a long waiting time, was considered. There was broad agreement that AI could facilitate *access to information* on supporting infrastructures (e.g. health services, activities, and legal support). The (final) quote, furthermore, raises an essential concern, namely whether AI might be more trusted or given more weight than individuals' testimonials in decision-making within the BAMF as well as by the courts.

Narrative of Agent 12: Meral F. From Iran (Status Decision Outcome: Rejection -> Tolerance)

Meral F. comes from Iran (for the purposes of the model, a country of origin with "lower priority" status) and could not take all the important documents with her. *"(…) that was difficult our way, because, without a passport, leaving home, (…). I was afraid of getting into prison, many many bad things happen, and especially for women, yes. Because, normally, rape, (…), it is the first consequence."* (Refugee from Iran, Interview, R3). During the hearing, Meral explains that she has been persecuted by state officials due to her active involvement in supporting women's rights in Iran. Although she reports receiving threats in her daily life, she does not feel safe sharing all details. Overall, the interviewer finds the report of the asylum seeker rather inconsistent and unclear; although she reported threats, the interviewer could not find sufficient evidence to support her statements. Based on the case report, the lack of documents, and the internal, rather restrictive guidelines within this specific BAMF branch, Meral receives a rejection after a while (see box 1). *"And every institution/ organization has a certain corporate culture, which doesn't necessarily have to be formalized or written down. But perhaps a department manager says, yes, you should take a particularly close look at the people (…), you take a particularly hard line."* (Expert 4, Participatory modelling, Group 2). Following her rejection, friends and some family members in Iran manage to send Meral some of her documents. Furthermore, she receives legal advice from an organization specialized in refugee law in Germany. This support helps her to formulate her arguments and empowers her to talk about her experiences with violence, and her fear (see box 2a/b). *"So the woman cannot, (…) she didn't say anything about the rape because she didn't want to say it to herself, didn't dare or so. Then she is rejected, then she appeals against this rejection in court (…). Then the judge is asking, "did you present/say that? And then she says, no, I didn't dare to do that."* (Expert 8, Participatory modelling, Group 4).

This case ("high administrator bias") could point to two different scenarios. On the one hand, according to the experts' perspectives, the tension (as in Meral's case) between what is said, what is not said and "what should have been said" is likely to evolve, among many other reasons, due to traumatic experiences, lack of support beforehand, and/or a "bad interpreter". In a context where there is a "high administrator bias", and possibly an AI-generated output rather supporting this bias, this may further exacerbate the problem that refugees' testimonial is based on how well they "perform" (see also van der Kist 2025), instead of providing them space to give a comprehensive account of past experiences and well-founded fear of persecution, which lies at the core of the hearing. Furthermore, experts expressed the concern that this "missing information" in the data set could again create further bias, which might be relevant for more complex systems, such as "case-matching" AI-based technologies (Ozkul 2023). On the other hand, one expert raised the concern that, even if an "optimally functioning AI" would be used, it remains unclear whether the AI's output can "overrule" this (administrator) bias:

> So AI should not have any political instrumentalization intentions (…), but hierarchies do that, they do that and that's really interesting. (…) Politically instrumentalized hierarchies are actually significant power factors, it doesn't mean that everything is right in every individual case, but the framework conditions describe it in such a way that it is extremely difficult for those affected to succeed in the system, as we can see from the recognition rates. Where there are heaps of positive recognition in the asylum procedure, for certain countries of origin, this is preceded by a political decision. (…) Quite independently of the individual narratives that are fed into the asylum applications in detail. But otherwise, if the assessment in the asylum procedure is only based on the individual narratives, then it is usually negative. Then the quotas are and that is due to these political guidelines. And I would like to see the authority that forgoes these political guidelines in favour of an optimally functioning AI. (Expert 8, focus group on possible AI integration)

The quote indicates that the potentials, or *hopes*, associated with AI, e.g. more objectivity, do not materialize automatically, given the (political) forces in play. This scenario puts into question a more general issue: to what extent are hierarchies reflected in the interpretation of AI-generated results, in how far street-level bureaucrats evaluate, or are trained to evaluate, these data and "weighing" them against their own perspective.

Both narratives illustrate (quite radically) that the *interplay of conditions* further deepens the power—and information asymmetry among refugees, decision-makers and, ultimately policymakers. Current and future (AI-based) assessment practices are likely to further undermine refugees' agency, especially due to the existing kafkaesque bureaucracy, and potentially further impact the asylum system's legitimacy by delegating responsibility to technology, neglecting the structural issues exacerbated through AI use.

From an "outsider perspective", it is hard to understand the processes as well as the assessment criteria. Refugees' agency has already been constrained and undermined in different ways through being confronted with vulnerabilities over a long-time span:

dealing with border controls, physical and mental violence as well as managing the economic implications. Past experiences, such as prior negative encounters with the officials in state institutions and current challenges, i.e. uncertainty regarding their future, waiting time and trauma, further influence individual decision-making and behaviour. It is not only crucial to take these vulnerabilities into account, but also the very structures *simultaneously* having a constraining, and disempowering impact. Participants considered support, possibly facilitated with AI technology, as very important regarding how refugees navigate through the asylum system. Related to this, transparency of decision-making processes was seen as fundamental, particularly with regard to knowing whether, and to what extent, an AI system had influenced the final decision, in order to enable intervention—for example, to clarify misunderstandings or to pursue legal action. When it comes to possibly appealing against the decision (cf. Nadim's case), this would of course require additional legal support.

The "insider perspective" that is, the standpoint of decision-makers and users of AI-based technologies—along with the persistent tension between asylum law, and the political objectives (Thränhardt 2023), are key factors to consider. Yet it remains unclear how exactly AI-generated results or recommendations influence decisions, particularly when organizational or political pressures favour different outcomes. Current approaches by political actors, implemented through street-level bureaucrats, tend to use AI primarily for legitimization (Späth 2025), invoking bureaucratic *values* such as efficiency, rationality, and objectivity (cf. "digital Weberianism", Muellerleile and Robertson 2018). This top-down mode of implementation disperses accountability among multiple actors being tasked with "making sense" of AI outputs, possibly of systems whose validity, or "meaningfulness" (e.g. systems like the DIAS), is highly contested. In the end, it remains highly questionable whether workload issues for street-level bureaucrats can be reduced, without compromising the quality of decision-making. Additionally, it is uncertain how far courts trust AI-assisted decisions made by the BAMF.

The asylum system (cf. Eule et al. 2020) as well as AI systems (cf. Cobbe et al. 2023) can be characterized as being operationalized by "many hands" (see also algorithmic value-chain model, Silva and Kenney 2018). Consequently, the prevailing implications cannot be seen from an "isolated" perspective, such as high workload within the BAMF or a controversial AI-based technology such as the DIAS, but in their intertwinement in the different processes. Importantly, AI-based technologies in this context should be understood as "epistemic technologies" (Alvarado 2023) because they co-shape both the epistemic content as well as the epistemic operation (ibid.), i.e. the assessment process, and thereby pre-structure decision-making for street-level bureaucrats. This occurs in a context in which "luck" can be considered a dominant, structural problem for refugees (Marshall 2025), and in which refugees' testimonial should be taken as the primary reference point. It is essential that the "promises" of AI, such as speeding up decision-making and reducing workload within the BAMF, should be weighed against the risk of creating additional forms of injustice towards vulnerable people, possibly further obscuring the decision-making processes, especially in case structural issues (e.g. different institutional practices across federal states, see Gundacker et al. 2025) remain untackled. Through the research participants' input, it has become clear that early stakeholder inclusion, especially considering "insider" as well as "outsider" perspectives of asylum bureaucracy, and a comprehensive technology assessment (Grunwald 2009, 2025), before any AI-based technology is implemented, are crucial. Striving for legitimacy is essential in this context, as AI use in asylum procedures directly affects fundamental rights and thus demands, next to participation, strong justification, transparency and oversight mechanisms. (Popovski and Turner 2012; Stewart 2024). Establishing those structures that foster dialogue, alongside legal safeguards, is a necessary step to address the complex challenges posed by the increasing use of AI in decision-making, and constitutes a core task of governance (Grimmelikhuijsen and Meijer 2022).

Conclusion

AI integration, as Dignum (2023) emphasizes, must be examined in relation to the structures of power, participation, and access to technology that determine who influences decisions, which data and knowledge are used, and how interactions between decision-makers and those affected are structured and maintained. Designing and applying the ABM—through both the parameter sensitivity analysis and narratives—illustrate what one expert described as how *"everything is somehow connected to one another"* (Expert 4, Participatory modelling, Group 2). This refers not only to the *formal sequence of processes* but also to *their quality*, including: the role of documents, support and information infrastructures for refugees, their agency being influenced by personal resources and health status, organizational challenges characteristic of asylum bureaucracy (e.g. the role of the interpreter and the federal state) and legitimization practices. Currently, AI development and implementation is designed only by a narrow set of stakeholders, relying on "technological fixes", while accountability becomes dispersed across institutional structures. The *combination* of structural issues, controversial AI applications, such as the DIAS, and a lack of transparency in how these are embedded in the (final) decision-making process affect not only individual refugee agency, but also refugee collectives (those with similar backgrounds and "pathways") and the system level. Given AI's direct impact on fundamental rights, addressing its normative and institutional challenges is a core governance task, requiring participation, transparency, oversight, and thus support for early stakeholder engagement and technology assessment.

Taking the perspective of the affected person by following their "pathways" before, during, and after the asylum procedure as well as of those working closely with refugees has proved valuable for approaching the possible implications of AI use in this highly sensitive domain. The ABM's design—its structure and components—aimed to be close to the narratives of those with experiential knowledge, indicating different aspects of refugee agency (cf. de Haas 2024). Participatory research with professionals from various disciplines has also demonstrated the value of recognizing the interplay between subsystems and the overall process across different organizational levels.

Notably, an important limitation of the analysis is that the primary source of the "insider perspective" of bureaucracy, the perspectives of administrative staff, is missing. These perspectives are crucial to learn about how the interaction with technology evolves, and to what extent training about intercultural competence, for example, plays a role. Another important limitation is that for reasons of space, only two narratives (from the 135 that were simulated) could be discussed.

It should be emphasized that the model is flexible and open to incorporating additional and especially more refined parameters. Future work could detail the processes of entering the job market or filing an appeal to the hardship commission. A further step could be to analyse the relative likelihood of the pathways followed by individual agents studied in the qualitative analysis (Neumann et al. 2023), for example, under what conditions "critical junctures" occur, which may be particularly useful for guiding targeted support or policy actions.

Acknowledgement Research presented in this chapter has been funded by the German VolkswagenStiftung under grant agreement number 98 560.

References

Affolter, L. (2021). *Asylum matters: On the front line of administrative decision-making.* Palgrave.

Ahrweiler, P. (2017). Simulationsexperimente realexperimenteller Politik—der Gewinn der Zukunftsdimension im Computerlabor. In S. Boeschen, M. Gross, & W. Krohn (Eds.), *Experimentelle Gesellschaft* (pp. 199–237). Nomos.

Alvarado, R. (2023). AI as an epistemic technology. *Science and Engineering Ethics, 29*(32), https://doi.org/10.1007/s11948-023-00451-3

Andreetta, S., & Borrelli, L. M. (2024). *Governing migration through paperwork: Legitimation practices, exclusive inclusion and differentiation.* Berghahn Books.

Boettcher, V. S., & Neuner, F. (2022). The impact of an insecure asylum status on mental health of adult refugees in Germany. *Clinical Psychology in Europe, 4*(1), e6587. https://doi.org/10.32872/cpe.6587

Bogumil, J., & Kuhlmann, S. (2022). Verwaltungsverflechtung als "missing link" der Föderalismusforschung: Administrative Bewältigung der Flüchtlingskrise im deutschen Mehrebenensystem. *Der moderne Staat—dms. Zeitschrift für Public Policy, Recht und Management, 15*(1), 84–108. https://doi.org/10.3224/dms.v15i1.0

Borgonovo, E., et al. (2022). Sensitivity analysis of agent-based models: A new protocol. *Computational and Mathematical Organization Theory, 28*, 52–94. https://doi.org/10.1007/s10588-021-09336-y

Boshuijzen-van Burken, C., Gore, R., Dignum, F., Royakkers, L., Wozny, P., & Shults, F. L. (2020). Agent-based modelling of values: The case of value sensitive design for refugee logistics. *Journal of Artificial Societies and Social Simulation, 23*(4), 6. https://doi.org/10.18564/jasss.4411

Bradby, H., Humphris, R., Newall, D., & Phillimore, J. (2015). *Public health aspects of migrant health: A review of the evidence on health status for refugees and asylum seekers in the European region.* World Health Organization, Regional Office for Europe.

Clegg, S., Cunha, M. P., Munro, I., Rego, A., & de Sousa, M. O. (2016). Kafkaesque power and bureaucracy. *Journal of Political Power, 9*(2), 157–181. https://doi.org/10.1080/2158379X.2016.1191161

Cobbe, J., Veale, M., & Singh, J. (2023). Understanding accountability in algorithmic supply chains. In *Proceedings of the 2023 ACM Conference on Fairness, Accountability, and Transparency (FAccT '23)*. https://ssrn.com/abstract=4430778

Corbin, J., & Strauss, A. (2008). *Basics of qualitative research: Techniques and procedures for developing grounded theory* (3rd ed.). Sage.

Dahlvik, J. (2018). *Inside asylum bureaucracy: Organizing refugee status determination in Austria. IMISCOE research series.* Springer. https://doi.org/10.1007/978-3-319-63306-0

de Haas, H. (2024). *Changing the migration narrative: On the power of discourse, propaganda and truth distortion.* IMI Working Paper No. 181/PACES Project Working Paper No. 3. University of Amsterdam.

Dignum, V. (2023). Responsible artificial intelligence: Recommendations and lessons learned. In D. O. Eke, K. Wakunuma, & S. Akintoye (Eds.), *Responsible AI in Africa* (pp. 159–174). Palgrave Macmillan. https://doi.org/10.1007/978-3-031-08215-3_9

Eule, T., Borrelli, L. M., Lindberg, A., Wyss, A., & Remmler, H.-P. (2020). *Hinter der Grenze, vor dem Gesetz.* Hamburger Edition HIS.

Gilbert, N., Ahrweiler, P., Barbrook-Johnson, P., Narasimhan, K. P., & Wilkinson, H. (2018). Computational modelling of public policy: Reflections on practice. *Journal of Artificial Societies and Social Simulation, 21*(1), 14. https://doi.org/10.18564/jasss.3669

Grimmelikhuijsen, S., & Meijer, A. (2022). Legitimacy of algorithmic decision-making: Six threats and the need for a calibrated institutional response. *Perspectives on Public Management and Governance, 5*(3), 232–242. https://doi.org/10.1093/ppmgov/gvac008

Grunwald, A. (2009). Technology assessment: Concepts and methods. In A. Meijers (Ed.), *Philosophy of technology and engineering sciences* (pp. 1103–1146). North Holland.

Grunwald, A. (2025). Technology assessment contributing to AI management in society. In C. H. Hoffmann (Ed.), *Artificial intelligence, entrepreneurship and risk* (pp. 135–153). Springer VS. https://doi.org/10.1007/978-3-658-45544-6_9

Gundacker, L., Kosyakova, Y., & Schneider, G. (2025). How regional attitudes towards immigration shape the chance to obtain asylum: Evidence from Germany. *Migration Studies, 13*(1), mnae002. https://doi.org/10.1093/migration/mnae002

Hinsch, M., & Bijak, J. (2022). Principles and state of the art of agent-based migration modelling. In *Towards Bayesian model-based demography* (pp. 43–68). Springer. https://doi.org/10.1007/978-3-030-83039-7_3

Klabunde, A., & Willekens, F. (2016). Decision-making in agent-based models of migration: State of the art and challenges. *European Journal of Population, 32*(1), 73–97. https://doi.org/10.1007/s10680-015-9362-0

Kosyakova, Y., & Brücker, H. (2020). Seeking asylum in Germany: Do human and social capital determine the outcome of asylum procedures? *European Sociological Review, 36*(5), 663–683. https://doi.org/10.1093/esr/jcaa013

Latour, B. (2005). *Reassembling the social: An introduction to actor-network-theory.* Oxford University Press.

León-Medina, F. J. (2017). Analytical sociology and agent-based modeling: Is generative sufficiency sufficient? *Sociological Theory, 35*(3), 157–178. https://doi.org/10.1177/0735275117726642

Lulamae, J. (2022). Kontroverse Dialekterkennung: Das BAMF und sein Pilotprojekt. AlgorithmWatch. Retrieved September 15, 2025, from https://algorithmwatch.org/de/dialekterkennung-bamf/

Marshall, E. (2025). Reconsidering the asylum lottery: Refugee determination and the structure of luck. *Social & Legal Studies.* https://doi.org/10.1177/09646639241312092

Muellerleile, C., & Robertson, S. L. (2018). Digital Weberianism: Bureaucracy, information, and the techno-rationality of neoliberal capitalism. *Indiana Journal of Global Legal Studies, 25*(1), Article 9.

Mulcaire, J., Smetham, D., Holt, L., Zard, S., Brady, F., & O'Driscoll, C. (2024). Impact of the asylum determination process on mental health in the UK and EU+: A systematic review and thematic synthesis. *BMJ Public Health, 2*(2): e000814. https://doi.org/10.1136/bmjph-2023-000814

Neumann, M., Dirksen, V., & Dickel, S. (2023). On the construction of plausible futures in interpretive agent-based modelling. In M. Neumann (Ed.), *An interpretive account to agent-based social simulation: Using criminology to explore cultural possibilities* (pp. 185–202). Routledge. https://doi.org/10.4324/9781003393207-9

Neumann, M., & Lotzmann, U. (2017). Simulation for interpretation: A methodology for growing virtual cultures. *Journal of Artificial Societies and Social Simulation, 20*(3). https://doi.org/10.18564/jasss.3317

Ozkul, D. (2023). *Automating immigration and asylum: The uses of new technologies in migration and asylum governance in Europe*. Refugee Studies Centre, University of Oxford.

Ozkul, D. (2025). Constructed objectivity in asylum decision-making through new technologies. *Journal of Ethnic and Migration Studies, 51*(14), 3629–3648. https://doi.org/10.1080/1369183X.2025.2513161

Palmiotto, F. (2024). When is a decision automated? A taxonomy for a fundamental rights analysis. *German Law Journal, 25*(2), 210–236. https://doi.org/10.1017/glj.2023.112

Popovski, V., & Turner, N. (2012). Legitimacy as complement and corrective to legality. In R. Falk, M. Juergensmeyer, & V. Popovski (Eds.), *Legality and Legitimacy in Global Affairs* (pp. 329–342). Oxford University Press. https://doi.org/10.1093/acprof:oso/9780199781577.003.0015

Quimby, B., & Beresford, M. (2022). Participatory modeling: A methodology for engaging stakeholder knowledge and participation in social science research. *Field Methods, 35*(1), 73–82. https://doi.org/10.1177/1525822X221076986

Riedel, L., & Schneider, G. (2017). Dezentraler Asylvollzug diskriminiert: Anerkennungsquoten von Flüchtlingen im bundesdeutschen Vergleich, 2010–2015. *Politische Vierteljahresschrift, 58*, 21–48. https://doi.org/10.5771/0032-3470-2017-1-21

Schittenhelm, K., & Schneider, S. (2017). Official standards and local knowledge in asylum procedures: Decision-making in Germany's asylum system. *Journal of Ethnic and Migration Studies, 43*(10), 1696–1713. https://doi.org/10.1080/1369183X.2017.1293592

Schock, K., Rosner, R., & Knaevelsrud, C. (2015). Impact of asylum interviews on the mental health of traumatized asylum seekers. *European Journal of Psychotraumatology, 6*(1). https://doi.org/10.3402/ejpt.v6.26286

Silva, S., & Kenney, M. (2018). Algorithms, platforms, and ethnic bias: An integrative essay. *Phylon (1960-), 55*(1–2), 9–37. https://www.jstor.org/stable/26545017

Späth, E. (2025). AI use in the asylum procedure in Germany: Exploring perspectives with refugees and supporters on assessment criteria and beyond. In P. Ahrweiler (Ed.), *Participatory artificial intelligence in public social services. Artificial intelligence, simulation and society*. Springer. https://doi.org/10.1007/978-3-031-71678-2_6

Squazzoni, F. (2008). The micro-macro link in social simulation. *Sociologica, 2*(1), 1–26. https://doi.org/10.2383/26576

Stewart, L. S. (2024). Fair and efficient asylum procedures and artificial intelligence: Quo vadis due process? *Computer Law & Security Review, 55*, 106050. https://doi.org/10.1016/j.clsr.2024.106050

Szczepanska, T., et al. (2022). GAM on! Six ways to explore social complexity by combining games and agent-based models. *International Journal of Social Research Methodology, 25*(4), 541–555. https://doi.org/10.1080/13645579.2022.2050119

Thränhardt, D. (2023). Welcome culture and bureaucratic ambiguity: Germany's complex asylum regime. In C. Finotelli & I. Ponzo (Eds.), *Migration control logics and strategies in Europe* (pp. 277–296). Springer. https://doi.org/10.1007/978-3-031-26002-5_14

van der Kist, J. (2025). Algorithmically constructed shibboleths: The technological mediation of automated dialect recognition in asylum procedures. *Geopolitics*, 1–36. https://doi.org/10.1080/14650045.2025.2530417

Zeit Online. (2025). *Mehr Richter und KI für mehr Tempo bei Asylverfahren.* Retrieved March 12, 2025, from https://www.zeit.de/news/2025-03/10/mehr-richter-und-ki-fuer-mehr-tempo-bei-asylverfahren.

Chapter 5
Gamifying Fairness: Exploring Algorithmic Decision-Making in Estonia's Welfare System

Maris Männiste, Triin Vihalemm, and Avo Trumm

Abstract Artificial intelligence and algorithmic systems are increasingly used to help make decisions about public service provision and state benefits for citizens. Delegating decision-making to machines raises ethical and social concerns and important questions about responsibility, accountability, transparency, and the quality of such decision-making (see, for example, Allhutter et al. 2020). Countries also have different policy contexts where these systems are situated, which can impact the attitudes towards AI-supported decision-making and understanding of fairness in particular contexts. By using a "serious games" approach, we aimed to understand how a selected automated assessment system might be reviewed and improved with real-world stakeholders to incorporate concerns of fairness into it. For this purpose, we conducted half-day-long workshops with master students (n = 18) from different social science-focused curriculums who, by taking the roles of consultants or clients in an unemployment insurance fund, played out the various possible scenarios for clients when an algorithm is used to assess the needs of the clients. The chapter analyzes the workshop results with master students as real-life stakeholders inspired by the serious games approach and discusses further opportunities for better integration of AI-based tools into social service provision in Estonia.

M. Männiste (✉)
Lecturer in Critical Data Studies, Institute of Social Studies, University of Tartu, Tartu, Estonia
e-mail: maris.manniste@ut.ee

T. Vihalemm
Professor of Communication Research, Institute of Social Studies, University of Tartu, Tartu, Estonia
e-mail: triin.vihalemm@ut.ee

A. Trumm
Researcher of Information Management and Analysis, Institute of Social Studies, University of Tartu, Tartu, Estonia
e-mail: avo.trumm@ut.ee

P. Ahrweiler and N. Gilbert (eds.), *Participatory Modelling and Simulation to Improve AI-based Public Social Services*, Artificial Intelligence, Simulation and Society,
https://doi.org/10.1007/978-3-032-15283-1_5

Introduction

Artificial intelligence (AI) and automated decision-making (ADM) are increasingly shaping public service provision and the allocation of state benefits and services (Dencik and Kaun 2020; Algorithm Watch 2019; AI Watch 2020; Lighthouse Reports 2024). These technologies are often assumed to enhance efficiency, consistency, and scalability in decision-making processes (Veale and Brass 2019) and primarily adopted to meet the organizational goals of cost-efficiency and administrative stream-lining (Valli Buttow and Weerts 2022; Dencik and Kaun 2020). However, delegating decision-making to AI is not without challenges, raising ethical and social concerns related to algorithmic bias, responsibility, accountability, transparency, and decision-making quality, particularly in the social welfare domain (Alston 2019; Eubanks 2018; Allhutter et al. 2020; Whiteford 2021; Rinta-Kahila et al. 2024; Lighthouse Reports 2024; Akhtar and Frank Jørgensen 2024; Amnesty International 2024).

One of the central concerns in mitigating the risks associated with algorithmic systems is fairness (Starke et al. 2022), a fundamental principle in trustworthy AI frameworks (OECD 2019). Algorithmic fairness is generally defined as ensuring that automated decisions do not produce unjust, discriminatory, or disparate consequences (Shin and Park 2019; Mitchell et al. 2021). However, fairness is context-dependent, shaped by national policy frameworks and societal attitudes, which influence perceptions of fairness and trust across different settings (Starke et al. 2022). The context of utilization of AI or algorithmic solutions shapes citizen perception towards algorithmic technologies and trust towards state institutions (Kaun et al. 2024; Steedman et al. 2020; Kaun and Masso 2025). Therefore, depending on the domain, there are also specific factors that influence the perception of citizens who are being subjected to AI or algorithmic assessment what is considered to be fair in particular situations. Previous research suggests that opportunities for appeal and control over algorithmic decisions are critical for mitigating algorithmic discrimination (Sun and Tang 2021), and explanations of algorithmic decisions can enhance public understanding of fairness in benefits and services distribution (Starke et al. 2022). Furthermore, the extent to which algorithms account for qualitative information and context appears to be a crucial factor in shaping fairness perceptions, further underscoring the complexity and subjectivity of algorithmic fairness and the need for context-sensitive approaches when implementing AI-driven decision-making in public services. Thus, as Ahrweiler et al. (2024) note, there is no approach that would be perceived fair everywhere.

This chapter will investigate the stakeholders', who are represented by social science master students' perspectives on fairness in algorithmic decision-making in unemployment career counseling services by employing a gamification approach and more concretely by using serious games. The algorithm used in the serious game was loosely based on our previous research regarding the decision support tool OTT used by the Estonian Unemployment Insurance Fund (see for more detailed overview Vihalemm et al. 2025; Weitz et al. 2024). In a workshop with University of Tartu master students from social science-focused curriculums, participants adopted the roles of consultants or clients to simulate scenarios involving an automated assessment system. Through this approach, we aimed to uncover actionable insights into how concerns about fairness can be integrated into the design and implementation of AI-supported assessment systems for social services. The whole process of the study is schematically drawn in Fig. 5.1.

The chapter is structured as follows: In Sect. "Introduction", we will give a short overview of the case-specific game design and agent-based modelling (further ABM) approach. Sect. "Estonian ABM and Serious Game for Improving Social Assessment Practices" will introduce the main results from the serious game. The chapter ends with a summary that highlights the main findings from using the serious game approach.

Estonian ABM and Serious Game for Improving Social Assessment Practices

The next chapters will give an overview of the ABM that was created to simulate the assessment and support process of the Estonian Unemployment Insurance Fund (further EUIF) and the serious game conducted with Estonian master students from social science-focused curriculums. The game was developed by Martha Bicket from Surrey University and was also accompanied by the ABM model that in the AI FORA project aims to be *"of a theorem-checking device for the ruleset derived from the one in place in the empirical system under investigation"* (Ahrweiler et al. 2024). The purpose of the agent-based model used in this case study was to simulate and explore the dynamic effects of algorithm-based support level assessments on consultant-client interactions, under varying fairness logics. The utilization of ABM approach was already pre-planned by the general project design. The use of method was chosen because it suited well for the inclusion of students and integration with the academic seminars.

The Estonian Model Description

The ABM was specifically designed to model the career counselling services provided to job-seekers by the EUIF. The chapter presents the key elements of the ABM following the framework proposed by Dilaver and Gilbert (2023), which has also been applied to other AI FORA case studies (see Ahrweiler et al. 2024).

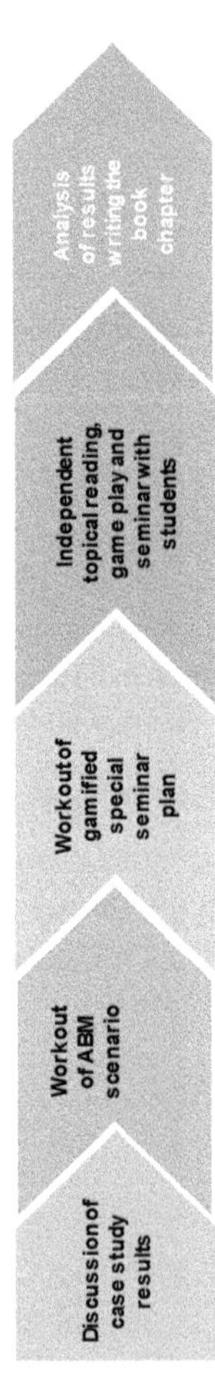

Fig. 5.1 Study procedure

Table 5.1 Attributes used in Estonian decision system

Work experience	Number of years of previous work experience
Fluency—Estonian	Yes/no
Fluency—other	Number of additional languages client is fluent in
Driving license	Yes/no
Education	The client's highest level of completed education
Dependents	Number of people who rely on the client as a primary source of income or for care
Health	Presence and severity of health conditions that may affect the client's ability to work
Time-since-employment	The number of months since the clients last employment

The Agents

The agents in the Estonian ABM simulation were jobseekers ("clients") applying for career counselling support, and consultants who assess and assist them. The consultants' objective was to allocate resources effectively to maximize client employment outcomes. Clients were initialized with the attributes described in Table 5.1. The attributes included work experience, Estonian language fluency, fluency in other languages, driving license, the highest level of completed education, number of dependents (including children as well as elderly people a person may need to care for), health status and time passed since the last employment. These attributes reflected some of the attributes also considered in the decision-system OTT but also included attributes like health status that is not considered in the real-life model because of the data protection regulations.

Consultants could then draw on these applicant attributes to calculate an assessment result that granted the client access to several counselling sessions and/or additional training.

Environment

The environment consisted of locations where applicants can go to in every round: at home, at work, or waiting in a queue to meet with a consultant. The number of consultant desks available was defined at the start of the simulation based on the chosen number of consultants.

The global attributes that defined the simulation environment and the dynamics between consultants and clients included round number, number of clients, number on consultants, number of new clients, and job threshold.

Actions and Interactions

At the start of the simulation and at the beginning of each new round, a new group of applicants was initialized at home. Clients were randomly assigned to consultants for an initial meeting, during which their support needs were assessed.

Consultants assess clients using an algorithm that applies a set of rules based on the client attributes. While an initial ruleset is provided, the simulation framework allows for adjustments such as modifying the scoring algorithm, changing input attributes, or redefining assessment thresholds.

At the end of each round, clients may have an opportunity to secure employment.

Scoring Algorithm

The probability of finding a job is positively influenced by the following factors: higher number of years of work experience, completion of training courses, greater number of career counselling sessions attended, possession of a driving license, higher educational attainment, fewer dependents, shorter periods of unemployment, clients remain with the same consultant until they find employment. The simulation concludes once the maximum number of rounds, defined at setup, is reached.

At the end of each round, clients had the opportunity to get a job. A client's chances of getting a job were positively influenced by the following factors: Number of years of work experience, attended a training course, number of career counselling meetings attended, driving license, higher education levels, fewer dependents, and less time spent unemployed. Applicants stayed with the same consultant until they find a job. The run ended when the maximum number of rounds defined at setup had elapsed.

The Goal and Design of the Serious Game

The role of the Estonian ABM model in the AI FORA project was to act as a tool for checking whether the rules used in the assessing system make sense and lead to the expected results. In our case, this involved testing the rules behind how job seekers are assessed by an algorithm, loosely based on the OTT decision-support system used by the Estonian Unemployment Insurance Fund. However, these rules may not reflect how things work in practice, they may seem unfair or may not lead to the desired outcomes. For the purpose to improve the rules, it is important to involve the people who are affected by or work with the system. Thus, the gamification workshop, using a serious game, was designed in cooperation with Martha Bicket from Surrey University and held in Tartu October 2024 to explore the perception of fairness and possible improvements for the systems. The serious game lasted altogether 4 hours.

Participants in this serious game's session covered a range of expertise, skills, and experiences based on their previous work experience and the specific master curriculum. The group of participating master's students was heterogeneous by age. The youngest was 28 and the oldest 52 years old. 9 female and 9 male students participated. The participation in the research was part of an elective master's course, "Artificial Intelligence and Social Justice: A Special Gamified Seminar" (SVUH.00.287), and their participation was voluntary. They all had prior knowledge about potential problems related to artificial intelligence and automated decision-making in the public sector context. All participants were inexperienced with using any kind of unemployment insurance fund services and had not worked in a specific public sector organization. Participants' backgrounds varied and included specialist working in public sector institutions (e.g., analysts, managers) as well as in private sector organization (e.g., journalists, analysts).

Participants taking part in the workshop played either the role of jobseekers ("clients") or EUIF consultants. All participants part of the clients group were divided into three profiles (Natalja, Mattias, Andres) that presented different kinds of vulnerabilities (young jobseeker, jobseeker with serious health issues, jobseeker with multiple dependents) that are not assessed or were considered difficult to assess through the decision-support system based on our previous research (Vihalemm et al. 2025) and thus may impact the length of unemployment as well as the needs in relation to the work. The division of the profiles in the groups was not done evenly. Those playing clients (n = 15) received information about the profile of the character they are playing, and consultants (n = 3) were given information about what data to collect, what to do with it, and the result of the assessment, which determines how much support the client will get. During the 1-on-1 assessment meetings with employment consultants, students playing clients answered the consultants' questions based on the prewritten profiles. All the clients received the result (written descriptions what happens next with their profile) based on the scores calculated. The result of the assessment was calculated by the "notetaker" whose role was played by the researchers. The clients did not recieve the calculated score itself, only the description based on the score.

The students who played real-life stakeholders were supported by three researchers who had dual roles during the serious game: 1) they supported the players who had adopted the consultant role as "note-takers" and calculated during the game the algorithm scores based on the information provided by the clients and gave out the decisions based on the scores on the consultants meeting notes, and 2) they facilitated three rounds of smaller focus group discussions as well as the decision-making regarding any choices in the algorithm. All the decisions on if and how to change the algorithm in rounds 2 and 3 were made in the bigger group discussions and had to be agreed by all participants.

The social assessment simulation was repeated in three iterations. During each iteration, certain factors were changed based on the agreements during the bigger group discussion. During the first iteration, participants had no knowledge about the algorithm (Table 5.2) used to calculate the scores, and the algorithm was revealed and explained to them during the first focus group session.

Table 5.2 Initial algorithm and result categories

	Scoring system	Example	Example score
Work experience	Number of years of previous work experience	E.g. if the client has 1.5 years of work experience, they get 1.5 points	1.5
Language	3 points for fluency in Estonian +1 point for fluency in each additional language	E.g. if the client's native language is Estonian and they speak some English, they get 3 points for fluent Estonian	3
Driving license	3 points for a driving license	E.g. if the client has no driving license, they get 0 points here	0
Education	Score based on the client's highest level of completed education only: Master's degree or higher = 5 points Bachelor's degree = 3 points Completed school only = 1 point	E.g. if the client has a master's degree they get 5 points	5
		Total score	9.5

Result categories for the initial algorithm:

Total points > 20	Green
10 < total points < 20	Yellow
Total points < 10	Red

For the second and third rounds, participants could suggest changes in the algorithm. The changes for the second and third rounds were chosen from the premade list (see Table 5.3) of the possible changes in the algorithm. During the second round, they could choose a maximum of two changes, and for the third round they could, if they chose to, apply all the possible changes. Most of the added variables had preassigned scores, and one, health, was subjectively decided by the consultant during the assessment process. This also led to the fact that participants with the same profile could have different results in some groups based on the consultant's subjective assessment.

The data collection from the serious game was based on participants' diaries (filled out after each iteration by both, the clients and consultants), three rounds of focus group discussions, and group discussions after each round.

Table 5.3 Premade list of changes to the algorithm

Suggested change	Scoring
Work experience	(a) If previous experience is less than 1 year -> 0 points. (b) If experience is more than 1 but less than 3 years -> 1 point. (c) If experience is more than 3 but less than 10 years -> 3 points. (d) If the client has more than 10 years of work experience -> 5 points. N.B. If the work experience scoring is changed, then the category thresholds will need to be updated to the following: | Total points > 10	Green
5 < total points < 10	Yellow
Total points < 5	Red	
Caring responsibilities	-3 points per child or adult being cared for by the client.
Health	Assign a score on a scale of 0 to -10 where 0 indicates no health problems and -10 indicates severe health issues which are a significant impediment to finding work.
Time elapsed since last employment	-0.5 points per month

In analyzing the discussion transcripts and diaries, we used qualitative thematic analysis about what was said in discussions about fairness perceptions, trust, and the effects of algorithm design changes, and also observations from participant interactions in the game. No quantitative outputs were tracked, the study was exploratory and qualitative by its nature. No statistical analysis was conducted based on the collected data.

Conclusions

The serious game workshops provided a unique opportunity to explore how students as stakeholders perceive algorithm-based social assessment tools and what kind of changes they propose. Throughout the sessions, participants—taking on the roles of consultants and clients—engaged in multiple scenarios reflecting real-world challenges in decision-making based and supported by the assessment algorithm.

One of the key findings from the workshop was that while adding more variables—such as health conditions and caring responsibilities—improved the algorithm's ability to assess needs more accurately, it also shifted participants' focus on individual circumstances rather than the fair allocation of resources. As the algorithm became more nuanced in recognizing vulnerabilities, participants playing the role of clients engaged more deeply with their profiles, emphasizing their specific needs over broader systemic fairness. This suggests that while increasing the number of variables may lead to more precise assessments, it can also encourage a more individualistic approach rather than a collective perspective on welfare distribution.

Additionally, when variables such as health conditions were introduced, the same profile could receive vastly different results depending on how the consultant assessed the case. This highlighted a crucial challenge in algorithmic fairness: certain criteria are inherently difficult to evaluate objectively, as they depend on multiple, inter-related factors. Participants noted that the final assessment was not only shaped by the algorithm's design but also by how much information a client was willing to disclose—particularly regarding personal aspects like health status, caregiving responsibilities or motivation, as our previous research has shown (Vihalemm et al. 2025) This underscores a key limitation in algorithmic social assessments: not all essential factors can be quantified or fairly compared across different cases.

Participants emphasized the need for an agile and adaptable model that allows for real-time adjustments during consultant-client interactions. Rather than relying solely on a predefined set of variables, they suggested that consultants should have the ability to add additional factors based on the meeting, ensuring that the assessment captures individual circumstances more accurately. This would enable the scoring system to update dynamically, reflecting new information and preventing rigid or incomplete evaluations. As one participant reflected during the focus group session:

"The job market is changing fast, and if the person is considered to find a new job fast mainly because he/she has worked a long time in the same position, then it does not go with the current policies which say that you should learn new things, be agile."

Participants highlighted that ensuring fairness in the assessment process requires a more job-specific approach rather than a generalized evaluation of employability. They noted that formal education is not a critical factor in some professions and prior-itizing it in assessments could create unnecessary barriers for qualified candidates. Instead, they advocated for a skills-based matching system, where individuals are connected to job opportunities based on their actual competencies rather than tradi-tional qualifications. This approach was seen to increase fairness by recognizing diverse career pathways and ensuring that job seekers are evaluated on relevant criteria for the roles they pursue.

During the third round, where the algorithm accounted for all possible variables, participants reflected on the limitations of merely expanding the dataset. Instead of continuously adding new variables, they proposed a decision-tree model, where new questions emerge dynamically based on prior responses. This approach, they argued, would allow for more context-sensitive assessments while preventing an overly rigid or exhaustive system. Their feedback highlights an important consideration for algo-rithmic tools: rather than relying solely on static pre-defined criteria, adaptive models that evolve based on case complexity may provide a more responsive and fair assess-ment framework. Moreover, their responses reflected that in social assessment situ-ations, algorithms are seen as supportive tools for the consultant rather than separate individual actors in the process.

The results highlighted the role of consultant subjectivity in assigning resources, particularly in evaluating family-related factors and health conditions. Participants noted that similar client profiles received different scores depending on how individual consultants interpreted and weighted these factors. This variability led to inconsistencies in resource allocation, as some consultants assigned higher importance to caregiving responsibilities or health limitations while others prioritized different aspects of employability. Such discrepancies underscore the challenges of standardizing fairness in algorithmic assessments and highlight the need for clearer guidelines or support mechanisms to ensure greater consistency in decision-making across different consultants.

Participants also raised concerns about institutional capacity in evaluating complex social factors. They pointed out that certain criteria, such as health or caregiving responsibilities, require domain-specific knowledge that a single public institution may lack. A fair and reliable assessment requires cross-sector collaboration, where different institutions contribute their expertise to ensure well-informed decisions.

Participants expressed concerns about an overreliance on the algorithm, emphasizing the need for human-machine collaboration rather than automated decision-making. They pointed out that while the system provides valuable insights, consultants should not blindly follow its recommendations but instead use it as a supportive tool. The ability to ask additional questions and interpret contextual factors beyond what the machine suggests was seen as crucial for ensuring fair and accurate assessments. This highlights the importance of consultants' expertise and judgment, ensuring that algorithmic evaluations remain aiding rather than replacing human decision-making in unemployment services.

"It's also a question about whether the consultant just takes into account what the machine says or really asks additional questions to understand the other factors affecting the job search."

Finally, discussions revealed a potential risk in making algorithmic decision-making fully transparent to citizens. While participants acknowledged the importance of algorithmic explainability in social assessments, they also noted that more digitally literate users might learn how to "trick" the system. This raises questions about the balance between transparency and system integrity, particularly in contexts where access to benefits depends on algorithmic evaluations. These insights suggest that designing AI-driven tools requires technical refinement and careful consideration of human behavior and ethical implications.

Summary

This chapter investigated how perceptions of fairness in algorithmic decision-making are shaped in the context of unemployment services, using a serious game methodology accompanying the ABM, involving master's students from different social science-focused curriculums as possible stakeholders. Literature on algorithmic fairness emphasizes its importance in building trustworthy AI, particularly in welfare domains where decisions affect citizens' access to benefits and services (Alston 2019; OECD 2019). Fairness, however, is not a fixed or universal concept—it is shaped by cultural, institutional, and situational contexts (Starke et al. 2022). This chapter contributes to the literature by offering empirical insights into how fairness is understood and evaluated when participants actively engage with simulated decision-making processes in a controlled but dynamic setting.

The serious game workshop allowed participants to take on the roles of consultants or clients within an unemployment service scenario. Through multiple rounds, adjustments were made to the algorithm, such as adding variables like health status and caregiving responsibilities, which revealed how participants engaged with fairness not as a fixed outcome, but as a process of negotiation and interpretation. A key observation was that increasing the number of variables (e.g., adding health variables or caring responsibilities) helped tailor decisions to individual needs but also led to a shift in focus from system-wide equity to personal justification. This reflects a tension between individualized fairness and collective justice, echoing concerns in the literature that expanding data inputs may not always lead to greater fairness, especially if structural inequalities remain unaddressed (Allhutter et al. 2020; Mann 2020). In addition, the importance of human judgment emerged strongly. Students viewed algorithms as tools to assist and not replace the consultants. They stressed the need for discretion, especially when dealing with sensitive or ambiguous criteria. Concerns about full transparency were also raised, as some feared it could allow users to manipulate the system, highlighting the delicate balance between accountability and system integrity (Akhtar and Frank Jørgensen 2024). Thus, flexibility and adaptability emerged as crucial values. Participants proposed the use of dynamic models, such as decision trees, that would allow new questions to appear based on previous answers—better capturing the nuance of real-world interactions. This suggestion aligns with calls in the literature for AI systems that are responsive and situated, rather than rigid or overly reductionist (Shin and Park 2019). Furthermore, participants emphasized that algorithms should act as support tools rather than decision-makers, reinforcing the idea that human judgment, discretion, and empathy remain vital in welfare assessments.

Our research indicates that the use of a serious game was not just valuable in understanding how stakeholders perceive data and can also improve people's digital literacy and understanding about the algorithms, especially in a context where algorithms often remain black-boxed (Pasquale 2015) and invisible for the people subject to the assessments and decision-making. In an educational context, serious games provide an interactive and immersive learning experience that goes beyond theoretical instruction, enabling students to apply concepts in simulated real-world scenarios, experiment with decision-making, and immediately observe the potential consequences of their choices. This experiential approach can foster deeper engagement, enhance critical thinking skills, and support the long-term understanding of complex ideas.

To sum up, this case study demonstrates that serious games offer a promising participatory method for exploring fairness in ADM systems. The modelling experience highlighted the importance of transparency, contextual fairness, and interaction design. Future iterations should involve real service users and frontline workers and explore institutional embedding of such participatory models in policy development. Also, the future experimentation could include testing the sensitivity of client outcomes to different weightings in the support score or simulating longer-term trajectories under more complex advisor-client dynamics.

Acknowledgement Research presented in this chapter has been funded by the German VolkswagenStiftung under grant agreement number 98 560.

References

Ahrweiler, P., Gilbert, N., Juranyi, Z., Bicket, M., Coll, A. S., Kampis, G., & Wurster, D. (2024, May). Using ABM and serious games to create "better AI". In *2024 Annual Modeling and Simulation Conference (ANNSIM)* (pp. 1–16). IEEE. https://doi.org/10.23919/ANNSIM61499.2024.10732031

Akhtar, M., & Jørgensen, R. F. (2024). A rights-based approach to automated decision-making in the public sector. In M. Balcerzak & J. Kapelańska-Pręgowska (Eds.), *Artificial intelligence and international human rights law* (pp. 69–85). Edward Elgar Publishing.

Amnesty International. (2024, November 13). *Denmark: Coded injustice: Surveillance and discrimination in Denmark's automated welfare state—Amnesty International.* https://www.amnesty.org/en/documents/eur18/8709/2024/en/

Alston, P. (2019). Report of the special rapporteur on extreme poverty and human rights. A/74/48037. https://www.ohchr.org/EN/NewsEvents/Pages/DisplayNews.aspx?NewsID=25156

Allhutter, D., Cech, F., Fischer, F., Grill, G., & Mager, A. (2020). Algorithmic profiling of job seekers in Austria: How austerity politics are made effective. *Frontiers in Big Data, 3*, 5. https://doi.org/10.3389/fdata.2020.00005

Dencik, L., & Kaun, A. (2020). Datafication and the welfare state. *Global Perspectives, 1*(1), 12912.

Dilaver, O., & Gilbert, N. (2023). Unpacking a black box: A conceptual anatomy framework for agent-based social simulation models. *Journal of Artificial Societies and Social Simulation, 26*(1).

Eubanks, V. (2018). *Automating inequality: How high-tech tools profile, police, and punish the poor.* St Martin's Press.

Kaun, A., Larsson, A. O., & Masso, A. (2024). Automation scenarios: Citizen attitudes towards automated decision-making in the public sector. *Information, Communication & Society, 28*(7), 1177–1194. https://doi.org/10.1080/1369118X.2024.2375261

Kaun, A., & Masso, A. (2025). *The data welfare state.* Sage Publications Ltd.

Lighthouse Reports. (2024, November 27). *Sweden's suspicion machine—Lighthouse reports.* https://www.lighthousereports.com/investigation/swedens-suspicion-machine/

Mann, M. (2020). Technological politics of automated welfare surveillance: Social (and data) justice through critical qualitative inquiry. *Global Perspectives, 1*(1), 12991.

Mitchell, S., Potash, E., Barocas, S., D'Amour, A., & Lum, K. (2021). Algorithmic fairness: Choices, assumptions, and definitions. *Annual Review of Statistics and its Application, 8*(1), 141–163.

OECD. (2019). *Recommendation of the council on OECD legal instruments artificial intelligence.* https://oecd.ai/en/ai-principles (updated 2024).

Pasquale, F. (2015). *The black box society: The secret algorithms that control money and information.* Harvard University Press.

Rinta-Kahila, T., Someh, I., Gillespie, N., Indulska, M., & Gregor, S. (2024). Managing unintended consequences of algorithmic decision-making: The case of Robodebt. *Journal of Information Technology Teaching Cases, 14*(1), 165–171. https://doi.org/10.1177/20438869231165538

Shin, D., & Park, Y. J. (2019). Role of fairness, accountability, and transparency in algorithmic affordance. *Computers in Human Behavior, 98,* 277–284. https://doi.org/10.1016/j.chb.2019.04.019

Starke, C., Baleis, J., Keller, B., & Marcinkowski, F. (2022). Fairness perceptions of algorithmic decision-making: A systematic review of the empirical literature. *Big Data & Society, 9*(2), 20539517221115189. https://doi.org/10.1177/20539517221115189

Steedman, R., Kennedy, H., & Jones, R. (2020). Complex ecologies of trust in data practices and data-driven systems. *Information, Communication & Society, 23*(6), 817–832. https://doi.org/10.1080/1369118X.2020.1748090

Sun, L., & Tang, Y. (2021). Data-driven discrimination, perceived fairness, and consumer trust—The perspective of consumer attribution. *Frontiers in Psychology, 12,* 748765. https://doi.org/10.3389/fpsyg.2021.748765

Valli Buttow, C., & Weerts, S. (2022). Public sector information in the European Union policy: The misbalance between economy and individuals. *Big Data & Society, 9*(2), 20539517221124587. https://doi.org/10.1177/20539517221124587

Veale, M., & Brass, I. (2019). Administration by algorithm? Public management meets public sector machine learning. In K. Yeung & M. Lodge (Eds.), *Algorithmic Regulation* (pp. 121–149). Oxford University Press. https://doi.org/10.1093/oso/9780198838494.003.0006

Vihalemm, T., Männiste, M., Trumm, A., & Solvak, M. (2025). Specialists and algorithms: Implementation of AI in the delivery of unemployment services in Estonia. In P. Ahrweiler (Eds.), *Participatory artificial intelligence in public social services. Artificial intelligence, simulation and society* (pp. 97–117). Springer. https://doi.org/10.1007/978-3-031-71678-2_5

Weitz, K., Schlagowski, R., André, E., Männiste, M., & George, C. (2024, May). Explaining it your way-findings from a co-creative design workshop on designing XAI applications with AI end-users from the public sector. In *Proceedings of the 2024 CHI Conference on Human Factors in Computing Systems* (pp. 1–14). https://doi.org/10.1145/3613904.3642563

Whiteford, P. (2021). Debt by design: The anatomy of a social policy fiasco–or was it something worse? *Australian Journal of Public Administration, 80*(2), 340–360. https://doi.org/10.1111/1467-8500.12479

Chapter 6
Targeted Subsidies Plan:
An Agent-Based Modeling Approach

Hassan Bashiri

Abstract This chapter reports on an agent-based modeling project to simulate the implementation of a targeted subsidies plan (TSP) in Iran, which was conducted as one of the case studies in the Artificial Intelligence for Assessment (AI-FORA) research project. The model aims to examine the dynamics of the targeted subsidies plan and assess the effectiveness of related policies, such as paying subsidies to the lower deciles of households, and their impact on income inequality and improving the welfare of low-income households. In this model, households are considered the key agents. Based on the targeted subsidies plan, households are divided into different income deciles according to various parameters such as income, assets, number of household members, foreign trips, and bank transactions (a total of 260 information fields). Each year, a budget is allocated by the government for the TSP, and subsidies are paid to low-income deciles (in this simulation, to the 4 low-income deciles). In the early years of the plan's implementation, equal subsidies were paid to different deciles, but in the past few years, the plan has purposefully calculated a different subsidy to be paid to each decile. Additionally, in this simulation, the dynamic behaviors of households, including income generation, consumption, and savings, as well as sudden income jumps or bankruptcy, are considered to be closer to the reality of society. Finally, the impact of the policy on income distribution, poverty reduction, and household welfare is analyzed. In future work, in this research, we will try to examine the relationships between households and add the effects of macroeconomic parameters, such as inflation, in the simulation.

Problem Statement

The Targeted Subsidy Plan (TSP), implemented by the Iranian government since late 2010, is one of the largest economic projects in the country's history. The plan was announced to reform the subsidy system and reduce socio-economic inequalities.

H. Bashiri (✉)
Department of Computer Science, Hamedan University of Technology, Hamedan, Iran
e-mail: bashiri@hut.ac.ir

© The Author(s) 2026

P. Ahrweiler and N. Gilbert (eds.), *Participatory Modelling and Simulation to Improve AI-based Public Social Services*, Artificial Intelligence, Simulation and Society,
https://doi.org/10.1007/978-3-032-15283-1_6

By eliminating indirect subsidies of goods and services and distributing direct cash subsidies to low-income households, the plan aimed to optimize resource allocation and support vulnerable groups (Bashiri 2025). However, challenges on a macro scale, such as economic instability, inflation, devaluation of the national currency, sanctions, and problems related to the accurate identification of eligible households at the implementation level, have created obstacles to the realization of the plan's goals.

At the implementation level, artificial intelligence, as a tool in data analysis and data-driven decision-making, plays an important role in improving the processes of identifying eligible households carried out in the Ministry of Cooperatives, Labor and Social Welfare, The Iranian Welfare Database (IWDB), launched in 2014, has enabled more accurate household decile classification by collecting comprehensive information from more than 60 data sources, including government organizations and the Central Bank (Bashiri 2025). However, the complexity of socio-economic interactions and the variability of household behavior require the use of advanced modeling approaches that can analyze and simulate the long-term effects of subsidy policies. Agent-based modeling has been chosen as an appropriate approach for analyzing such policies due to its ability to represent heterogeneous behaviors, inter-agent interactions, and systematic dynamics.

Research Literature

In the past decade, agent-based modeling as a computational approach has gained attention as a tool for modeling complex systems, especially in social and economic science research. Unlike traditional modeling methods that mainly work on the assumption of homogeneity of agents and equilibrium at the macro level, this modeling style allows the simulation of complex systems, where interactions between heterogeneous agents with simple behavioral rules and dynamics are important. This feature has made agent-based modeling an efficient tool for analyzing phenomena in which heterogeneity, nonlinear interactions, and evolutionary dynamics play a key role (Bonabeau 2002). For these reasons, agent-based modeling has increasingly been used in the field of economic and social policy analysis.

One application of agent-based modeling is to examine the dynamics of income distribution and economic inequality. Scholars have used this approach to explore how various policy instruments, ranging from taxation to direct transfers and welfare initiatives, affect the allocation of income within a population (Tesfatsion and Judd 2006). These simulations typically represent households, firms, and governmental bodies as autonomous agents whose interactions, such as market exchanges, tax payments, and subsidy receipts, evolve over time. Within the sphere of subsidy interventions, Happe et al. (2006) applied agent-based modeling to assess the implications of agricultural subsidies in developing nations. Their findings suggest that while well-targeted subsidies can contribute to narrowing income disparities, the overall impact is strongly mediated by broader economic conditions, including inflationary pressures and the structural characteristics of markets.

In the Iranian context, Bakhshodeh (2013) explored statistical techniques for identifying deserving households and likewise underscored the importance of precise data. Although this study did not utilize agent-based modeling, it provided a foundational framework for data-driven analyses that could inform and strengthen future agent-based simulations.

Also, a study by Doshmangir et al. (2015) examined the effects of subsidy policies on the health behaviors of Iranian households and showed that cash subsidies can change consumption behaviors, but their long-term effects depend on macroeconomic factors (Doshmangir et al. 2015).

Recently, with the advancement of artificial intelligence technologies, combining agent-based modeling with machine learning algorithms has attracted attention to improve economic simulations. For example, Zhang and his team in 2020 used agent-based modeling and machine learning to map out how food subsidies were distributed in China, and it made their predictions more accurate (Tian et al. 2021). Collectively, these types of achievements demonstrate the high potential of agent-based modeling when trying to explain complex policies, such as the targeted subsidies plan in Iran.

Purpose of the Model in the Case Study

The purpose of modeling in this study is to examine the dynamics of the targeted subsidies plan and assess the effectiveness of related policies, such as paying subsidies to the lower deciles, and their impact on income inequality and improving the welfare of low-income households. The following subjects were considered in the modeling:

- **Household heterogeneity:** Households are the most important factor in this modeling, and various characteristics, including income, assets, household size, and consumption patterns, reflecting the socio-economic diversity in Iran, are considered for households.
- **Targeted subsidies:** The allocation of cash subsidies to four low-income groups, with variable amounts based on income level and household size, is the most important government measure, which is paid monthly and based on the credit or budget allocated for the targeted subsidies plan. In practice, 260 indicators are used for calculating deciles. In this modeling, several key indicators were included in the model.
- **Economic dynamics:** examining the dynamic behavior of households, including income generation, consumption and savings patterns, sudden income jumps or bankruptcies, and the impact of subsidy policies on economic mobility.

- **Policy evaluation:** analyzing the impact of the targeted subsidies plan on income distribution, poverty reduction, and overall household well-being, by moving households between deciles. Household deciles are reclassified each year based on the data collected. Therefore, households may move between income deciles.

The model was developed as part of the international project "Artificial Intelligence for Assessment (AI-FORA)" and aims to help policymakers design more effective subsidy programs by simulating different scenarios. The model source code and details are published in the CoMSES Model Repository (Bashiri 2023).

Model Description

Model Design

The agent-based model is implemented using NetLogo software, and the basic model includes adjustable n households as agents, by default 230 households, representing 23 million Iranian households, and it is showable on the computer screen. This scale was chosen to maintain computational efficiency while reflecting the diversity of households. The key features of the model are as follows:

- **Agents (households):** Each household has characteristics such as income, assets, household size, and monthly expenses. We analyzed 2% of the household records from the Iranian Welfare Database (IWDB), which is publicly available to researchers, and based on the analyzed information, income and assets were assigned to households as a power-law distribution to match the distributions found in the Iranian Welfare Database. Household size was also modeled based on a normal distribution with a mean of 4. Fig. 1 presents the characteristics of the household agent and the distribution of income in households. The model was defined in such a way that the power distribution was maintained in the income distribution. In our model, as shown in the code description provided in Fig. 2, 75% of households have an income of 0–3000 dollars, and only 25% have an income of 3000–10,000 dollars.

- **Household grouping:** Households are classified into 10 groups (deciles) based on income and wealth, with group 1 comprising the lowest-income households

```
household-own [
   income       ; monthly income of the household
   deposit      ; wealth of the household
   group        ; the group number that the household belongs to
   subsidy      ; subsidy amount that the household receives each month
   family-size  ; size of the household based on its income
   expenses     ; monthly expenses of the household
]
```

Fig. 1 Characteristics of the household agent

```
to income-distribution

  let min-value 0        ; minimum income
  let max1 3000          ; maximum income is 10000$ but in order to gernerate random numbers based on power-law we divided the incomes to two ranges
  let max2 10000         ; ranges [0 - 3000][3000 - 10000] only 1/4 households have incomes in the [3000 - 10000]
  let count-low 0        ; number of low-income households
  let count-high 0       ; number of high-income households

  while [count-low + count-high < num-of-households] [
    let index random-float 4
    ifelse index <= 3[
      let x random-float 1
      let value min-value + (max1 - min-value) * x
      set income-lists lput value income-lists
      set count-low count-low + 1
    ][
      let x random-float 1
      let value max1 + (max2 - max1) * x
      set income-lists lput value income-lists
      set count-high count-high + 1
    ]
  ]

end
```

Fig. 2 Implementation of income distribution

and group 10 comprising the highest-income households. The grouping method is shown in Fig. 3. For simplicity, we considered assets in the form of a single number called a deposit. In the IWDB, each household's assets, including property, car, shop, company, or business unit, are calculated, and a portion is considered as living necessities for each family.

- **Subsidy allocation:** Cash subsidies are distributed to the first four groups (low-income). Group 1 ($200 per person), Group 2 ($150), Group 3 ($100), and Group 4 ($50). These amounts are distributed monthly. In practice, the subsidy distribution is done in the country's current currency, the Rial, but to create a common understanding, these numbers were defined hypothetically and in dollars. In the simulation settings section, all these values can be changed to better characterize

```
to-report grouping            ; calculate the group number based on income and wealth

  let group-num 0
  ifelse income <= 500 and deposit <= 4000
  [ set group-num 1 ]
  [ ifelse income <= 1000 and deposit <= 6000   [ set group-num 2 ]
    [ ifelse income <= 1500 and deposit <= 9000     [ set group-num 3 ]
      [ ifelse income <= 2000 and deposit <= 12000      [ set group-num 4 ]
        [ ifelse income <= 3000 and deposit <= 15000       [ set group-num 5 ]
          [ ifelse income <= 4000 and deposit <= 25000        [ set group-num 6 ]
            [ ifelse income <= 5500 and deposit <= 30000         [ set group-num 7 ]
              [ ifelse income <= 7000 and deposit <= 40000          [ set group-num 8 ]
                [ ifelse income <= 8500 and deposit <= 50000           [ set group-num 9 ]
                  [ set group-num 10 ]
                ]
              ]
            ]
          ]
        ]
      ]
    ]
  ]

  report group-num
end
```

Fig. 3 Grouping households into 10 deciles based on income and assets

the effect of the income distribution policy. The declared values are considered default.

- **Time:** The model is run over 10 years, with a monthly distribution of subsidies and an annual assessment of households to review the grouping.

Model Workflow

The workflow of the model includes the following steps:

1 **Initiation**: In the initial step, income, assets, and household size are assigned to each household based on the distributions extracted from 2% of the actual data published by the Ministry of Cooperatives, Labor, and Social Welfare.
2 **Grouping**: Households are divided into 10 income and asset groups based on decile indicators. In the modeling, each income decile is displayed in a different color.
3 **Subsidy distribution**: This step, which is repeated every month, allocates cash subsidies to four low-income groups. With the explanation that the amount of cash subsidy for each income decile is different, and each family receives a subsidy based on the decile in which it is contracted, and the household size. In Fig. 4, we show how household size affects the amount of subsidy received. Based on the value that the user sets in the model for the subsidy per decile in the UI and the household size, the subsidy per household is calculated.

4 **Consumption and savings**: Part of the dynamics is modeled in this step. Households consume their subsidies and income for expenses and savings.
5 **Annual review**: At the end of each year, households are assessed based on new income and assets, and their grouping is updated.
6 **Display of changes**: Changes in household grouping are publicly displayed.

```
; calculate and pay subsidies for households in groups 1, 2, 3, and 4
ask household with [group = 1] [
    set subsidy family-size * subsidy-group-1
    set subsidies-group-1 subsidies-group-1 + subsidy
]
ask household with [group = 2] [
    set subsidy family-size * subsidy-group-2
    set subsidies-group-2 subsidies-group-2 + subsidy
]
ask household with [group = 3] [
    set subsidy family-size * subsidy-group-3
    set subsidies-group-3 subsidies-group-3 + subsidy
]
ask household with [group = 4] [
    set subsidy family-size * subsidy-group-4
    set subsidies-group-4 subsidies-group-4 + subsidy
]
```

Fig. 4 How do we calculate the subsidy for the first 4 groups of households

Model Implementation

The model is implemented using NetLogo 6.4.0 and includes global variables (such as subsidy budget, year, and month) and household-specific characteristics (such as income, assets, expenses, and subsidy group). Key functions include:

- **Setup society:** Initialize households and distributions.
- **Go:** Execute monthly operations and pay subsidies.
- **Enrichment rate:** Percentage of households that become rich one time due to factors such as inflation, rent, investment, or inheritance.
- **Bankruptcy rate:** Percentage of households that become bankrupt due to factors such as capital loss, fraud, economic failure, or misinvestment.

Input Data

The model data behavior is derived from a 2% random sample of the Iranian Welfare Database, which includes the distribution of household size, income, and assets. The data is analyzed using Python libraries such as Pandas, NumPy, and Matplotlib to reflect real-world patterns in the model. The details of the analysis of these data are detailed in Bashiri (2025).

Figure 5 shows the user interface of the agent-based modeling for the targeted subsidies plan within the framework of the AI-FORA research project. The interface consists of a central panel in which 230 households (as the default number of households) are displayed in various colors, each color representing an income decile (from black for the lowest income decile 1 to blue for the highest income decile 10). By running the model, applying household deciles, allocating subsidies to low-income deciles, spending, saving, and possible bankruptcy of households, as well as household income jumps, the dynamics of the social and economic system are modeled. The outputs include analytical graphs such as income distribution and household size distribution based on input data and derived from real society data, as well as subsidy distribution, wealth distribution, and dynamic decile graphs that visually present dynamic data with histograms and time series, respectively.

Also, in the NetLogo environment, it is possible to set parameters such as the number of households, subsidy amount, and subsidy group size, which allows policymakers to examine the impact of different scenarios. The graphs show the heterogeneous distribution of income and wealth, which is consistent with the actual data from the Iranian Welfare Database, and the time series of subsidy distribution highlights the impact of targeted policies on low-income groups. Due to the screen limitation in displaying the model, the UI of the simulation environment is provided in NetLogo. Figure 5 shows the overall view of the model.

As can be seen in Fig. 6, the number of households, which is selected as a default of 230 households, can be adjusted at the beginning of the modeling. The user also sets the subsidy amount to the first four income deciles and selects the rate of enrichment

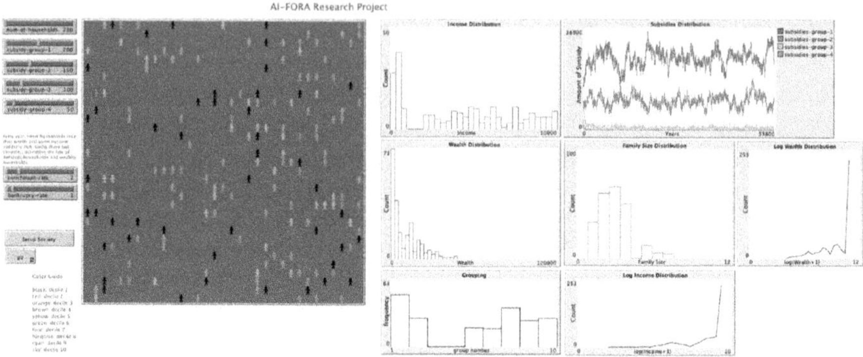

Fig. 5 The user interface of the NetLogo model of the Targeted Subsidies Plan

or bankruptcy of households in the community, which is usually a low number, and finally starts running the model. In Fig. 7, the household size distribution (middle right) is roughly normal or Poisson in shape, with a greater concentration around the median values (4–6 members). The income distribution (top left) is long-tailed, meaning that most households have relatively low incomes, but a small number of households have very high incomes. The wealth or asset distribution (bottom left) shows even more skewness than income, indicating that wealth is concentrated in the hands of a small group of households. The logarithmic distributions of income and wealth (bottom right and bottom middle) show a more linear pattern in the upper-middle portions after logarithmic transformation, consistent with the properties of power-law distributions.

The Grouping plot (bottom left) shows the distribution of households by grouping defined in the model.

Model Results and Findings

Running the model over 10 years provides several analyses into the impact of the targeted subsidies plan:

- **Economic mobility:** The model showed that subsidy policies lead to limited economic mobility among households. Especially in recent years, with rising inflation and limited subsidy growth, and the devaluation of the national currency, subsidies have had a very small impact on household welfare. According to data published by the Statistical Center of Iran, in March 2018, the inflation difference between the first and tenth deciles was zero, but in February 2024, inflation was 45% for the tenth decile and 55% for the first decile.

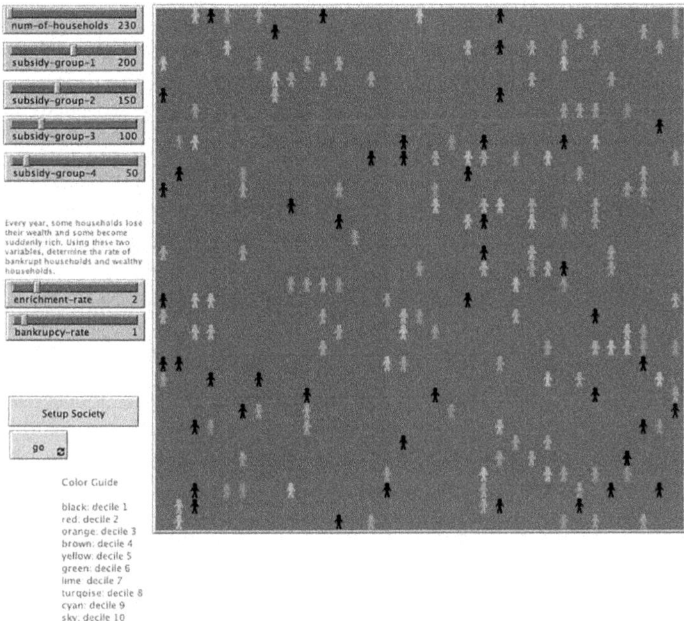

Fig. 6 View of the simulation environment and input parameters to the model

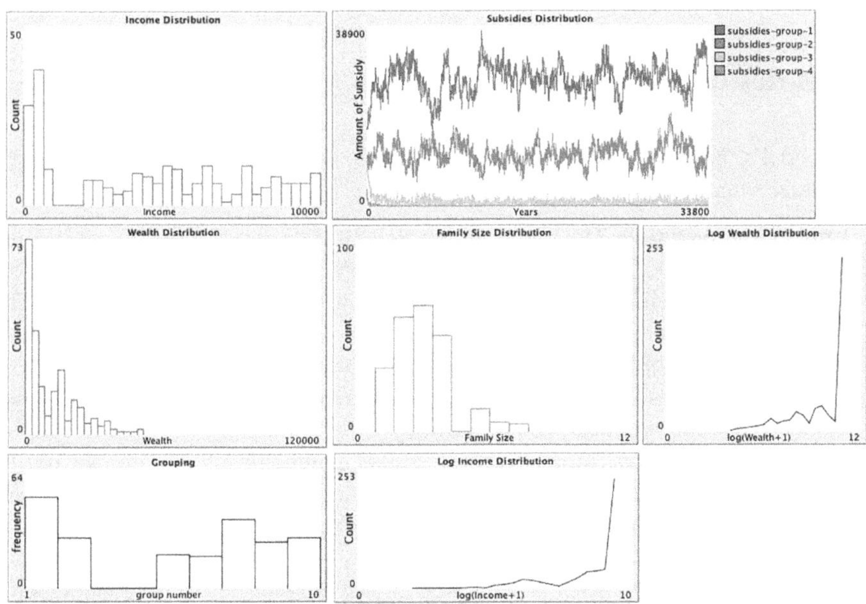

Fig. 7 Distributions and output

- **Impact on low-income groups:** Households in groups 1 to 4 receive cash subsidies in proportion to the number of household members, which, in the early years before inflationary concerns and devaluation of the national currency, reduced financial pressures on these households and led to improved welfare. Despite the implementation of the TSP, a substantial income gap persists between the lower-income deciles and the higher-income groups of deciles.
- **Income distribution:** While the income distribution graphs indicate a modest reduction in inequality, this improvement appears marginal and has been constrained by exogenous factors beyond the scope of the TSP—most notably, inflationary pressures, international sanctions, and the ongoing depreciation of the national currency.
- **Household dynamics:** The annual review of household mobility across income deciles reveals that the subsidy policy has contributed to a degree of economic stabilization for low-income groups. However, it has fallen short of addressing the deeper, structural dimensions of inequality that underpin long-term income disparities.

The model's visual outputs—including income distribution histograms and time-series graphs depicting subsidy allocations—offer a nuanced lens through which to examine the multifaceted effects of the policy over time. These tools enable a more granular understanding of both the program's immediate impacts and its broader socioeconomic implications.

Model Results to Policies

The model's findings for policymaking in the targeted subsidies plan can be summarized under the following headings:

- **Improving targeting:** The model shows that allocating subsidies to low-income groups is effective. This is the goal pursued by the targeted subsidies plan. At the same time, identifying eligible households is the bottleneck of this plan. The most important value that the TSP has created is the data that is aggregated in the Iranian Welfare Database and collected from more than 60 organizations in the form of 260 information fields. This data is the fuel for artificial intelligence models. Cleaning the data, pre-processing it, and ultimately using it to classify households is very essential. Recording and maintaining this data can be the input for artificial intelligence and machine learning models for the purposes of predicting income behavior, bankruptcy, tax evasion, the impact of household deciles on student success, and the like.
- **Resistance to externalities:** The limited impact of subsidies on reducing income inequality indicates the need for complementary policies to combat inflation and economic sanctions. In other words, any change in the macroeconomic environment directly affects the subsidy rates of target groups, the prices of energy carriers, and the number of households in each income decile.

- **Transparency and public trust:** The implementation of the targeted subsidies plan has been implemented with high success in terms of acceptance, public trust, and transparency. We have discussed this claim in Bashiri (2025). The reason for this trust is the data that is collected every year. Annual review and public display of grouping changes have increased public trust in the subsidy system.
- **Model extension:** The model has the potential to be extended to test alternative policies, such as non-cash subsidies or educational programs, which could increase the overall effectiveness of the scheme.

By providing a dynamic simulation environment, this model allows policymakers to test different scenarios and predict the long-term effects of subsidy policies.

Conclusion

In this chapter, we present a framework based on agent-based modeling for simulating the targeted subsidies plan in Iran. In modeling issues such as household heterogeneity, the subsidy allocation process and household dynamics were simulated based on the targeted subsidies plan, and recommendations were made to strengthen this plan, which is referred to as the Iranian economic surgery. The findings show that targeted cash subsidies, rather than indirect subsidies, have a positive impact on the welfare of low-income groups. At the same time, limitations caused by external factors such as inflation, sanctions, and devaluation of the national currency have made the targeted subsidies plan less effective. Also, in this research, considering the high potential that the Iranian Welfare Database has created as a valuable source of data used in household decile classification, we suggest integrating technologies such as artificial intelligence and agent-based modeling in policymaking as the next steps of this research.

Acknowledgement Research presented in this chapter has been funded by the German VolkswagenStiftung under grant agreement number 98 560.

References

Bakhshodeh, M. (2013). Proxy means tests for targeting subsidies scheme in Iran. *Iranian Journal of Economic Studies, 2*(2), 25–46. https://doi.org/10.22099/ijes.2013.2718

Bashiri, H. (2025). Social assessment for the targeted subsidies plan as a social service provision in Iran: AI application in the targeted subsidies plan. In P. Ahrweiler (Ed.), *Participatory artificial intelligence in public social services*. Springer. https://doi.org/10.1007/978-3-031-71678-2_7

Bashiri, H. (2023, September 21). The Targeted Subsidies Plan Model (Version 1.0.0). CoMSES Computational Model Library. https://www.comses.net/codebases/883171d8-1dcc-4740-992b-2d7f785a9194/releases/1.0.0/

Bonabeau, E. (2002). Agent-based modeling: Methods and techniques for simulating human systems. *Proceedings of the National Academy of Sciences, 99* (Suppl_3): 7280–7287. https://doi.org/10.1073/pnas.082080899

Doshmangir, L., Doshmangir, P., Abolhassani, N., Moshiri, E., & Jafari, M. (2015). Effects of targeted subsidies policy on health behavior in Iranian households: A qualitative study. *Iranian Journal of Public Health, 44*(4): 570.

Happe, K., Kellermann, K., & Balmann, A. (2006). Agent-based analysis of agricultural policies: An illustration of the agricultural policy simulator AgriPoliS, its adaptation and behavior. *Ecology and Society, 11*(1). http://www.jstor.org/stable/26267800

Tesfatsion, L., & Judd, K. L. (Eds.). (2006). *Handbook of computational economics* (Vol. 2). Elsevier.

Tian, S., Lu, Y., Ge, X., & Zheng, Y. (2021). An agent-based modeling approach combined with deep learning method in simulating household energy consumption. *Journal of Building Engineering, 43*, 103210. https://doi.org/10.1016/j.jobe.2021.103210

Chapter 7
Agent-Based Modelling of the Indian Public Distribution System in AI FORA

Ashly Ann Jo, Ebin Deni Raj, and Sumathi Srinivasalu

Abstract The Public Distribution System (PDS) in India is one of the world's largest food security programs, serving over 800 million citizens. Yet, the system continues to face critical challenges, including corruption, leakage, and inequitable service delivery. This chapter presents an Agent-Based Model (ABM), developed under the AI FORA (Artificial Intelligence for Fair, Open, and Responsible Automation) initiative, to simulate the complex behavioural and logistical dynamics of the PDS. Implemented in NetLogo, the model incorporates beneficiaries, ration shop operators, suppliers, trucks, and inspectors within a spatially embedded district-level environment. By embedding Responsible AI metrics, the simulation evaluates fairness, transparency, and accountability under varying operational conditions. Scenario-based experiments examine the effects of inspection frequency, corruption propensity, and supply delays on both system efficiency and ethical performance. Findings highlight pathways for digital governance and demonstrate the value of AI-driven simulation as a testbed for designing equitable, accountable, and effective welfare policies.

Introduction

The Public Distribution System (PDS) is one of India's most ambitious social welfare programs, ensuring food security for millions of low-income households by providing essential commodities—such as rice, wheat, sugar, and kerosene—at subsidized rates through a vast network of Fair Price Shops (FPS) (Khera, 2011). Administered jointly

A. A. Jo (✉) · E. D. Raj
Indian Institute of Information Technology Kottayam, Valavoor, India
e-mail: ashlyannjo.phd2112@iiitkottayam.ac.in

E. D. Raj
e-mail: ebindeniraj@iiitkottayam.ac.in

S. Srinivasalu
University of Madras, Chennai, India

P. Ahrweiler and N. Gilbert (eds.), *Participatory Modelling and Simulation to Improve AI-based Public Social Services*, Artificial Intelligence, Simulation and Society,
https://doi.org/10.1007/978-3-032-15283-1_7

by central and state governments, the PDS covers all states and union territories and reaches more than 800 million people. Despite its expansive reach, the system faces chronic challenges that compromise effectiveness. Stock diversion, ghost beneficiaries, pilferage, ration denial, and bureaucratic opacity continue to undermine the goals of equitable and efficient distribution (Dreze & Khera, 2015; Khera, 2011).

The core complexity of the PDS lies in its decentralized, multi-actor structure, where decisions and behaviours at the micro level—by ration dealers, suppliers, beneficiaries, and inspectors—aggregate to influence macro outcomes such as coverage, corruption levels, and public trust. Traditional analytical methods fall short in capturing this layered interactivity and nonlinear dynamics (Bonabeau, 2002). To explore these intricacies, we employ an Agent-Based Modelling (ABM) approach, which allows for the representation of individual agents, their behaviours, interactions, and emergent patterns in a simulated environment. ABM is particularly suited to systems where heterogeneity, local decision-making, and adaptive behaviour are central—as in the Indian PDS (Epstein & Axtell, 1996).

In the AI FORA (Artificial Intelligence for Assessment) project, we apply ABM to simulate and evaluate the Indian PDS using NetLogo (Wilensky & Rand, 2015). The model represents key actors—beneficiaries, ration shop employees, suppliers, trucks for logistical movement, and government officials responsible for inspections. Each agent follows simple decision rules, yet their collective behaviour yields insights into systemic outcomes such as fairness in ration allocation, transparency in operations, and accountability through effective governance. The simulation environment mirrors real-world processes, including stock delivery, corruption risk at shops, and random inspections, enabling a realistic and dynamic assessment of the system (see Fig. 7.1).

The objectives of this agent-based simulation are threefold. First, it seeks to ensure fairness, defined as equitable ration distribution to all eligible beneficiaries. This is crucial in a country as socio-economically diverse as India, where procedural delays or corrupt practices disproportionately affect marginalized groups. Second, the model promotes transparency through inspection mechanisms and information visibility, modelled by tracking whether ration shops are inspected and whether their activities align with protocol. Third, it evaluates accountability by linking agent behaviour (e.g., corruption or inefficiency) to consequences via inspection,

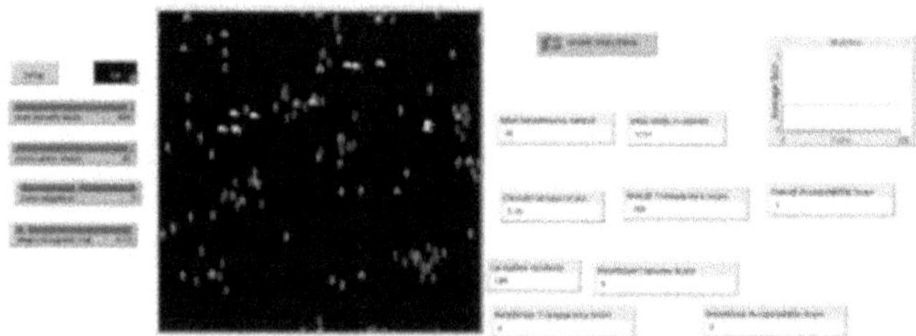

Fig. 7.1 NetLogo interface showing agents and interactions, including beneficiaries (blue), FPS (red/pink), suppliers (orange), officials (green triangles), and trucks (yellow)

reporting, and feedback loops. Together, these three pillars—fairness, transparency, and accountability—form the foundation of a Responsible AI framework tailored to public sector governance (Jobin et al., 2019, Mittelstadt et al., 2016).

The Indian case study in AI FORA models a representative district-level PDS network, abstracting real-world configurations while preserving essential behaviours and structures. It does not explicitly simulate policy interactions (such as community engagement or workshops), which are covered in a separate chapter. Instead, the focus here is on modelling logic, simulation dynamics, and insights from experimental runs. Embedding AI principles within a simulation-based governance framework illustrates how digital tools can support not only efficiency but also ethical and equitable service delivery.

In summary, this chapter provides a modelling-driven perspective on rethinking India's PDS. It offers a testbed for exploring how algorithmic interventions, monitoring protocols, and logistical efficiencies can shape outcomes, and it generates insights that can guide data-informed policy experimentation and AI-driven optimization in large-scale welfare systems.

Purpose of the Agent-Based Model in the Indian Case Study

The decision to use an Agent-Based Model (ABM) for India's Public Distribution System (PDS) arises from the system's intrinsic complexity and behavioural heterogeneity. Unlike equation-based or system dynamics models, ABMs provide a bottom-up framework to simulate decentralized decision-making, individual-level interactions, and emergent outcomes in complex adaptive systems. The PDS involves a distributed network of stakeholders—beneficiaries, ration dealers, suppliers, logistics providers, and inspectors—each with distinct motivations, constraints, and behavioural tendencies. ABM allows these actors to be modelled explicitly as autonomous entities with individual rules, while still capturing the system-level phenomena emerging from their interactions.

A key advantage of ABM over traditional approaches is its ability to incorporate corruption as a behavioural attribute rather than a static input. Corruption in the PDS is neither uniform nor constant; it varies across shops, regions, and individuals. ABM enables corruption risk to be represented probabilistically, dynamically influenced by factors such as inspection frequency, stock replenishment, and perceived enforcement. This nuanced representation is difficult to achieve in aggregate-level models.

The model is designed to address several critical questions:

- How do localized corruption incidents at ration shops impact overall fairness in distribution?
- What is the effect of inspection frequency and targeting strategy on transparency and accountability?

- How does coordination between suppliers and ration shops influence stock availability and beneficiary satisfaction?
- Under what conditions does the system show resilience versus breakdown (e.g., due to widespread diversion or logistical bottlenecks)?

The simulation also integrates Responsible AI metrics—fairness, transparency, and accountability—as real-time performance indicators. These metrics are not retrospective analytics but evolve as the simulation progresses and are embedded in agent behaviour. This enables the model to serve as a testbed for ethical and operational interventions, including AI-driven inspection schedules or predictive analytics to identify high-risk shops.

Beyond academic insights, the purpose of this ABM is to inform governance. It provides a risk-free environment to explore policy alternatives, understand failure modes, and identify leverage points for intervention. The long-term vision is to incorporate such models into digital policy sandboxes, where AI tools are evaluated for technical performance and alignment with public values and institutional constraints. In this way, the model advances AIFORA's broader objective: designing and evaluating AI systems that are fair, open, and responsible in domains directly affecting human well-being.

Agents

Agent-Based Modelling (ABM) enables the simulation of complex systems by defining discrete, autonomous entities—called agents—each with its own behavioural logic, goals, and interactions. In the AI FORA case study of the Indian Public Distribution System (PDS), we construct a simulation that captures the decentralized and interdependent behaviours of five key agent types: beneficiaries, ration shop operators, suppliers, trucks, and officials. Additionally, a sixth class—administrative or policy agents—is proposed for future versions to introduce adaptive and AI-driven oversight mechanisms. Each agent type plays a crucial role in determining the emergent performance of the food distribution ecosystem in terms of fairness, transparency, and accountability (see Fig. 7.2).

Beneficiaries

Beneficiaries represent ration cardholders entitled to subsidized food. Their actions and outcomes form the foundation of fairness assessment.

- Location Assignment: Each beneficiary is placed at a fixed home location on the simulation grid, enabling proximity-based routing and load balancing across shops.

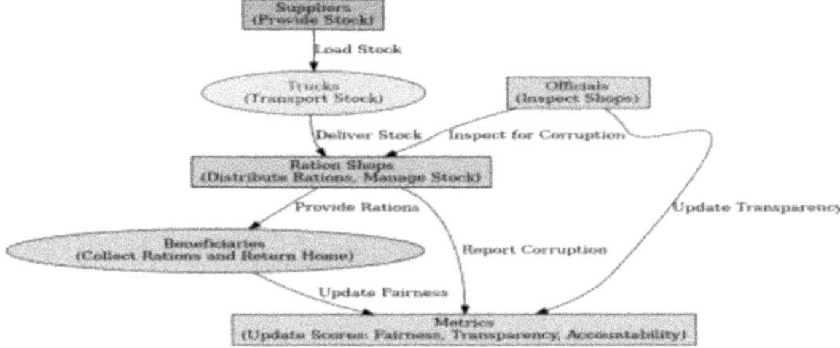

Fig. 7.2 PDS Workflow Diagram: The supply chain and AI-driven monitoring process for public ration distribution, involving suppliers, trucks, shops, officials, beneficiaries, and metric tracking

- Movement Behaviour: They periodically travel to the nearest FPS to collect rations, with configurable frequency (e.g., monthly).
- Eligibility Quota: Each is entitled to a fixed ration (e.g., 5 kg of foodgrain), which must be fully delivered to count as successful.
- System Perception: Failed or incomplete transactions reduce fairness and transparency scores.

Beneficiaries do not directly influence others but act as sensitive indicators of system integrity. Fairness outcomes emerge from their interactions with suppliers, FPS operators, and officials.

Ration Shop Operators (FPS)

Ration shops serve as distribution hubs and are central to both service delivery and corruption risk.

- Inventory Management: Each FPS begins with stock that depletes with distribution; when below a threshold, it requests replenishment from a supplier.
- Corruption Risk: Each FPS has a corruption risk value between 0.0 (honest) and 1.0 (fully corrupt). During transactions, the shop probabilistically diverts part or all of a ration.
- Diversion Behaviour: Diversion reduces beneficiary entitlement, even when recorded inventory suggests adequacy.
- Service Capacity: Each shop has a limited throughput, serving only a set number of beneficiaries per tick.

FPS agents drive systemic performance. Their stochastic corruption behaviour creates patterns of leakage and accountability lapses observable across scenarios.

Suppliers

Suppliers act as institutional agents managing central stocks and dispatching to FPS.

- Fulfilment of Requests: On resupply requests, suppliers generate truck agents carrying fixed quantities.
- Stock Adequacy Assumption: In the base model, suppliers hold infinite or "adequate" stock, keeping focus on FPS and logistics. Future versions may introduce shortages or delays.

Suppliers resemble government depots or warehouses, affecting performance mainly through logistics and dispatch timing.

Trucks (Mobile Logistics Agents)

Trucks model foodgrain transportation from suppliers to FPS.

- Dynamic Instantiation: Created by suppliers in response to FPS requests.
- Shortest-Path Routing: Travel to shops via grid-based shortest paths.
- Fixed Capacity: Each carries a fixed load (e.g., 100 units); large shortfalls may require multiple trips.
- Lifecycle: Removed from the system after completing delivery.

Modelling trucks enables analysis of delivery bottlenecks, capacity constraints, and the benefits of route optimization or AI-assisted dispatch.

Officials

Officials audit FPS operations and enforce compliance.

- Mobility Strategy: Officials patrol randomly or according to rules, prioritizing historically high-risk shops.
- Inspection Protocol: They check for discrepancies between reported inventory and actual transactions.
- Corruption Detection: Misalignments (e.g., recorded distribution without actual delivery) are flagged.
- Transparency Impact: Shops inspected during beneficiary interactions contribute positively to transparency scores.

Officials introduce governance feedback. Their frequency and targeting directly influence credibility, oversight, and potential AI-driven auditing extensions.

Optional: Administrative/Policy Agents

Proposed for future versions, these agents simulate higher-level policy and AI-enabled oversight.

- Policy Modulation: Adjust system parameters such as inspection frequency or supply reallocation dynamically.
- AI-Based Targeting: Use historical corruption scores to optimize inspections and surveillance.
- Adaptive Behaviour: Learn from prior runs to evolve governance strategies over time.

Incorporating these agents would create a multi-level governance simulation, linking citizen, operational, and policy layers—aligned with AI FORA's vision of adaptive, ethical digital governance.

Environment and Global Attributes

The simulation operates within a two-dimensional grid-based environment designed to represent a stylized administrative district in India. This environment is not geographically accurate but captures key structural characteristics necessary for modelling the Public Distribution System (PDS). The grid provides a spatial substrate on which agents interact, move, and make decisions based on proximity and availability. The spatial layout plays a crucial role in influencing access to services, frequency of interactions, and the efficiency of operations. It also enables the capture of spatial disparities in access to rations, a key equity concern in large and diverse countries like India.

Spatial Elements

The spatial environment consists of several fixed and dynamic entities, each contributing to the realism and operational logic of the model.

- Households: Each beneficiary agent is assigned a unique, fixed location on the grid. This spatial anchoring reflects the geographic dispersion of ration card holders across a district. The distance from each household to nearby Fair Price Shops (FPS) directly affects travel time and access. In remote or underserved areas, increased travel distance may discourage collection and lead to underutilization.
- FPS Locations: Ration shops are strategically positioned to ensure geographic coverage and manageable service loads. Their placement is designed to simulate a realistic mix of urban density (with multiple beneficiaries per shop) and rural dispersion (with fewer shops and higher travel distances). The positioning

of FPS also influences congestion levels, stock depletion rates, and inspection effectiveness.

- Supplier Nodes: These represent central warehouses or depots and are typically positioned along the edges or corners of the simulation grid to reflect logistical remoteness. Suppliers serve as static nodes that respond to stock requests from FPS locations. Their positioning affects delivery time, frequency of resupply, and overall system responsiveness.
- Paths: Agent movement follows the shortest-path logic, typically based on grid-based or Euclidean distance algorithms. Beneficiaries walk to their nearest FPS, while trucks and officials move along optimal routes to minimize travel time. Travel time impacts not only individual experience but also system performance—particularly when trucks are delayed, or officials must travel long distances to reach high-risk shops.

The spatial configuration allows the model to simulate and test various geographic scenarios, such as:

- *Urban Concentration:* High-density neighbourhoods with many beneficiaries per shop, leading to congestion, long queues, rapid stock depletion, and increased pressure on FPS staff. This can degrade service quality and amplify the impact of corruption.
- *Rural Sparsity:* Scenarios where a single FPS must serve a dispersed rural population, increasing beneficiary travel time and affecting fairness. Sparse distribution of FPS can result in logistical delays, underutilization of entitlements, and lower inspection coverage.

These configurations help evaluate the resilience and responsiveness of the PDS under diverse conditions. The flexible spatial structure allows for policy experimentation, such as testing the impact of adding new FPS locations or optimizing official movement.

Global Attributes

Global attributes are overarching indicators that track the evolving state of the simulation over time. These attributes are updated at each tick (simulation time step) and provide quantitative feedback on system performance, agent behaviour, and emerging trends. They are essential for monitoring the impact of dynamic decisions and environmental factors on key outcomes.

- Total beneficiaries served: Cumulative count of beneficiaries who have successfully collected their full ration entitlement. This metric provides a baseline for evaluating system reach and delivery efficiency. It serves as a key proxy for fairness and access.

- Stock levels: Real-time inventory values are maintained for each FPS. These values influence service availability and help determine when restocking is necessary. Low stock levels may trigger restock requests or result in partial service, directly affecting beneficiary outcomes.
- Corruption incidents: Number of verified corruption cases detected through inspections. These incidents are logged when officials find discrepancies between reported and observed stock or transaction records. The frequency and geographic spread of incidents help identify high-risk zones.
- Inspection count: Total number of inspections conducted by officials. This reflects the system's monitoring effort and is correlated with the transparency metric. A higher number of inspections may signal stronger enforcement, but it also consumes operational resources.
- Responsible AI Metrics:
    – fairness score: Measures the proportion of beneficiaries who received their full entitlement. It is sensitive to stock availability, corruption, and access.
    – transparency score: Tracks whether FPS locations have been inspected during beneficiary interactions. It reflects visibility and oversight.
    – accountability score: Assesses the proportion of transactions occurring at low-risk FPS locations (corruption risk <0.2). It indicates the system's success in steering distribution toward trusted nodes.

Tracking these global attributes allows real-time visualization and scenario analysis. They serve as key performance indicators for policymakers, modellers, and AI system designers aiming to optimize the fairness, efficiency, and governance of the PDS. When plotted over time, these metrics provide diagnostic signals for system improvement, risk management, and adaptive policy interventions.

Actions and Interactions

The simulation proceeds through discrete time steps, or "ticks," during which agents perform specific actions that contribute to the evolving state of the system. These actions and interactions are designed to reflect the real-world dynamics of a functioning PDS network. The following sequence outlines the operational loop:

1. Beneficiaries move to the nearest shop to collect rations: Each eligible beneficiary travels from their home to the closest Fair Price Shop. This movement is determined using the shortest-path algorithm. Travel success and ration access depend on whether the shop has sufficient inventory. If the shop is out of stock or corrupt, the beneficiary may return home without receiving their full entitlement.
2. Ration shops distribute or request new stock: FPS agents serve arriving beneficiaries, reducing their stock accordingly. If a shop's inventory falls below a threshold, it triggers a resupply request to the nearest supplier. If the shop is flagged as corrupt, there is a probability that the agent may divert some or all of the stock instead of distributing it fairly.

3. Trucks transport goods between suppliers and shops: Upon receiving a resupply request, supplier nodes dispatch truck agents to carry stock to the respective FPS. These trucks move through the grid and complete deliveries, after which they are removed from the simulation. Delivery delays may occur due to grid congestion or distance.
4. Officials conduct random inspections: Inspector agents move through the grid and conduct checks at selected FPS locations. Their visits help verify the integrity of distribution records. If discrepancies are found between reported and actual distributions, the system logs a corruption incident. Inspected shops contribute to higher transparency scores.
5. Metrics update at each tick: Following all agent actions, the system updates global attributes and performance metrics. These updates include stock levels, number of beneficiaries served, corruption incidents, and Responsible AI metrics (fairness, transparency, accountability). This continuous feedback loop helps model the evolving impact of agent behaviour on the system.

This cycle repeats across the simulation's run duration, enabling detailed analysis of temporal patterns, system bottlenecks, and the effect of policy interventions or behavioural assumptions.

Scoring Algorithm

To evaluate AI FORA-aligned performance, the model calculates three Responsible AI metrics: fairness, transparency, and accountability. These metrics are computed dynamically based on agent behaviour, transaction outcomes, and inspection events. They serve as ethical performance indicators, providing insights into whether the system is achieving its intended social and governance objectives.

Fairness

Fairness measures whether beneficiaries receive their full ration entitlement during each interaction with a Fair Price Shop. The metric captures the extent to which the system succeeds in delivering promised services without bias, denial, or loss.

For each beneficiary i:

Fairness $\_ i = 1$ if full ration received; 0 if partial or none received.

The system-wide fairness score at each tick is computed as the average across all N beneficiaries:

Fairness Score $= (1/N) \sum (Fairness \_ i) from i = 1 to N.$

This score is sensitive to factors such as FPS stock availability, corruption, and system congestion. A declining fairness score may indicate systemic bottlenecks, diversion of stock, or undersupply in specific areas.

Transparency

Transparency assesses whether transactions are conducted in an environment subject to oversight and verification. It reflects whether officials are actively inspecting FPS during beneficiary interactions, thus ensuring visibility and discouraging corrupt behaviour. For each beneficiary i:

Transparency $\_i = 1$ if FPS serving i was inspected; 0 otherwise.

The system-wide transparency score is computed as:

Transparency Score $= (1/N) \sum (Transparency \_i)$ from $i = 1$ to N.

This metric reveals whether monitoring mechanisms are functioning effectively. A low transparency score suggests that FPS are operating without sufficient oversight, increasing the risk of undetected malpractice.

Accountability

Accountability captures the extent to which the system channels transactions through low-risk (trustworthy) ration shops. It reflects the system's ability to minimize the influence of high corruption-risk FPS on the ration distribution process.

For each beneficiary i:

Accountability $\_i = 1$ if FPS corruption risk < 0.2; 0 otherwise.

The overall accountability score is then:

Accountability Score $= (1/N) \sum (Accountability \_i)$ from $i = 1$ to N.

High accountability implies that beneficiaries are primarily served by shops with low corruption risk. A declining accountability score could signal growing reliance on high-risk FPS or ineffective targeting and enforcement by officials.

Together, these three metrics enable a quantitative assessment of ethical and operational performance in the model. They also provide feedback loops for dynamic policy experimentation, allowing researchers and decision-makers to test interventions—such as increasing inspection frequency or reallocating supply—while monitoring their impact on fairness, transparency, and accountability.

Simulation Experiments and Results

Experimental Design

To evaluate the model under different operational and governance conditions, a series of simulation experiments were conducted. These experiments aim to examine how variations in key parameters affect system performance in terms of fairness, transparency, and accountability. The main experimental parameters include corruption probability levels, the number and frequency of inspections, and stock replenishment delays. FPS agents are initialized with varying levels of corruption risk, ranging from 0.0 (fully honest) to 1.0 (fully corrupt). Experiments explore how the system behaves when the average corruption level across all shops is low, medium, or high, thereby testing the model's resilience to systemic dishonesty. Officials may inspect FPS on a regular, random, or risk-targeted basis. By varying the frequency and strategy of inspections, the model simulates the effect of increased oversight on corruption detection and metric improvements. The time taken by trucks to deliver stock after an FPS raises a request is also varied to simulate logistical efficiency. Delays may occur due to distance, congestion, or truck availability. Scenarios with both prompt and delayed replenishment are evaluated to assess their impact on ration availability and beneficiary satisfaction.

Each simulation scenario is run for a fixed number of ticks (e.g., 500–1000) to allow enough time for patterns to emerge. All key metrics are recorded at each tick to track the temporal evolution of system behaviour.

Results Overview

The simulation experiments produced three key findings regarding the ethical and operational performance of the PDS system under varying conditions.

Regular Inspections Reduce Corruption Incidents In scenarios where officials inspected FPS frequently and in a targeted manner, the number of recorded corruption incidents decreased significantly. In high-inspection environments, corruption events were reduced by up to 50% compared to low-inspection baselines, and the transparency score improved steadily over time. These results demonstrate the importance of proactive oversight mechanisms to suppress unethical behaviours.

Improved Stock Logistics Enhance Fairness Simulations with minimal stock delivery delays showed consistently high fairness scores. Beneficiaries received their full entitlements more reliably, with fairness scores above 0.85. When delays were introduced, fairness dropped by 20–30%, revealing the sensitivity of the system to logistical performance. Efficient replenishment of FPS inventory is thus essential for maintaining equitable access.

Metric Trends Reflect System Health Visualization of metric data over simulation ticks offers insight into the system's dynamic state. Fairness trends show how service quality evolves in response to operational stress. Transparency increases with inspection coverage. Accountability improves as high-risk shops are identified and circumvented. These metrics provide valuable diagnostic signals for policy adaptation and system resilience.

These findings affirm the model's ability to represent the complexities of the PDS and underscore the potential of agent-based simulations as tools for policy design and evaluation.

Summary and Learnings

The Agent-Based Model of the Indian Public Distribution System (PDS) developed under the AI FORA initiative offers substantial insights into the inner workings of welfare distribution networks and their responsiveness to policy interventions. The simulation has shown that even minor changes in operational parameters—such as increasing the frequency of inspections or reducing stock replenishment delays—can lead to significant improvements in key Responsible AI metrics: fairness, transparency, and accountability.

In particular, the model underscores the systemic impact of behavioural patterns among frontline agents, such as ration shop operators, and the critical role of enforcement agents in curbing corrupt practices. It has revealed how corruption, when left unchecked, can cascade through the system and severely degrade service delivery. Conversely, strategically deploying officials for inspection can generate self-correcting feedback loops, gradually improving system performance.

Moreover, the simulation has helped identify bottlenecks, such as logistical delays in stock movement and the unequal distribution of FPS locations, which disproportionately affect beneficiaries in remote areas. These findings support the case for integrating digital monitoring tools and real-time data into the PDS to detect anomalies early and deploy corrective measures proactively. Ultimately, this model serves as a foundational prototype for using computational simulations to analyse ethical dimensions in public sector service delivery.

Outlook and Future Work

The current model provides a simplified but powerful representation of the PDS, and several promising directions exist for extending its capabilities in subsequent research phases. Future enhancements may include:

Integration with Real-Time PDS Datasets: By linking the simulation with actual administrative data (such as FPS-level ration allotments, beneficiary transaction logs, or mobile POS systems), the model can be calibrated and validated against real-world conditions. This will enhance predictive accuracy and support scenario planning for specific districts.

Dynamic Learning Agents: Future versions could introduce adaptive behaviours, such as ration shopkeepers who learn to evade inspections or change their strategies based on past enforcement. Similarly, beneficiaries could develop preferences or trust scores, altering how they engage with the system. These additions would reflect a more realistic decision-making landscape.

Scaling to Pan-India Simulations: With appropriate optimization and parallel processing, the model could be scaled to simulate state-level or national PDS networks. This would allow policy experiments that compare region-specific outcomes and test interventions at scale, incorporating geographic, socio-economic, and infrastructural heterogeneity.

Coupling with Policy Dashboards or Digital Twins: The model can be embedded within decision support systems that offer visual dashboards to policymakers. Alternatively, it could be linked to a digital twin of the PDS to enable real-time simulations, policy stress tests, and AI-assisted recommendations.

These directions would not only increase the technical sophistication of the model but also deepen its utility as a tool for ethical, data-driven, and context-sensitive governance of public distribution systems.

Acknowledgements Research presented in the chapter has been funded by the German Volkswa-genStiftung under grant agreement number 98 560.

References

Bonabeau, E. (2002). Agent-based modeling: Methods and techniques for simulating human systems. *Proceedings of the National Academy of Sciences, 99*(suppl_3), 7280–7287.

Dreze, J., & Khera, R. (2015). Understanding leakages in the public distribution system. *Economic and Political Weekly, 50*(7), 39–42.

Epstein, J. M., & Axtell, R. (1996). *Growing artificial societies: Social science from the bottom up.* Brookings Institution Press.

Jobin, A., Ienca, M., & Vayena, E. (2019). The global landscape of AI ethics guidelines. *Nature Machine Intelligence, 1*(9), 389–399.

Khera, R. (2011). Trends in diversion of grain from the public distribution system. *Economic and Political Weekly*, 106–114.

Mittelstadt, B. D., Allo, P., Taddeo, M., Wachter, S., & Floridi, L. (2016). The ethics of algorithms: Mapping the debate. *Big Data & Society, 3*(2), 1–21.

Wilensky, U., & Rand, W. (2015). *An introduction to agent-based modeling: Modeling natural, social, and engineered complex systems with NetLogo.* MIT Press.

Chapter 8
Policy Learnings and Policy Change for AI-Based Social Services

Albert Sabater, Beatriz López, and Roger Campdepadrós

Abstract This chapter examines the development and application of AI in social services through stakeholder engagement within the AI FORA project, drawing on meetings held in May 2022 and 2023 with diverse participants, including marginalized communities, social workers, policymakers, technologists, and academics. Focusing on Spain as a case study, we identify key challenges and opportunities in AI-driven social service provision, emphasizing the importance of compositional (demographic and socioeconomic factors), contextual (local systems and biases), and collective (community trust and participation) dimensions. Our findings reveal that AI risks exacerbating inequities when these factors are overlooked. However, stakeholders pointed out that context-aware AI applications, designed with adaptability, transparency, and participatory oversight can mitigate these risks. The chapter highlights three key policy lessons: (1) AI systems must evolve through continuous auditing and community input, (2) predictive tools should account for local realities to avoid bias, and (3) participatory governance is essential to ensure equity.

Introduction

In this chapter, we explain how we have engaged with several stakeholders that are related to various AI-based social services to understand common policy views and assess whether the development and application of AI in social services is guided by policy learnings and policy change. As part of the AI FORA[1] project, two separate

---

[1] https://www.ai-fora.de/

A. Sabater (✉) · B. López · R. Campdepadrós
University of Girona, Girona, Spain
e-mail: albert.sabater@udg.edu

B. López
e-mail: beatriz.lopez@udg.edu

R. Campdepadrós
e-mail: roger.campdepadros@udg.edu

P. Ahrweiler and N. Gilbert (eds.), *Participatory Modelling and Simulation to Improve AI-based Public Social Services*, Artificial Intelligence, Simulation and Society,
https://doi.org/10.1007/978-3-032-15283-1_8

meetings on May 6, 2022, and May 4, 2023, with various stakeholders are taken as the main sources of information and deliberation. The stakeholders that came to the meetings represented various segments of the population: (1) marginalized or vulnerable groups (community organizations of migrants and advocacy groups for workers); (2) professionals who administer social services and have firsthand experience with the practicalities and challenges of integrating AI into their work (social workers and service providers); (3) government officials responsible for the implementation of AI in social services (policy makers); (4) engineers, data scientists, and AI specialists who design and build AI systems (AI technologists and developers, mostly academics); and (5) scholars who study the social, ethical, and legal implications of AI (social scientists).

All these stakeholders were able to provide a comprehensive picture of the advantages and disadvantages of using AI in social services for our Spanish case study. The two meetings employed a mixed-method approach with gamification techniques, focus groups, and simulation to facilitate productive dialogue between stakeholders. The participant pool was stratified into distinct breakout groups such as social workers, service providers, and policymakers to discuss practical implementation hurdles, and another one with technical and social scientists to debate frameworks for AI-based social assessment that were mostly (active) observers before and after meetings and working sessions to integrate multiple perspectives in the research. Gamification and focus groups included discussions guided by scenario-based situations to elicit specific reactions (e.g., coronavirus game, unemployment game, and self-sufficiency game), which allowed not only the actual improvement of initial AI specifications of rulesets, but were also useful to break down disciplinary silos, translate technical concepts into practical consequences, and ground abstract ethical principles in the lived realities of service delivery.

This chapter provides further detail about these issues dealth with by stakeholders, and is purposively organized as follows: first, we provide an overview of three key challenges for AI implementation in social services: the compositional, contextual, and collective factors. Second, we stress that one size does not fit all when it comes to using AI for social services. And, third, we look at some of the main obstacles and ways forward.

Compositional, Contextual and Collective Factors

The use of AI in social services in Spain and elsewhere, from housing and employment to migration assistance or integration, generally lies in a common expectation, namely that it will enhance precision, efficiency, and scalability in the social provision (Criado et al., 2025). However, its success depends on three fundamental challenges, namely that social service provision is inherently place-specific, shaped by who lives there (compositional factors), local systems and resources (contextual factors), and community trust and collaboration (collective factors). Hence, our case study has revealed that the risks posed by AI in social services are significant, particularly when compositional, contextual, and collective factors are overlooked (Tangi et al., 2023). Compositional factors such as the demographic and socioeconomic makeup of affected communities determine how AI systems interpret and act upon real-world needs, often with consequences that diverge sharply from intended outcomes. Contextual elements, including entrenched institutional biases and infrastructural limitations, further complicate deployment, while collective dynamics, such as community trust and power imbalances, mediate whether AI entrenches or alleviates existing inequities.

Without deliberate safeguards, algorithmic discrimination, privacy violations, and an over-reliance on automated decision-making (ADM) risk compounding harm, thus eroding trust in social services, especially among vulnerable populations already subject to most systemic exclusion. In other words, the implementation of AI applications for social service delivery that ignore these factors risk exacerbating inequities rather than resolving them. These issues were central to our discussions among policymakers, academics, and civil society organizations. For example, biased risk-assessment tools were seen by many as a way to disproportionately flag low-income families for punitive interventions, while opaque data-sharing practices were looked at to expose sensitive personal information (Eubanks, 2018). These were only a few examples that reflected a disconnect between AI's current design and the complex realities of the communities it serves.

Therefore, the first lesson from the policy workshops was that the path forward demands context-aware AI applications that harmonize innovation with adaptability, transparency, and participatory oversight. Most stakeholders viewed that this requires systems capable of evolving in response to unintended consequences, with mechanisms for continuous auditing and recalibration as social needs shift. In this sense, transparency must extend beyond technical explainability to meaningful accountability, thus ensuring that affected communities understand how decisions are made and how to challenge them. The second lesson from stakeholders was that while AI-driven tools such as predictive analytics for early intervention or data-driven resource allocation offer powerful ways to optimize social services, their design and deployment must address place-based realities. For instance, AI may help target services to high-need populations, but without safeguards, it may replicate biases embedded in historical data or overlook marginalized groups for which data availability is limited. The third lesson was that decision-support systems must integrate grassroots insights to ensure that AI applications complement rather than replace human judgment and community expertise. Stakeholders clearly pointed out that participatory oversight must be embedded in AI governance from the outset as a way to transform passive stakeholders into active co-designers of technological solutions.

Further, a key problem identified by most stakeholders was that attempting to mitigate one factor without the others can be ineffective or counterproductive. For example, creating a technically "unbiased" algorithm for a compositionally diverse community (compositional factor) will fail if deployed without the trust of that community (collective factor) or within a biased institutional context (contextual factor). Therefore, any solution requires an approach where progress in one dimension actively enables and strengthens progress in the others, thereby creating a positive feedback loop that leads to equitable outcomes. The meetings with stakeholders clearly demonstrated that an important way to accomplish this is by implementing a participatory oversight (collective factor), which ensures that context-aware AI (contextual factor) is designed with and for the specific community it serves (compositional factor). Since the compositional, contextual, and collective factors are deeply intertwined and measures to mitigate risks in one area almost invariably create mutually reinforcing effects in the others, it is crucial to have transparency and accountability (contextual/collective) that not only allow communities to understand and challenge decisions, but also build trust (collective) and ensure that the system evolves to meet real-world needs (compositional).

Beyond the Algorithm: A Participatory Framework

The Interdependent Triad

Policymakers often treat AI as a singular, ready-made solution for improving precision, efficiency, and scalability in social services (Dowding & Taylor, 2024). However, addressing complex social challenges requires far more than generic algorithmic tools. For AI to produce meaningful results, it must be grounded not only in a far greater understanding of compositional factors (who is affected, including demographics and vulnerabilities), contextual factors (local systems, data infrastructure, and service gaps), and collective factors (community trust and participatory norms), but also for AI to meaningfully improve social services, its deployment must be place-specific and consciously adapted across key functional areas such as data-driven targeting and resource allocation, predictive analytics and early intervention, decision-support systems for policy development, and evaluation for continuous improvement.

How AI Can Improve Resource Allocation

AI applications can improve resource allocation when its deployment adapts to local ecosystems, but effective targeting demands more than algorithmic processing of datasets. It requires a multidimensional understanding of who needs services (compositional), what local capacity exists (contextual), and how communities define equitable distribution (collective). Compositionally, algorithms can be tuned to recognize varying needs across demographic groups, for instance, by adjusting housing assistance models for migrant and non-migrant communities with distinct kinship structures. Contextually, resource allocation systems must integrate with existing service infrastructures, whether well-funded urban social services or under-resourced rural ones. Collectively, communities should be able to co-design delivery metrics in order to ensure that AI-based social services prioritize their definitions of "effective" service rather than top-down efficiency benchmarks. This also means that public administrations must work with academics to design targeting models that weight sociodemographic variables differently across contexts.

Contextualizing AI-Based Social Service

Needless to say, civil society plays a crucial role in contextualizing these models through ground-level knowledge about which vulnerable groups are systematically excluded from official datasets. Therefore, the so-called data-driven policymaking gains value when evidence incorporates place-based knowledge. For instance, compositionally speaking, dashboards should disaggregate data by sociodemographic and other relevant factors to expose inequities. Contextually, models must account for local variations such as how fairness or prejudice manifests differently across localities. The collective dimension can also emerge when participatory data collection (e.g. community-led surveys) supplements administrative datasets.

Understanding Compositional Vulnerabilities

It is understood that AI models, including predictive ones, are useful and achieve greater preventive potential only when they account for compositional vulnerabilities (e.g., housing availability for migrants), contextual data ecosystems (e.g., integration of migrant records where legally permitted), and collective early warning systems (e.g., community worker insights). Academics can help address compositional blind spots by developing subpopulation-specific risk indicators, while civil society organizations can provide contextual insights about which informal support networks already exist in neighborhoods to name one example. Importantly, the collective factor becomes operational when AI models incorporate community feedback loops to continuously adjust risk thresholds based on lived experience from the potential recipients of social services. This interdependence is key: the collective factor of community worker input provides the contextual grounding that makes the compositional prediction actionable. In turn, this actionability builds trust (collective), ensuring the system evolves to meet the real-world needs of the specific populations (compositional) it was designed to protect.

Decision-Support Systems to Maintain Legitimacy

It is clear that policy AI tools such as agent-based models (ABM) can be used to balance compositional complexity (representing needs of diverse groups), contextual constraints (matching recommendations to local service delivery capacities), and collective governance (maintaining public legitimacy). For instance, in our gamification and simulation that aimed to maximize individual and aggregate well-being by allocating limited social service resources among applicants, stakeholders demonstrated that by playing and interacting with the simulation, they gained awareness of historical biases and discriminatory practices in social service allocation within their national context and actively sought to mitigate such risks. These observations suggested that collaborative decision-making processes also foster consensus on evaluation standards and promote more consistent implementation of the assessment tool. In other words, compositionally, policy teams have the capacity to audit training data for representation gaps like including informal settlement residents in housing-need assessments.

Contextually, the metrics used can reflect local priorities, whether geographic deprivation indices or community-defined inclusion benchmarks. Collectively, the impacted groups may have a veto power over algorithmic criteria affecting them to make sure that participation is effective and not against them. Although academics have shown that disaggregated metrics for social assessment that capture compositional disparities in service outcomes are useful, they need to be complemented by civil society organizations, which provide contextual grounding by monitoring unintended consequences that quantitative metrics might miss or might be unable to capture with only observational data. Thus, the collective element is a crucial step toward participatory evaluation methods that complement AI-driven analytics with community scorecards and narrative feedback. This creates a reinforcing dynamic where collective oversight strengthens contextual fit, which in turn ensures compositional fairness, thus building the public trust essential for the tool's viability and legitimacy.

Continuous Evaluation

A continuous evaluation is necessary as AI feedback loops become transformative only when they capture the collective dimension over time and a bridge is built between AI models and observable measurements on compositional and contextual realities, using previous literature and theoretical justification. Participatory methods, where communities adjust algorithmic weights (collective), directly tie compositional outcomes to contextual constraints. This process builds trust (collective) through transparency, ensures the system meets real-world needs (compositional), and adapts to local realities (contextual). As shown in the AI FORA approach, within the sphere of social service provision, the evaluation of algorithmic systems must be redesigned as a dialogic process of organizational learning, rather than a summative audit of performance indicators. Conventional metrics, such as caseload processing times or aggregate expenditure data, constitute a superficial engagement with compositional outcomes, while remaining agnostic to the contextual determinants of service delivery.

In order to overcome this, a paradigm of participatory evaluation is paramount. This approach institutionalizes collective oversight by integrating mechanisms such as community review panels and co-design workshops for algorithmic weight calibration. Such deliberation allows for the formal incorporation of tacit, place-based knowledge, ensuring that quantitative models are dynamically adjusted to reflect nuanced compositional realities (e.g., the specific vulnerabilities of transient populations) and are constrained by the operational limits of the local service ecology (contextual). This recursive feedback loop between the system and its stakeholders fosters the production of more granular and valid data, enhances the contextual parameters of the model, and, crucially, builds institutional legitimacy (collective). Only after the participative component is completed, and measurements are justified and defined, do policymakers and researchers proceed to the next step where data and AI models are deployed publicly to establish a positive feedback loop wherein algorithmic refinement, institutional adaptation, and enhanced community trust are mutually constitutive, thereby orienting continuous improvement toward the normative goal of equitable social outcomes (Sabater et al., 2025).

Overcoming Obstacles

Since the AI FORA approach involved multiple groups with diverse backgrounds and perspectives, balancing the discussions was challenging. Nonetheless, there were no major conflicts or difficulties in finding common ground. Generally, the approach succeeded in finding common ground precisely because it institutionalized structured deliberation mechanisms from the outset. Rather than treating diversity of perspectives as an obstacle, the process leveraged it as a diagnostic tool. An example is when technologists or academic proposals for scoring metrics were tested against social workers. This created what participants termed as "constructive friction", where apparent disagreements were useful to detect blind spots in the system design as well as hybrid approaches that incorporated both clear rules and discretionary override provisions (for instance, for exceptional cases validated by frontline staff). Because policy workshops, like real-world scenarios, always entailed translation work happening behind the scenes, social workers also acted as facilitators in their crucial role as "contextual interpreters", while simultaneously helping non-technical participants articulate their needs in ways that could inform model design.

However, the workshops revealed that technical complexity was not merely a communication challenge, but, more generally, a systemic barrier requiring structural solutions (Birhane, 2021). Generally, concepts were presented at three levels: technical specifications, policy implications, and real-world analogies for community representatives. For instance, algorithmic bias was simultaneously explained as (1) a statistical skew in training data, (2) a potential source of service inequities, and (3) being like a library that only stocks books about certain neighborhoods or localities. This approach allowed participants to engage at their comfort level while gradually building shared understanding. Most importantly, the explanations given were not unidirectional as social workers also gave feedback on how to interpret qualitative indicators like housing instability signals that never appear in structured datasets. It is clear that as participants' technical literacy grew, the nature of discussions evolved from passive reception to active co-design in a way that clearly highlighted that we must create pathways for non-technical stakeholders to reshape technical systems.

In summary, the policy workshops within the two separate meetings on May 6, 2022, and May 4, 2023, with various stakeholders proved to be extremely useful to analyze the extent to which developing context-aware AI systems requires institutionalizing three working principles: First, deliberative prototyping means testing models through scenario-based discussions and simulations with mixed stakeholder groups before any AI implementation. Second, contextualize outputs among stakeholders to discuss and further improve prototypes. Third, participatory stress-testing to evaluate AI systems against (un)usual cases, sometimes only identified by frontline social workers. Since there was always the very real possibility of power imbalance between those developing and deploying AI systems in practice, and the communities that are subject to them, the analysis of the compositional, contextual, and collective dimensions are not theoretical ideals, but practical necessities that emerge through structured engagement processes. The challenge moving forward is scaling these into standard practice, thus ensuring AI systems remain as adaptable as the complex social realities they aim to serve with multidisciplinary teams of researchers, practitioners, policy makers, and citizens alike.

Acknowledgment Research presented in this chapter has been funded by the German VolkswagenStiftung under grant agreement number 98 560.

References

Birhane, A. (2021). Algorithmic injustice: A relational ethics approach. *Patterns, 2*(2), 100205. https://doi.org/10.1016/j.patter.2021.100205.

Criado, J. I., Alcaide-Muñoz, L., & Liarte, I. (2025). Two decades of public sector innovation: Building an analytical framework from a systematic literature review of types, strategies, conditions, and results. *Public Management Review, 27*(3), 623–652. https://doi.org/10.1080/147 19037.2023.2254310.

Dowding, K., & Taylor B. R. (2024). Algorithmic decision-making, agency costs, and institution-based trust. *Philosophy & Technology, 37*(2), 68. https://doi.org/10.1007/s13347-024-00757-5.

Eubanks, V. (2018). *Automating inequality: How high-tech tools profile, police, and punish the poor*. Picador, St. Martin's Press.

Sabater Coll, A., López, B., Campdepadrós, R., & Sánchez, C. (2025). Participatory action research for AI in social services: An example of local practice from Catalonia. In P. Ahrweiler (Ed.),

Participatory artificial intelligence in public social services: From bias to fairness in assessing beneficiaries. Springer. https://doi.org/10.1007/978-3-031-71678-2_4.

Tangi, L., van Noordt, C., & Rodriguez Müller, A. P. (2023). The challenges of AI implementation in the public sector. An in-depth case studies analysis. In *Proceedings of the 24th Annual International Conference on Digital Government Research* (pp. 414–422).

Chapter 9
Policy Perspectives on AI Use for Asylum-Related Assessment Processes in Germany

Elisabeth Späth, David Wurster, Blanca Luque Capellas, and Petra Ahrweiler

Abstract This chapter examines the use of artificial intelligence (AI) in asylum-related assessment processes in Germany, focusing on the interaction between research, policy, and frontline administration. Germany has a well-established framework for integrating scientific expertise into policymaking, yet the dissemination of findings to practitioners, particularly public administrators, remains underdeveloped. Drawing on insights from the AI FORA project, the chapter reports on an interactive policy workshop with policymakers, migration experts, and refugee council representatives. Key themes discussed during the workshop include fairness, efficiency, and data quality in asylum-related assessment processes, alongside concerns about power asymmetries and fragmented governance. While participants saw potential in AI for reducing bureaucracy, facilitating translations, and supporting labour market integration, they cautioned that its use could intensify existing challenges related to justice and equity, highlighting the need for careful oversight. The chapter argues that "better AI" must go hand in hand with "better governance", requiring legal safeguards, inclusive participation, and stronger refugee agency. The participatory dissemination approach adopted here demonstrates how collaborative engagement could enhance policy relevance, point out ethical dilemmas, and guide future frameworks for responsible AI use in sensitive contexts such as asylum governance.

E. Späth (✉) · D. Wurster · B. Luque Capellas · P. Ahrweiler
TISSS Lab, Institute of Sociology, Johannes Gutenberg University, Mainz, Germany
e-mail: espaeth@uni-mainz.de

D. Wurster
e-mail: dwurster@uni-mainz.de

B. Luque Capellas
e-mail: bluqueca@uni-mainz.de

P. Ahrweiler
e-mail: petra.ahrweiler@uni-mainz.de

P. Ahrweiler and N. Gilbert (eds.), *Participatory Modelling and Simulation to Improve AI-based Public Social Services*, Artificial Intelligence, Simulation and Society,
https://doi.org/10.1007/978-3-032-15283-1_9

Introduction

In Germany, policymakers engage with scientific expertise both through formal requests and unsolicited contributions. National and regional laws require the inclusion of experts—such as scientists, business leaders, and NGO representatives—when drafting legislation. This involvement typically takes the form of parliamentary hearings, commissioned evaluation reports, and expert discussions organised by ministries. Scientific advisory boards and enquiry commissions, often composed of academics and former politicians, provide comprehensive assessments of emerging policy challenges. Many ministries also operate research institutes employing large numbers of scientists, such as the Federal Environment Agency. Within this formal framework, scientific organisations proactively provide expertise. For example, the Max Planck and Helmholtz societies regularly publish policy briefs and host events for knowledge exchange (Heinze, 2013; Weingart, 2001). This reflects Germany's well-established institutional infrastructure for integrating science into policymaking.

University researchers frequently contribute to expert bodies and commissioned studies, though they less often produce targeted policy briefs. New formats are emerging to bridge this gap, such as pairing schemes and lab visits that connect researchers directly with policymakers. In addition, policy-relevant research projects at universities increasingly address practitioner audiences outside formal institutional pathways. The AI FORA project engages directly with public servants in social service agencies and policymakers. Research findings in such settings can inform institutional practices and support fair and transparent decision-making. Involving public administrators and ground-level decision makers is essential for several reasons. First, these actors *implement policies*. While high-level politicians design laws and frameworks, it is administrators who interpret, apply, and enforce them in daily practice (Ewert & Evers, 2014). Their decisions have direct consequences for asylum seekers, often involving discretion in complex or ambiguous cases. Understanding how AI tools could function in their workflows is crucial for assessing feasibility, risks, and practical outcomes. Second, frontline workers are the first to *interact with new technologies*: if AI systems are introduced into asylum procedures, they will be the ones operating, trusting, or questioning these tools (Kersing et al., 2022). Finally, policy feedback loops often start from below. Administrators, ideally, feed information upward, influencing internal guidelines, policy adjustments, and even future legislation. Their experiences shape what works and what requires reform, making their engagement vital for adaptive, evidence-informed governance (Bovens & Zouridis, 2002). As the use of AI-based technology in the context at hand is gaining increasing relevance and importance (Ozkul, 2023), it is of crucial importance that policymakers understand the ethical as well as practical implications of using AI in asylum-related assessment processes. Bridging the gap between refugees' lived experiences, technical and organisational capabilities, as well as expectations of public administration and those of policymakers becomes essential.

Dissemination of Research Findings to the Policy Community in Germany

The dissemination of findings from the German case study in AI FORA (Späth, 2025)[1] sought to bridge two gaps: first, incorporating policy perspectives into the research data and, second, presenting results in a form that could be discussed and potentially transferred across the policy arena, across different federal states and institutions. A key aim was to understand how challenges, such as bureaucratic inertia, and federal–local hierarchies could shape the engagement with, or adoption of, AI-based technologies.

To this end, an interactive policy workshop was organised.[2] Invitations were extended to national and regional policymakers, domain experts, and researchers specialising in migration and asylum governance as well as digitalisation. Ten participants attended the workshop: policymakers from the regional and federal levels, representatives from refugee councils, an organization focused on education and integration, as well as academic experts on migration policy. Dissemination was achieved through the co-design of a simplified model of the asylum system, charting the journey from "arrival in Germany" to "economic independence/naturalisation". This exercise employed Participatory Systems Mapping (Barbrook-Johnson & Penn, 2022) visualising processes before, during, and after the asylum procedure. Collaborative modelling with policymakers has proven to be important not only to confirm the quality and availability of data, but also to gain a broader as well as deeper understanding of the complexities of policy domains (Ahrweiler et al., 2019; Gilbert et al., 2018). In a first step, participants were asked to evaluate different stages of assessment processes using three suggested guiding criteria: *fairness, data quality, and efficiency*. In a second step, they were asked to reflect upon possible implications as well as potentials of AI-based technologies. In the following, some reflections are presented briefly.

Fairness, Data Quality, and Efficiency

Fairness was linked not only to the availability of information but also to refugees' ability to access, comprehend, and share relevant data with authorities and supporting organisations. Suggestions included creating low-barrier participation opportunities to counteract excessive bureaucracy and limited digitalisation. One major proposal was an AI-driven guidance tool that could inform refugees about processes and

---

[1] Empirical research zooming into the micro-scene of AI-based decision-making in the asylum procedure as well as post-asylum procedure assessment processes was conducted based on document analysis, qualitative interviews, focus groups, as well as participatory modelling with refugees, voluntary supporters, and professionals working in the field.

[2] The workshop took place 2–3 July 2024 at Johannes Gutenberg University Mainz as a satellite to the European Workshop on Algorithmic Fairness (EWAF'24).

connect them to relevant organisations based on their needs, ideally offering immediate placement—a "digital guidance and counselling package" covering the entire process. Another recurring theme in the discussion was that refugees' legal status outcome are often shaped by "luck", depending on the federal state in which the asylum procedure takes place. Participants also noted limited political momentum to address this situation.

Concern was expressed about the arrival and distribution of refugees across federal states. Participants called for a more targeted distribution, balancing local demands with refugees' individual backgrounds.[3] Participants also emphasised the need for greater involvement of migrants, particularly those with refugee backgrounds, in public administration. Besides, they noted that the margin of discretion present in many post-asylum procedure assessment processes, such as in foreigners' offices, heightens the risk of unfair treatment. There were divergent opinions, however, as to what extent digitalisation and AI-based technology could mitigate these issues.

On *data quality*, participants highlighted the need for accurate personal data (age, gender, documents, etc.) and the importance of proper management, protection, and evaluation. Fragmented data collection across governmental levels—state, federal, and municipal—was seen as both inefficient and error-prone. Divergent organisational structures, privacy rules, and security standards exacerbate these problems. As a result, poor data quality could undermine fairness, for example, in respect to accessing integration courses. Furthermore, workshop participants emphasised that stakeholders (e.g. hardship commissions, NGOs or foreigner offices) evaluate data quality differently, i.e. some actors are more sceptical towards assessments or reports, often due to intransparent decision-making beforehand.

The participants identified *efficiency* as the overarching problem, as asylum-related assessment processes are lengthy and overly complex from the outset, involving a high number of different actors as well as regulations, and differences in respect to technical infrastructures. While recognition of educational and professional qualifications as well as work permits was described as inefficient and opaque, participants saw opportunities for AI to support faster recognition of qualifications and more effective career counselling, thereby facilitating earlier access to the labour market.

Overall, participants viewed AI as potentially helpful in reducing bureaucracy and offering translations in multiple contexts, from document processing to communication with authorities. Translation was directly linked to all three evaluation criteria: efficiency, data quality, and fairness.

---

[3] This has been realised by the Match'In project by the Universities of Hildesheim and Erlangen-Nuremberg, 2021–2025 (see Policy paper by Reinhold et al., 2025).

Policy Reflections on "Better AI" and "Better Governance"

A central message from the workshop was that it would be ethically unacceptable to use technology merely to "optimize an unfair system", thereby intensifying issues related to justice and equity. While some AI tools already in use are classified as "high-risk" technologies under the EU AI Act (Brouwer, 2024; PICUM, 2024) and require special scrutiny, many other potential applications that could support refugees and administration staff demand consideration as well as critical evaluation. As Discussions underscored that focusing solely on technical optimisation or ethical principles is insufficient, especially when these principles lack enforcement (cf. Hagendorff, 2020; Maclure & Morin-Martel, 2025). Related to this, addressing legal aspects necessitates a critical reflection on cultural and structural factors impacting decision-making processes, such as hierarchical and federalist organisation. From these reflections, several governance lessons emerge:

Institutionalised Dialogue Multi-stakeholder engagement is essential to move beyond "legal loopholes", build legitimacy and establish corresponding legal safeguards (Grimmelikhuijsen & Meijer, 2022; Popovski & Turner, 2012). Dialogue should occur early and continuously, protecting democratic values and human rights.

Inclusive Participation Involvement must extend beyond policymakers, legal experts, and technology providers. Refugees and migrants—through councils and self-organised groups—need to be included. Their lived experience offers indispensable expertise for ensuring transparency, bias prevention as well as efficiency, such as in terms of improving information infrastructures.

Strengthening Refugee Agency Refugees should have access not only to information and support, but also to transparent decision-making processes. Low-barrier pathways to participation are necessary for equitable treatment, regardless of origin or legal status. Improving access to employment and healthcare was emphasised as fundamental by policymakers, professionals, volunteers, and refugees alike. Building digital infrastructures offering immediate placement as well as AI applications that facilitate communication and information-sharing, such as translation tools, should be prioritised.

Conclusion

The joint evaluation of AI FORA findings with the policy community demonstrated the importance of acknowledging complexity and interdependence in asylum-related assessment processes. Policymaking must address not only individual processes but also the tensions and recurring issues that cut across domains. Participants suggested that future collaborative modelling should combine a broad "zooming out" perspective on systemic interrelations with a "zooming in" focus on specific barriers, such as access to employment. This dual approach could help design policies where AI applications complement fair and transparent governance. The participatory approach adopted by AI FORA, bringing together diverse stakeholders and addressing both risks and opportunities, enabled to explore some of the challenges and trade-offs regarding AI in asylum governance. Dissemination of scientific findings in this way can foster critical reflection and connects research with practice, pointing out relevant ethical dilemmas. Ultimately, future policies on AI in the asylum context should aim to create frameworks that uphold democratic values, protect human rights, and strengthen refugee agency.

Acknowledgements We thank the Mercator Science-Policy Fellowship-Program for connecting AI FORA researchers with policymakers. Research presented in the chapter has been funded by the German VolkswagenStiftung under grant agreement number 98 560.

References

Ahrweiler, P., Frank, D., & Gilbert, N. (2019). Co-designing social simulation models for policy advice: Lessons learned from the INFSO-SKIN study. In *2019 Spring Simulation Conference (SpringSim)* (pp. 1–12). IEEE. https://ieeexplore.ieee.org/document/8732901

Barbrook-Johnson, P., & Penn, A. S. (2022). Participatory systems mapping. In P. Barbrook-Johnson & A. S. Penn (Eds.), *Systems mapping* (pp. 61–78). Palgrave Macmillan. https://doi.org/10.1007/978-3-031-01919-7_5

Bovens, M., & Zouridis, S. (2002). From street-level to system-level bureaucracies: How ICT is transforming administrative discretion and constitutional control. *Public Administration Review, 62*(2), 174–184. https://doi.org/10.1111/0033-3352.00168

Brouwer, E. (2024). EU's AI act and migration control: Shortcomings in safeguarding fundamental rights. Retrieved September 15, from *Verfassungsblog.* https://doi.org/10.59704/a4de76df20e0de5a

Bullock, J., Young, M. M., & Wang, Y.-F. (2020). Artificial intelligence, bureaucratic form, and discretion in public service. *Information Polity, 25*(4), 491–506. https://doi.org/10.3233/IP-200223

Ewert, B., & Evers, A. (2014). Blueprints for the future of welfare provision? Shared features of service innovations across Europe. *Social Policy and Society, 13*(3), 423–432. https://doi.org/10.1017/S1474746414000074

Gilbert, N., Ahrweiler, P., Barbrook-Johnson, P. Narasimhan, K., & Wilkinson, H. (2018). Computational modelling of public policy: Reflections on practice. *Journal of Artificial Societies and Social Simulation, 21*(1), 14. https://doi.org/10.18564/jasss.3669.

Grimmelikhuijsen, S., & Meijer, A. (2022). Legitimacy of algorithmic decision-making: Six threats and the need for a calibrated institutional response. *Perspectives on Public Management and Governance, 5*(3), 232–242. https://doi.org/10.1093/ppmgov/gvac008

Hagendorff, T. (2020). The ethics of AI ethics: An evaluation of guidelines. *Minds & Machines, 30*, 99–120. https://doi.org/10.1007/s11023-020-09517-8

Heinze, R. G. (2013). Federal government in Germany: Temporary, issue-related policy advice. In K. H. Goetz et al. (Eds.), *Policy analysis in Germany.* Policy Press. https://doi.org/10.51952/9781447306269.ch010.

Kersing, M., van Zoonen, L., Putters, K., & Oldenhof, L. (2022). The changing roles of frontline bureaucrats in the digital welfare state: The case of a data dashboard in Rotterdam's work and income department. *Data & Policy, 4*, e24. https://doi.org/10.1017/dap.2022.16

Maclure, J., & Morin-Martel, A. (2025). AI ethics' institutional turn. *Digital Society, 4*, 18. https://doi.org/10.1007/s44206-025-00174-x

Ozkul, D. (2023). *Automating immigration and asylum: The uses of new technologies in migration and asylum governance in Europe*. Refugee Studies Centre: University of Oxford.

PICUM. (2024). A dangerous precedent: How the EU AI Act fails migrants and people on the move. Retrieved September 15, from https://picum.org/blog/a-dangerous-precedent-how-the-eu-ai-act-fails-migrants-and-people-on-the-move

Popovski, V., & Turner, N. (2012). Legitimacy as complement and corrective to legality. In R. Falk, M. Juergensmeyer, & V. Popovski (Eds.), *Legality and legitimacy in global affairs* (pp. 329–342). Oxford University Press. https://doi.org/10.1093/acprof:oso/9780199781577.003.0015

Reinhold, S.A., Euler, K., Bendel, P., Kasparick, D., & Schammann, H. (2025). *Match'in: Policy paper. Passgenaue Verteilung für Schutzsuchende und Kommunen im Zuweisungsverfahren*. Stiftung Mercator. https://doi.org/10.25528/224.

Späth, E. (2025). AI use in the asylum procedure in Germany: Exploring perspectives with refugees and supporters on assessment criteria and beyond. In P. Ahrweiler (Ed.), *Participatory artificial intelligence in public social services* (pp. 119–146). Springer. https://doi.org/10.1007/978-3-031-71678-2_6

Third European Workshop on Algorithmic Fairness (EWAF'24). (2024, July 1–3). Mainz. Retrieved September 15, from https://2024.ewaf.org

Weingart, P. (2001). Paradoxes of scientific advice to politics. In OECD (Ed.), *Social sciences for knowledge and decision making* (pp. 79–94). OECD.

Chapter 10
Bridging Data and Policy: Disseminating Scientific Insights in Estonia's AI-Driven Welfare Governance

Avo Trumm, Maris Männiste, and Triin Vihalemm

Abstract This chapter gives an overview of the results of a multi-stakeholder policy workshop held in Estonia in December 2024. The participants were experts from the National Statistical Board, Research Council, Social Insurance Board, Foresight Centre of the Estonian Parliament, Health Board, Tartu City Government, and Centre of IT Impact Studies (University of Tartu). The workshop was inspired by the Estonian case study of an AI-based decision-support system applied in the Estonian Unemployment Insurance Fund which illustrates the complexity of integrating AI into public welfare systems. While Estonia's digital infrastructure provides a strong foundation, the success of AI-driven decision-making depends on robust data ecosystems and interoperable standards, ethical and participatory governance models, ongoing education, and stakeholder engagement. Future research should explore longitudinal impacts of AI tools on welfare outcomes, develop standardized frameworks for bias assessment, and expand participatory design practices. Estonia's experience offers valuable lessons for other countries navigating the intersection of data, AI, and social policy.

Introduction

In the evolving landscape of digital governance, the dissemination of scientific findings to policymakers will play a pivotal role in shaping responsive, ethical, and effective public policies. In Estonia, a country renowned for its digital innovation, this process is particularly significant in the context of welfare provision.

A. Trumm (✉) · M. Männiste · T. Vihalemm
Institute of Social Studies, University of Tartu, Tartu, Estonia
e-mail: avo.trumm@ut.ee

M. Männiste
e-mail: maris.manniste@ut.ee

T. Vihalemm
e-mail: triin.vihalemm@ut.ee

P. Ahrweiler and N. Gilbert (eds.), *Participatory Modelling and Simulation to Improve AI-based Public Social Services*, Artificial Intelligence, Simulation and Society,
https://doi.org/10.1007/978-3-032-15283-1_10

119

The dissemination of scientific findings to policymakers in Estonia involves a multi-layered and evolving system. First, institutions such as the Estonian Research Council, Enterprise Estonia, and various ministries—such as the Ministry of Education and Research and the Ministry of Economic Affairs and Communications—form the core framework connecting key actors.

Second, a ministerial network of science advisers helps bridge the gap between researchers and policymakers. These advisers interpret and translate scientific evidence into formats that are relevant and accessible for policy development. In addition, several policy advisory networks are active, integrating scientific insights into policymaking through advisory bodies and expert panels, often involving researchers from universities and think tanks.

As a result, the Estonian government actively collaborates with local tech companies and research institutions to develop and implement AI solutions. These partnerships frequently involve the direct sharing of scientific findings with policymakers through joint projects and pilot programmes.

Finally, the Estonian Research Council plays a key role in promoting communication and dialogue among politicians, entrepreneurs, and researchers. It also coordinates and strengthens cooperation among stakeholders involved in scientific communication (Estonian Research Council, 2020).

The Artificial Intelligence for Assessment (further AI FORA) project aims to foster participatory and fair AI applications in public social services. In Estonia, the project culminated in a policy workshop that brought together experts from diverse fields to discuss the implications of data-driven decision-making in welfare services, and this chapter explores how scientific insights from the Estonian case study of the AI FORA project were responded to the stakeholders and policymakers.

The workshop brought together eight experts from various public and R&D institutions, including:

- The Estonian Statistical Board.
- The Estonian Research Council.
- The Social Insurance Board.
- The Foresight Centre of the Estonian Parliament.
- The Estonian Health Board.
- The Tartu City Government.
- The Centre of IT Impact Studies.

The workshop was structured around moderated discussions and practical exercises, with participants engaging in three rounds of dialogue focused on: a) principles of data-driven decision-making in social protection, b) roles and competencies of professionals working with AI, and c) contextual and ethical considerations in algorithmic decision-making. The example of decision-support tool OTT of the Estonian Unemployment Insurance Fund (further EUIF) as the focus of the Estonian AI FORA case study was used as a central reference point of discussions. However, the participants were asked to expand their thoughts beyond this case.

Main Results

The following section highlights the main ideas discussed during the workshop in the chronological order in which they emerged during the discussions and interprets them in a wider academic and political context.

Data as the Foundation of Policy Innovation

A central theme of the workshop was the quality and governance of data. Participants unanimously identified data-related challenges as the primary barrier to effective AI-supported decision-making. Lack of comprehensive data and limited access across institutions, inconsistent classifications and metadata, complicating integration and analysis, as well as insufficient data integrity and outdated datasets were highlighted. These concerns echo findings from the Estonian Foresight Centre, which emphasized the need for a national data strategy that aligns technical infrastructure with societal goals (Õunapuu et al., 2022; Keskus, 2022).

Ethical and Legal Considerations in a Datafied Society

The workshop highlighted the tension between privacy and the right to information and all kinds of ethical considerations were intensively discussed.

Estonia has made strides in developing tools like the consent service and data tracker, which enhance transparency and user control (Gstrein & Beaulieu, 2022). However, strict privacy regulations can hinder the personalization of public services. Participants also stressed the need for a balanced approach that respects both individual autonomy and the collective benefits of data use. '*If the right to privacy is a fundamental right, so is the right to information*' declares the report about the future of the data society, and introducing a weighing obligation into the Public Information Act could help reconcile these rights. The Data Protection Inspectorate's dual role—protecting privacy while promoting data access—also needs clarification (Keskus, 2022). The simulation game conducted with university students (see Männiste et al., in this book for details) illustrated that individuals are more willing to share data when it leads to tangible benefits, such as increased access to services.

Human-Centric AI and Stakeholder Involvement

Human-centricity was a key term highlighted by the experts. On the one hand, it involves the issues of privacy and data protection described above, and on the other hand, it opens multiple aspects related with the use of algorithms and automated decision-making.

The workshop participants emphasized that the algorithms underlying the decision-making 'machine' should not only be transparent and understandable but also offer opportunities for stakeholder involvement in their development. This collaborative approach leads to more effective and ethical solutions as it harnesses diverse perspectives and expertise. Moreover, human-centred AI fosters trust and acceptance among users. When people understand and see the value of AI systems, they are more likely to adopt and support these technologies (Interaction Design Foundation, 2024). The interviews with the employment consultants of EUIF, carried out in the frames of the Estonian case study, clearly approved this argument (Vihalemm et al., 2025).

Algorithmic and Human Biases: Dual Challenges

The workshop addressed both algorithmic and human biases in welfare decision-making. Algorithmic bias arises from poor data quality, flawed design, or misinterpreted causal relationships (Kordzadeh & Ghasemaghaei, 2021; Williams et al., 2018). The Bias Network Approach (Arriagada-Bruneau et al., 2025) was cited as a promising method for identifying and mitigating such biases.

Human bias, including selective adherence to algorithmic advice and reliance on stereotypes, was considered an even greater risk in complex welfare decisions (Alon-Barkat & Busuioc, 2023). The hybrid model used by EUIF—where algorithms provide initial assessments and human specialists make final decisions—was seen as a pragmatic compromise that leverages the strengths of both systems.

Contextual Use of Algorithms in Welfare Provision

Participants discussed when and how to use AI tools effectively. The conceptual model of AI use in social services, developed within AI FORA Estonian case study (see Vihalemm et al., 2025), served as a framework for this discussion. The discussion concluded that full automation is suitable for routine, binary decisions (e.g., traffic fines, birth grants), but hybrid models are preferable for complex or ambiguous cases, where human discretion is essential.

It is also relevant to evaluate cost-efficiency: while AI systems require significant investment, they can reduce long-term operational costs and improve service delivery (Alhosani & Alhashmi, 2024; Vatamanu & Tofan, 2025). However, participants cautioned that not all decisions benefit from automation, especially when the impact on individual well-being is marginal or when the cost of implementation outweighs the benefits.

Education and Capacity Building

A major barrier to effective AI use is the lack of data and algorithm literacy among both public servants and citizens. The White Book of Data and Artificial Intelligence (2024–2030) notes that over 30 per cent of data-related positions in the public sector remain unfilled (Ministry of Economic Affairs and Communications; Ministry of Justice; Ministry of Education and Research; Government Office, 2024). Workshop participants emphasized the need for interdisciplinary training that bridges technical, ethical, and policy domains, the importance of public education to build trust and understanding of data governance, and the value of cross-sector collaboration between developers, policymakers, and service providers.

Conclusions

The workshop about data-driven decision-making was inspired by the Estonian case study of AI-based decision-support system applied in the Estonian Unemployment Insurance Fund but raised a wider set of issues related to use of data and algorithms in welfare provision. The high-level expertise of the eight participants of the workshop covered multiple competences related to collecting and processing data, ethics and data protection, e-governance, welfare policy design, and provision of social benefits and services. The invited experts engaged actively and constructively throughout the workshop, contributing a wide range of valuable ideas during the co-creation process. Given that all participants represented key institutions involved in the design and implementation of AI-driven welfare policies, it is reasonable to anticipate that the insights and proposals shared during the discussions will inform and influence real-world policy development.

The Estonian AI FORA case study illustrates the complexity of integrating AI into public welfare systems. While Estonia's digital infrastructure provides a strong foundation, the success of AI-driven decision-making depends on robust data ecosystems and interoperable standards, ethical and participatory governance models, ongoing education, and stakeholder engagement.

Future research should explore longitudinal impacts of AI tools on welfare outcomes, develop standardized frameworks for bias assessment, and expand participatory design practices. Estonia's experience offers valuable lessons for other countries navigating the intersection of data, AI, and social policy.

In AI FORA, dissemination was not a peripheral activity but a core component of the project's methodology. The project aimed to ensure that the development and application of AI tools in welfare services were informed by ethical, social, and technical considerations. Dissemination contributed for *raising awareness* among stakeholders about the capabilities and limitations of AI in welfare provision, *facilitating dialogue* between data scientists, ethicists, and public administrators, *translating complex findings* from agent-based modelling simulations into actionable policy recommendations, and *encouraging participatory governance* by involving stakeholders in the design and evaluation of AI tools.

Acknowledgement Research presented in this chapter has been funded by the German VolkswagenStiftung under grant agreement number 98 560.

References

Alhosani, K., & Alhashmi, S. M. (2024). Opportunities, challenges, and benefits of AI innovation in government services: A review. *Discover. Artificial Intelligence, 4*(18), https://doi.org/10.1007/s44163-024-00111-w

Alon-Barkat, S., & Busuioc, M. (2023). Human–AI interactions in public sector decision making: "Automation bias" and "selective adherence" to algorithmic advice. *Journal of Public Administration Research and Theory, 33*(1), 153–169. https://doi.org/10.1093/jopart/muac007

Keskus, A. (2022). *Andmeühiskonna tulevik. Stsenaariumid aastani 2035. [the future of the data society: Scenarious up to 2035].* Tallinn: Arenguseire Keskus.

Arriagada-Bruneau, G., López, C., & Davidoff, A. (2025). A bias network approach (BNA) to encourage ethical reflection among AI developers. *Science and Engineering Ethics, 31*(1), https://doi.org/10.1007/s11948-024-00526-9

Estonian Research Council. (2020). Development plan 2027. https://etag.ee/wp-content/uploads/2021/01/ETAG-arengukava-2027_eng.pdf

Gstrein, O., & Beaulieu, A. (2022). How to protect privacy in a datafied society? A presentation of multiple legal and conceptual approaches. *Philosophy and Technology, 35*, 3. https://doi.org/10.1007/s13347-022-00497-4

Interaction Design Foundation. (2024). What is Human-Centered AI (HCAI)? Interaction Design Foundation-IxDF. https://www.interaction-design.org/literature/topics/human-centered-ai

Kordzadeh, N., & Ghasemaghaei, M. (2021). Algorithmic bias: Review, synthesis, and future research directions. *European Journal of Information Systems, 31*(3), 388–409. https://doi.org/10.1080/0960085X.2021.1927212

Vatamanu, A. F., & Tofan, M. (2025). Integrating artificial intelligence into public administration: Challenges and vulnerabilities. *Administrative Sciences, 15*(4), 149. https://doi.org/10.3390/admsci15040149

Vihalemm, T., Männiste, M., Trumm, A., & Solvak, M. (2025). Specialists and algorithms: Implementation of AI in the delivery of unemployment services in Estonia. In P. Ahrweiler (Ed.), *Participatory artificial intelligence in public social services: From bias to fairness in assessing beneficiaries* (pp. 97–117). Springer. https://doi.org/10.1007/978-3-031-71678-2_5

Ministry of Economic Affairs and Communications, Ministry of Justice, Ministry of Education and Research, Government Office. (2024). White book of data and artificial intelligence of Estonia 2024–2030. https://www.mkm.ee/sites/default/files/documents/2024-02/Tehisintellekti%20ja%20andmete%20valge%20raamat%202024-2030.pdf

Williams, B. A., Brooks, C. F., & Shmargad, Y. (2018). How algorithms discriminate based on data they lack: Challenges, solutions, and policy implications. *Journal of Information Policy, 8*, 78–115. https://doi.org/10.5325/jinfopoli.8.2018.0078

Õunapuu, T., Olesk, M., Raun, M., Kaldur, K., Tiits, M., & Tatar, M. (2022). *Andmed tulevikuühiskonnas [data in the future society].* Uuring. Tallinn: Arenguseire Keskus. https://www.ibs.ee/wp-content/uploads/Andmed-tulevikuuhiskonnas-2022.pdf

Chapter 11
Translating Evidence to Practice—A Trojan Horse Approach

David Wurster, Blanca Luque Capellas, Izabel Sabino De Sousa, and Erik W. Johnston

Abstract The gap between evidence discovery and using evidence-based decision-making is widened when those roles are filled by different groups. To bridge this gap and to more regularly translate evidence to practice we found that authentically including policymakers and other relevant stakeholders directly in the model building process, through events like policy modelling workshops, is a promising intervention we have coined as a trojan horse approach. Repeatedly, we have found that people are more likely to act on something if they discovered it themselves. Participatory co-modelling is thus a powerful intervention to reduce the discovery/usage gap. The 2024 Annual Modeling and Simulation Conference (ANNSIM) Workshop on Policy Modeling for Social Good, framed within the AI FORA US case study, brought together an interdisciplinary cohort of researchers, practitioners, and policymakers to explore how participatory modelling can inform public policy in domains such as healthcare, climate change, and social equity. This chapter synthesizes the workshop's core themes, discussions, and takeaways, emphasizing methodological advances, institutional enablers and barriers, and ethical imperatives. This paper contributes to the growing literature on computational social science and evidence-based decision-making. The integration of modelling and simulation (M&S) into policymaking presents transformative potential for addressing complex social challenges and responding to complex demands by various stakeholders.

D. Wurster (✉) · B. Luque Capellas
TISSS Lab, Institute of Sociology, Johannes Gutenberg University, Mainz, Germany
e-mail: dwurster@uni-mainz.de

B. Luque Capellas
e-mail: bluqueca@uni-mainz.de

I. S. De Sousa · E. W. Johnston
School for The Future of Innovation in Society, Arizona State University, Tempe, USA
e-mail: isabinod@asu.edu

E. W. Johnston
e-mail: erik.johnston@asu.edu

P. Ahrweiler and N. Gilbert (eds.), *Participatory Modelling and Simulation to Improve AI-based Public Social Services*, Artificial Intelligence, Simulation and Society,
https://doi.org/10.1007/978-3-032-15283-1_11

Introduction

Contemporary policymaking increasingly requires tools that can grapple with complexity, uncertainty, and the rapid pace of social, technological, and environmental change. Modelling and simulation (M&S), long established in engineering and physical sciences, are now permeating social policy domains where decisions must account for human behaviour, structural inequities, and systemic feedback loops (Gilbert, 2005; Süsser et al., 2021; Malbon & Parkhurst, 2023). The 2024 Annual Modeling and Simulation Conference (ANNSIM) Workshop on Policy Modeling for Social Good,[1] framed within the AI FORA US case study and held in conjunction with the Annual Modeling and Simulation Conference, brought together practitioners and modellers to learn how M&S can better support policymakers and public interest outcomes.

As part of the AI FORA research project, the US case study leaders, together with other German and US researchers with expertise on policy modelling, were among the workshop organizers. The scientific findings dissemination carried out within the AI FORA US case study took place as a parallel workshop within the 2024 ANNSIM Conference. The workshop preparation involved reaching out to policymakers with substantive expertise in policy modelling. This served two primary purposes: first, to enhance the effectiveness and relevance of dissemination practices by integrating practitioner insights, and second, to complement the scientific perspective. Also, an intentional effort was made in contacting experts in policy modelling with researchers attending the entire ANNSIM conference to get them involved in the workshop. At the end, the workshop convened approximately 30 participants, representing a diverse intersection of policy practitioners and academic researchers from multiple disciplines—including computer science, public health, environmental studies, political science, and ethics—to discuss challenges and best practices in using M&S for policymaking.

The workshop lasted a full day and combined both lecture-based and interactive formats. The presentations included inputs from the organizers on policy modelling concepts developed, as well as talks from various participants showcasing several policy modelling examples. Interactive formats comprised systematic feedback from policymakers at the end of each session, a world café session discussing on the use of artificial intelligence for automated decision-making in policy domains (such as terrorism recidivism, unmanned drones, or granting asylum), as well as how simulation could support on this purpose. A closing panel was held at the final part of the workshop.

This chapter distils insights from the workshop, focusing on two key themes: (1) institutional practices and stakeholder engagement and (2) ethical and epistemological concerns. These themes collectively underscore the workshop's ambition to not only advance technical modelling practices but also reshape how these models interact with real-world decisions and how the inclusion of practitioners in

---

[1] The workshop summary can be downloaded from the AI FORA website: https://www.ai-fora.de/wp-content/uploads/Summary_Policy-Modeling-Workshop_ANNSIM-final.pdf.

the discovery process is a type of trojan horse intervention to translate evidence to practice.

Institutional Practices and Stakeholder Dynamics

Modelling does not occur in a vacuum, and it also should not occur in a silo. The effectiveness of M&S for social good depends on considering the systems associated with evidence-based decision-making including institutional arrangements, stakeholder relationships, and governance structures that mediate how models are developed and used.

Interdisciplinary Collaboration

The workshop underscored the importance of cross-sector collaboration between modellers, domain experts (working on the fields such as healthcare, climate change, or social equity), and policymakers. Successful policy modelling initiatives often involve iterative engagement between these actors. For instance, a talk on pandemic response modelling demonstrated how early engagement with public health departments shaped model assumptions and outputs to be more actionable (Tolk et al., 2022).

However, conversations throughout the workshop respected that the potential of M&S approaches was tempered by increasingly visible challenges. Differences in epistemological orientation, language, and incentives can hinder effective communication. When practitioners could not be directly involved, one proposed solution involved establishing "boundary spanners" or knowledge brokers who can translate between technical and policy communities (Bednarek et al., 2018). These roles are crucial for embedding models within decision-making processes rather than treating them as isolated analytical tools.

Institutional Incentives and Barriers

A recurring theme was the misalignment between timing, accountabilities, and incentives between academics and practitioners. Academic researchers often prioritize novelty and publication, while policymakers seek timely and interpretable insights. This tension can disincentivize modellers from engaging deeply with policy processes.

Participants suggested institutional innovations such as dedicated translational research centres, joint appointments between universities and government agencies, and funding mechanisms that support long-term partnerships. These structures could bridge the gap between model development and policy implementation, enhancing the real-world utility of M&S.

Additional barriers arise from administrative rigidity and fragmented knowledge practice. Even when models address urgent policy needs, uptake may be delayed by weak institutional embedding or resistance to iterative learning. A case presented during the workshop on transport modelling in Colombia illustrated this well: despite strong technical design, the model struggled to gain traction due to limited data and weak engagement from local authorities (Salazar-Serna et al., 2024). The experience underscored how failures in anticipation, narrow problem framing, institutional reluctance, and lack of continuity, the four stages outlined in Johnston et al., (2011) framework, can converge to obstruct the integration of evidence into practice (Johnston et al., 2011).

Ethical and Epistemological Considerations

Modelling for social good is not merely a technical endeavour—it is deeply political and ethical. The workshop encouraged critical reflection on whose perspectives are represented in models, what values they encode, and how their outputs influence decisions.

Value-Laden Assumptions

Every model entails simplifications and assumptions. Participants warned that these choices are not neutral; they reflect value judgments about what matters and what does not. For example, modelling housing policy based solely on economic efficiency may neglect concerns about displacement or cultural heritage (Saltelli et al., 2020). As such, transparency about model assumptions and limitations is paramount.

One recommendation involved the use of model provenance documentation, detailing the development process, assumptions, and stakeholder inputs. Such practices enhance accountability and allow users to scrutinize the ethical dimensions of modelling choices.

Power and Participation

Equitable participation in the modelling process was another ethical imperative. Models developed without input from affected communities risk reinforcing existing power imbalances. Conversely, inclusive modelling practices can empower marginalized voices and democratize policy analysis. The workshop featured several case studies where community-engaged modelling led to more nuanced and just policy recommendations. In one instance, indigenous communities co-developed a land-use model that incorporated traditional ecological knowledge alongside scientific data (Gordon (Iñupiaq) et al., 2023). This approach not only improved model accuracy but also strengthened community agency in policy dialogues. In contexts where institutional data may be scarce or biased, participatory modelling offers pathways to refine simulations and co-create context-sensitive insights, making models more meaningful and trustworthy (Moallemi et al., 2021).

Curiosity, Inclusion, and Empathy

Participatory modelling does more than respond to predefined questions—they challenge the assumptions that shape how problems are framed. By inviting the formulation of new questions, they redistribute agenda setting, enabling diverse actors to explore possibilities, visualize consequences, and surface alternatives excluded from traditional policy frames. The model thus becomes a shared space of inquiry. Agent-based modelling, as Johnston et al., (2007) observe, often leads to unintended discoveries—not only through (emerging) outputs but through the process itself—turning model design into an active site of knowledge production (Johnston et al., 2007).

Ensuring meaningful and low-barrier participation opportunities requires methodological choices that recognize multiple forms of knowledge and expression. This includes accessible language, visual tools, collaborative practices, and openness to non-technical and experiential insights. Participatory modelling is most effective when it engages diverse perspectives, fosters explicit knowledge exchange, and remains alert to institutional and power asymmetries (Hinrichs & Johnston, 2020; Voinov et al., 2016). The idea of focus stacking,[2] discussed during the workshop, supports the integration of multiple scales and viewpoints, reducing the risk of reductive models.

Equally important is the modelling process's capacity to foster trust and mutual recognition by enabling shifts in perspective. Participatory simulations, serious games, role-playing, and situated narratives—methods highlighted in the workshop—encourage participants to engage across differences and build relational understanding (Ahrweiler et al., 2025). This aligns with Krishnamurthy et al.'s (2013) notion of synthetic empathy: a designed capacity to recognize and legitimize others' positions within complex systems. While disagreement remains, the process generates a shared vocabulary and emotional grounding through which tensions can be navigated more constructively (Krishnamurthy et al., 2013).

---

[2] Focus stacking refers to building/examining the model through multiple levels of analysis (e.g., micro-level agent behaviours, meso-level interactions, macro-level system outcomes), often in a layered or sequential manner, to avoid missing dynamics that only appear at certain scales.

Policy Reflections on Participatory Modelling for Policymaking

What the participants valued the most was the opportunity of sharing perspectives between scientists and policymakers, underlining the fact that these communities historically have worked separately. The invited practitioners brought expertise in areas such as border security, defence operations, and science and technology policy. Their contributions emphasized the importance of designing models that reflect real-world complexity, use suitable levels of abstraction, and clearly communicate both insights and limitations. They also highlighted how interactive, engaging models can help users explore assumptions, understand outcomes, and provide feedback. Related to the policy demands arising from the workshop discussion, participants agreed that models need to be able to:

- support informed decision-making,
- prepare us/society for better future,
- simulate various scenarios evaluating the effectiveness of different policy interventions (especially to manage possible risks/threats),
- emphasize on ontology to better represent the real-world context of the model,
- reflect real world to see possible bias/ambiguities and handle/work with real-world data, while having the right level of abstraction,
- work with accurate data (data quality) as well as transparent, interpretable, and understandable (it is clear what the model shows and what it is not),
- visualize outcome, meaning (of the outcome), and usage of the model,
- be interactive to ensure inclusion/engagement with wider public (the public understands complex issues, and the policy people receive feedback from citizens),
- be interoperable.

Future Directions and Recommendations

Building on workshop discussions, several forward-looking recommendations emerged:

- **Enhance Interdisciplinarity**: Encourage curricula and research that bridge computational, social, and policy sciences.
- **Invest in Participatory Modelling**: Fund processes that meaningfully involve stakeholders, especially from underrepresented communities.
- **Standardize Documentation and Transparency**: Promote norms for ethical modelling, including reproducibility, model provenance, and open-source tools.
- **Align Incentives**: Reform academic and funding structures to reward translational impact and sustained policy engagement.
- **Build Capacity**: Support training programmes for both modellers and policymakers to better understand each other's worlds.

- **Foster a Modelling Culture**: Encourage institutional openness and long-term engagement with modelling as a tool for collective learning and informed decision-making.

Conclusion

The 2024 ANNSIM Workshop on Policy Modeling for Social Good, complementing the AI FORA US case study, illuminated the multifaceted role of modelling in shaping a more just and effective policy landscape. While technical sophistication is essential, the true power of M&S lies in its capacity to integrate diverse perspectives, foreground ethical concerns, build trusting relationships, establish a common language, and support collaborative problem-solving. By advancing interdisciplinary methodologies, fostering institutional innovation, and committing to inclusive practice, the modelling community can play a critical role in advancing social good.

This workshop marks a vital step towards institutionalizing modelling as a core component of realizing the potential evidence-based policymaking. Policy modelling represents an approach that moves beyond the outdated model of speaking truth to power by leveraging the trojan horse approach to include those with power directly into the processes of discovery. As global challenges become ever more interconnected and urgent, the imperative for thoughtful, ethical, and participatory modelling has never been clearer.

Acknowledgements Research has been funded by the German VolkswagenStiftung under grant agreement number 98 560.

References

Ahrweiler, P., Späth, E., Siqueiros García, J. M., Capellas, B. L., & Wurster, D. (2025). Inclusive technology co-design for participatory AI. In P. Ahrweiler (Ed.), *Participatory artificial intelligence in public social services. Artificial intelligence, simulation and society*. Springer. https://doi.org/10.1007/978-3-031-71678-2_2

Bednarek, A. T., Wyborn, C., Cvitanovic, C., Meyer, R., Colvin, R. M., Addison, P. F. E., Close, S. L., Curran, K., Farooque, M., Goldman, E., Hart, D., Mannix, H., McGreavy, B., Parris, A., Posner, S., Robinson, C., Ryan, M., & Leith, P. (2018). Boundary spanning at the science–policy interface: The practitioners' perspectives. *Sustainability Science, 13*(4), 1175–1183. https://doi.org/10.1007/s11625-018-0550-9

Gilbert, G. N., & Troitzsch, K. G. (2005). *Simulation for the social scientist* (2nd ed.). Open University Press.

Gordon (Iñupiaq), H. S. J., Ross, J. A., Bauer-Armstrong, C., Moreno, M., Byington, R., (Choctaw), & Bowman, N. (Lunaape/Mohican). (2023). Integrating indigenous traditional ecological knowledge of land into land management through indigenous-academic partnerships. *Land Use Policy, 125*, 106469. https://doi.org/10.1016/j.landusepol.2022.106469

Hinrichs, M. M., & Johnston, E. W. (2020). The creation of inclusive governance infrastructures through participatory agenda-setting. *European Journal of Futures Research, 8*(1). https://doi.org/10.1186/s40309-020-00169-6

Johnston, E., Kim, Y., & Ayyangar, M. (2007). Intending the unintended: The act of building agent-based models as a regular source of knowledge generation. *Interdisciplinary Description of Complex Systems—Scientific Journal, 5*(2), 81–91.

Johnston, E., Hu, Q., & Auer, J. C. (2011). Lost in translation: Overcoming barriers to integrating evidence with practice. *International Journal of Critical Infrastructures, 7*(4), 317–334. https://doi.org/10.1504/IJCIS.2011.045067

Krishnamurthy, R., Bhagwatwar, A., Johnston, E. W., & Desouza, K. C. (2013). A glimpse into policy informatics: The case of participatory platforms that generate synthetic empathy. *Communications of the Association for Information Systems, 33*(1).https://doi.org/10.17705/1CAIS.03321

Malbon, E., & Parkhurst, J. (2023). System dynamics modelling and the use of evidence to inform policymaking. *Policy Studies, 44*(4), 454–472. https://doi.org/10.1080/01442872.2022.2080814

Moallemi, E. A., de Haan, F. J., Hadjikakou, M., Khatami, S., Malekpour, S., Smajgl, A., Smith, M. S., Voinov, A., Bandari, R., Lamichhane, P., Miller, K. K., Nicholson, E., Novalia, W., Ritchie, E. G., Rojas, A. M., Shaikh, M. A., Szetey, K., & Bryan, B. A. (2021). Evaluating participatory modeling methods for co-creating pathways to sustainability. *Earth's Future, 9*(3), e2020EF001843. https://doi.org/10.1029/2020EF001843

Salazar-Serna, K., Cadavid, L., & Franco, C. (2024). Analyzing transport policies in developing countries with ABM. arXiv preprint arXiv:2404.19745.

Saltelli, A., Bammer, G., Bruno, I., Charters, E., Di Fiore, M., Didier, E., Nelson Espeland, W., Kay, J., Lo Piano, S., Mayo, R., Pielke Jr., R., Portaluri, T., Porter, T. M., Puy, A., Rafols, I., Ravetz, J. R., Reinert, E., Sarewitz, D., Stark, P. B., et al. (2020). Five ways to ensure that models serve society: A manifesto. *Nature, 582*(7813), 482–484. https://doi.org/10.1038/d41586-020-01812-9

Süsser, D., Ceglarz, A., Gaschnig, H., Stavrakas, V., Flamos, A., Giannakidis, G., & Lilliestam, J. (2021). Model-based policymaking or policy-based modelling? How energy models and energy policy interact. *Energy Research & Social Science, 75*, 101984. https://doi.org/10.1016/j.erss.2021.101984

Tolk, A., Pires, B. S., & Cline, J. C. (2022). Artificial societies enabling multidisciplinary policy evaluation–A health policy example. *Proceedings of the MODSIM World*.

Voinov, A., Kolagani, N., McCall, M. K., Glynn, P. D., Kragt, M. E., Ostermann, F. O., Pierce, S. A., & Ramu, P. (2016). Modelling with stakeholders—Next generation. *Environmental Modelling & Software, 77*, 196–220. https://doi.org/10.1016/j.envsoft.2015.11.016

Part III
Looking to the Future

Chapter 12
Better AI for Public Good: Participatory Modelling and Simulation in Social Services

Mahesh Sasikumar, Ashly Ann Jo, and Ebin Deni Raj

Abstract Exploring the future of Artificial Intelligence (AI) in public social services, this chapter outlines a vision for "Better AI"—systems that go beyond technological performance to embody ethical integrity, transparency, equity, and human-centred design. Drawing on the AI FORA initiative's participatory modelling and simulation practices, this work emphasizes deep stakeholder involvement throughout the AI lifecycle. We argue that integrating technical insights with collaborative methodologies is essential for aligning AI development with the public good. This chapter contributes the following: (1) a conceptual framework for "Better AI" grounded in participatory principles, (2) technical strategies including Inverse Generative Social Science (IGSS) and simulation-based foresight, and (3) a discussion of challenges and future research directions for ethically robust AI in social services. These contributions are positioned to inform both policy and technical communities striving for responsible AI innovation.

Introduction

The integration of Artificial Intelligence (AI) into public social services offers transformative potential—ranging from optimizing resource allocation and tailoring individual support to enhancing the reach and efficiency of essential public programmes (Kalasampath et al., 2025). Yet, as these technologies advance and proliferate, they bring with them a host of societal risks, including fairness concerns, opacity in

M. Sasikumar (✉) · A. A. Jo · E. D. Raj
Department of Computer Science and Engineering Indian Institute of Information Technology Kottayam, Kottayam, India
e-mail: mahesh.23phd11013@iiitkottayam.ac.in

A. A. Jo
e-mail: ashlyannjo.phd2112@iiitkottayam.ac.in

E. D. Raj
e-mail: ebindeniraj@iiitkottayam.ac.in

P. Ahrweiler and N. Gilbert (eds.), *Participatory Modelling and Simulation to Improve AI-based Public Social Services*, Artificial Intelligence, Simulation and Society,
https://doi.org/10.1007/978-3-032-15283-1_12

decision-making, accountability gaps, and the potential reinforcement of systemic inequities (Taylor et al., 2024). In sectors as sensitive and high-impact as public social services, the need for a more thoughtful and ethically grounded approach to AI is not merely aspirational—it is imperative.

This chapter contributes to the *Looking to the Future* section by advancing a vision of "Better AI": a form of AI development and deployment that goes beyond performance metrics to embed values such as human-centricity, transparency, equity, and adaptability. Drawing from the AI FORA initiative, we argue that participatory modelling and simulation are essential methodological pillars for realizing this vision. Through continuous stakeholder engagement—including service users, social workers, policymakers, and community members—AI FORA emphasizes the co-creation of AI systems that are context-aware, ethically robust, and socially responsive.

Our central argument is that achieving "Better AI" requires a shift in both mindset and methodology. Rather than treating ethical considerations as secondary, they must be built into the AI lifecycle from the outset. Participatory modelling and simulation offer a structured and iterative way to do so, enabling collaborative identification of biases, testing of interventions in simulated environments, and integration of diverse forms of knowledge—quantitative and qualitative alike.

To guide this exploration, the chapter is structured as follows:

- Section 2 introduces the conceptual foundations of "Better AI" within the AI FORA framework, emphasizing principles such as co-design, transparency, fairness, and adaptability.
- We then present technical and methodological strategies, including agent-based and inverse generative modelling, simulation for ethical foresight, and hybrid approaches that combine stakeholder insight with data-driven techniques.
- Next, we discuss the practical challenges and opportunities of applying these strategies to public social services, illustrated through real-world examples.
- Section 5 concludes with reflections on the implications of "Better AI" for future research, policy, and system design.

Ultimately, we aim to offer a forward-thinking yet grounded perspective—one that encourages a transition from AI systems that are merely intelligent to those that are also wise, just, and aligned with public interest.

Discussion

The journey towards "Better AI" in public social services demands a paradigm shift—from technology-centred development to a more holistic, ethically-grounded, and human-centred approach. AI FORA's focus on participatory modelling and simulation offers a structured methodology for navigating this multifaceted challenge. In this section, we articulate the foundational principles that define "Better AI" within the AI FORA framework and examine the technical and methodological strategies necessary to bring this vision to life.

"Better AI" is not merely an academic concern but a practical imperative for public systems that impact vulnerable populations. Moving beyond abstract metrics of accuracy or efficiency, it calls for AI systems that are transparent, inclusive, adaptive, and accountable (Dignum, 2019). This includes the co-design of models with stakeholders, proactive identification of ethical risks, and iterative refinement grounded in real-world feedback.

The discussion proceeds as follows: we first unpack the conceptual foundations of "Better AI," emphasizing its human-centric ethos. We then explore modelling and simulation strategies that support ethical foresight, equity assessments, and context-sensitive decision-making. These approaches are further illustrated through examples from public welfare domains—including food security programmes like the Public Distribution System (Kumar et al., 2021)—where participatory AI can help reconcile complex trade-offs between efficiency and inclusion.

Conceptual Foundations of "Better AI" in the AI FORA Context

At its heart, "Better AI," as promoted by AI FORA, is characterized by several interconnected principles:

Human-Centricity and Co-design: AI systems must be designed with and for the people they are intended to serve. Participatory modelling, a cornerstone of AI FORA, ensures that diverse voices—including service users, social workers, policymakers, and community representatives—are integral to the design, development, and validation process (Kalasampath et al., 2025). This mitigates the risk of developing solutions that are technically sound but practically unworkable or misaligned with user needs and values. However, co-design also presents challenges: when stakeholders have conflicting priorities—for example, policymakers prioritizing efficiency while community members emphasize inclusivity—facilitators must mediate trade-offs transparently and ensure that consensus does not dilute critical ethical safeguards (Mittelstadt et al., 2016).

Transparency and Explainability (XAI): For AI to be trusted, especially in high stakes public service decisions (e.g., benefit eligibility, risk assessment), its reasoning processes must be understandable to the extent possible. AI FORA advocates for the development and integration of XAI techniques tailored to different stakeholder groups, moving beyond "black box" models (Al-Muwawi et al., 2023). Simulation can play a role here by allowing users to explore how different inputs affect AI outputs, fostering understanding. The evaluation of XAI methods is crucial to ensure their effectiveness and trustworthiness. This involves assessing various conceptual properties such as compactness, correctness, fidelity, robustness, and comprehensibility (Mishra et al., 2024). Evaluation can be done through formal methods (algorithmic metrics) or empirical approaches (user-centred studies) (Poursabzi-Sangdeh et al., 2024). Key evaluation metrics for XAI also include the degree of interpretability, the quality of explanations, and their impact on user understanding and trust [6, 4]. These evaluations are particularly important in sensitive domains like cybersecurity, where XAI explains firewall systems' decisions (Al-Muwawi et al., 2023). However, a persistent challenge in XAI is the trade-off between accuracy and explainability: highly accurate models such as deep neural networks often sacrifice interpretability, while simpler, more interpretable models may offer reduced predictive performance. Navigating this trade-off requires careful contextual judgement about when and where transparency should take precedence.

Fairness, Accountability, and Ethical Robustness: "Better AI" must actively promote fairness and equity, guarding against the perpetuation or amplification of existing societal biases (Veale et al., 2018). The AI FORA approach involves using simulation to proactively assess potential fairness implications of AI models under various scenarios and demographic assumptions (Binns, 2018; Peters & Carman, 2024). It also stresses the importance of clear accountability frameworks, defining who is responsible when AI systems lead to adverse outcomes. Real-world scenarios can pose intricate accountability challenges—particularly when AI tools are deployed across multiple agencies (Anderson & Anderson, 2015). For example, in welfare fraud detection systems jointly managed by social security and law enforcement departments, it can be unclear whether responsibility lies with the algorithm developers, the implementing agency, or the officials making decisions based on AI recommendations (Eubanks et al., 2018). Such cases highlight the need for predefined accountability protocols, transparent documentation, and legal safeguards to ensure recourse for affected individuals (Whittlestone et al., 2019).

Adaptive and Iterative Development: Public social services operate in dynamic and evolving contexts. "Better AI" systems must therefore be designed not as fixed solutions but as adaptable frameworks, capable of continuous monitoring, evaluation, and improvement. This requires embedding structured feedback mechanisms into the AI lifecycle—where participatory inputs from stakeholders are regularly incorporated through iterative modelling, scenario testing, and simulation-based refinement. Such adaptability ensures that AI systems remain responsive to real-world changes, evolving needs, and emerging ethical considerations.

Technical Reflections: Modelling and Simulation Strategies

Realizing the principles outlined above requires specific technical and methodological commitments. AI FORA's approach offers concrete strategies.

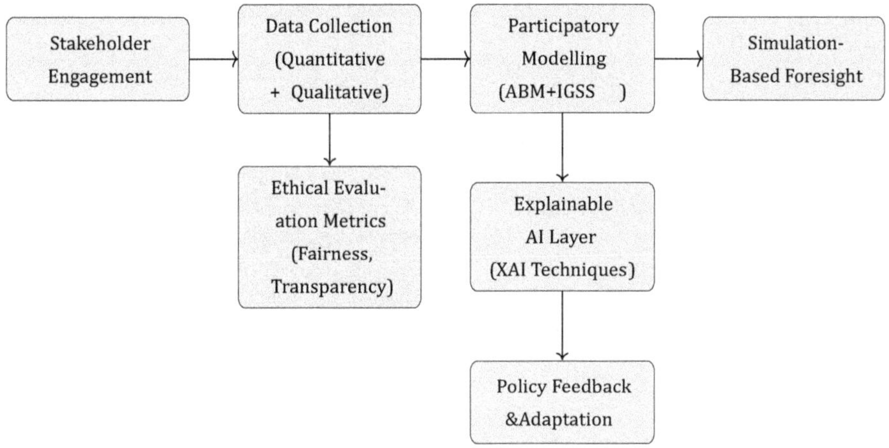

Fig. 12.1   Better AI system architecture for public services

Advanced Participatory Modelling Techniques

Conventional AI development frequently takes place in isolated technical environments, with minimal input from the communities the systems are meant to serve. AI FORA champions techniques such as agent-based modelling (ABM) combined with group model building sessions. These approaches enable stakeholders to collaboratively construct models of the social service system, embedding their tacit knowledge and diverse perspectives into the simulation framework. A powerful extension of this is Inverse Generative Social Science (IGSS). While traditional generative social science designs agents to produce macroscopic target patterns (the "forward problem") (Epstein, 2006), IGSS reverses this logic by starting with observed societal outcomes and evolving micro-level agent rules that could plausibly generate them (Epstein, 2023). Instead of manually designing agent behaviours, IGSS searches for families of agents that emerge through evolutionary processes. These agents are derived from basic building blocks of behaviour and interaction rules (Epstein, 2023).

This "backward problem" can be tackled using techniques from evolutionary computing—specifically, multi-objective genetic programming (MOGP) (Vu et al., 2019). MOGP is a method that evolves a population of candidate solutions (in this case, agent behaviour rules) over many generations. Each candidate is evaluated based on multiple objectives—such as how well it reproduces observed data patterns, minimizes bias, or aligns with policy goals. Unlike single-objective optimization, MOGP maintains a balance between competing priorities (e.g., accuracy versus interpretability) and seeks a diverse set of solutions along what is known as a Pareto front. In the IGSS context, this enables the discovery of multiple plausible

Table 12.1 Contrasting inverse generative social science (IGSS) and Traditional agent-based modelling (ABM)

Traditional ABM (Forward modelling)	Inverse generative social science (IGSS)
Begins with predefined agent rules to simulate social outcomes	Starts with real-world social outcomes and infers possible agent rules
Agent behaviours are manually coded by researchers	Agent behaviours evolve using algorithmic search (e.g., genetic programming)
Focuses on verifying hypotheses or theories	Aims to discover plausible micro-level mechanisms behind observed phenomena
Useful for scenario analysis and validation of known patterns	Useful for uncovering unknown causal structures and testing counterfactuals

behavioural strategies that could generate the same observed social patterns, offering rich insight into policy implications and alternative futures.

A practical example of this can be found in UK public health research, where IGSS was used to reverse-engineer individual drinking behaviours from population-level alcohol consumption trends. The resulting models were then used to simulate the potential effects of alternative alcohol pricing policies (Vu et al., 2019). This approach provides a novel and participatory way to understand complex social dynamics and co-design AI systems that aim to achieve specific public policy goals.

Technical Implementation Details of IGSS and XAI

Inverse Generative Social Science (IGSS)

The implementation of IGSS in our framework utilizes MOGP to reverse-engineer plausible agent behaviours from aggregate social outcomes. Specifically, we adopt the DEAP (Distributed Evolutionary Algorithms in Python) library to evolve agent rules using a population-based approach.

Each agent's decision policy is encoded as a tree-based expression of primitive functions (e.g., decision thresholds, weighted scoring rules) and terminal variables (e.g., household income, caregiving load). The MOGP algorithm simultaneously optimizes across three primary objectives:

- **Behavioural Fidelity:** How closely the macro-outcomes generated by the agent population match real-world data.
- **Ethical Alignment:** Reduction in bias across sensitive attributes (e.g., gender, caste).
- **Model Parsimony:** Simpler agent rules are preferred to enhance interpretability and reduce overfitting.

We run simulations for 100–200 generations with a population size of 500–1000, employing tournament selection, subtree crossover, and mutation. The evolved Pareto front yields diverse agent rule sets that are then tested in domain-specific scenarios, such as welfare eligibility refinement in urban India.

Explainable AI (XAI)

To support transparency and user trust, we integrate post-hoc explainability methods tailored for both technical auditors and non-technical users (Ghosh et al., 2025). Two primary techniques are employed:

- **SHAP (SHapley Additive exPlanations):** Used to quantify the marginal contribution of each input feature to a model's prediction. In our simulation case studies, SHAP was applied to logistic regression and tree-based eligibility models, highlighting which sociodemographic attributes most influence decisions.
- **Counterfactual Explanations:** These are scenario-based explanations that answer "what-if" questions, such as: "Had the applicant reported fewer dependents, would they have qualified for benefits?" This form of explanation is intuitive for end-users and aligns with the right to explanation principles in GDPR and India's DPDP Act.

To evaluate these XAI methods (Coroama & Groza, 2022a, 2022b; Nauta et al., 2023), we apply both formal and human-centred metrics:

- **Compactness and Fidelity:** Quantitative checks ensure the explanation aligns with model behaviour.
- **Comprehensibility and Trust:** We conducted pilot usability sessions ($n = 24$) to measure perceived clarity (on a 5-point Likert scale) and changes in trust scores ($\Delta U = +0.27$) after exposure to explanations.

This dual-layer XAI design—combining statistical interpretability with participatory usability testing—ensures that explainability is not only theoretically sound but practically meaningful across diverse stakeholder groups.

Challenges and Opportunities for "Better AI" in Public Services

The path to "Better AI" is not without its hurdles. Challenges include:

- **Data Governance and Privacy:** Public service data is highly sensitive. Robust data governance frameworks and privacy-preserving techniques (e.g., federated learning, differential privacy) are essential (Inampudi & Gaurav, 2024; Kathuria, 2021). Beyond technical solutions, there is also a pressing need to ensure these measures are transparent and comprehensible to both policymakers and the communities affected, reinforcing informed consent and trust.

- **Scalability and Generalizability:** Participatory approaches, such as stakeholder consultations or simulation-based co-design, can be time and resource-intensive. Scaling these methods without diluting stakeholder input or compromising contextual accuracy remains a major research challenge. For instance, in IGSS, generating diverse agent behaviours through evolutionary algorithms is computationally demanding and often specific to local data contexts.
- **Building Trust and Digital Literacy:** Effective participation depends not only on inclusion but also on understanding. Disparities in digital literacy among citizens and frontline workers may limit engagement with AI systems. Equipping users with the skills to interpret, question, and influence AI processes is crucial, especially where explainability and algorithmic transparency are vital.
- **Institutional Inertia:** Public sector institutions often operate under rigid legacy systems and established workflows that may resist paradigm shifts introduced by participatory AI models. Overcoming this requires capacity-building, cross-sector collaboration, and adaptive policy frameworks to encourage experimentation and responsible innovation.

The development of "Better AI" systems in the public domain is increasingly influenced by evolving legal and regulatory mandates. Frameworks such as the General Data Protection Regulation (GDPR) in the European Union and India's Digital Personal Data Protection (DPDP) Act establish critical guardrails for responsible AI usage.

GDPR mandates principles like data minimization, purpose limitation, and explicit consent, all of which align closely with the participatory ethos of AI FORA. Moreover, GDPR's provision for the "right to explanation" underscores the necessity for transparent and interpretable AI systems—key priorities in explainable AI (XAI).

India's DPDP Act introduces user consent norms, data fiduciary responsibilities, and cross-border data flow regulations (Inampudi & Gaurav, 2024). For participatory AI systems, this necessitates rigorous consent mechanisms, transparent documentation, and auditable decision trails, particularly when integrating qualitative community data (Chakrabarti et al., 2021; Bansal & Choudhary, 2024).

These regulatory frameworks are not merely compliance hurdles; they offer valuable scaffolding to embed ethical principles into system architecture from the ground up. Proactively engaging with these laws enhances both the credibility and sustainability of AI systems designed for public good.

Despite these challenges, the opportunities are immense. "Better AI," developed through the AI FORA lens, can lead to public social services that are more responsive, equitable, and ultimately, more humane. The iterative nature of participatory modelling and simulation allows for learning and adaptation, fostering a culture of continuous improvement.

A vivid illustration comes from a simulation-based redesign of social welfare targeting in Indian urban slums. Initial models focused narrowly on income thresholds. However, qualitative fieldwork revealed that caregiving burdens (e.g., elder care) were a better predictor of household vulnerability. By integrating these lived

Table 12.2 Key Tenets of "Better AI" vs. Conventional AI Development

Dimension	Conventional AI Development	"Better AI" (AI FORA Approach)
Primary goal	Performance, efficiency	Holistic Well-being, equity, Trust
Design process	Technology-driven, expert led	Human-centric, co-designed with stakeholders
Transparency	Often "black box"	Explainable, interpretable
Ethics	Reactive, add-on	Proactive, integrated by design
Evaluation	Technical metrics	Socio-technical impact, ethical audit
Adaptation	Periodic updates	Continuous,iterativevia Participation

insights into simulation models, eligibility algorithms were reweighted, improving aid distribution equity and service impact.

Another example is drawn from public health planning in the UK. Here, Inverse Generative Social Science was used to derive behavioural rules underlying alcohol consumption trends. This enabled policymakers to test alternative tax policies within a simulated environment, helping identify strategies that could shift social norms without disproportionately impacting vulnerable populations.

Conclusion

The development and deployment of Artificial Intelligence in public social services stand at a critical juncture. While the potential benefits are substantial, so too are the risks if AI is not guided by strong ethical principles and a deep understanding of its societal context. This chapter has argued for a vision of "Better AI," one that is actively shaped by participatory modelling and simulation as advocated by the AI FORA initiative.

Our technical reflections highlight that "Better AI" is not a futuristic ideal but an achievable goal, contingent upon a committed shift towards human-centricity, transparency, fairness, and adaptability. The AI FORA concepts provide a robust methodological toolkit—from co-design workshops and agent-based simulations to ethical foresight exercises—for building AI systems that are truly aligned with public values and the complex realities of social service delivery. The integration of advanced techniques like Inverse Generative Social Science further enriches this toolkit by allowing for the discovery of foundational mechanisms driving social patterns, offering a unique avenue for understanding and shaping AI's impact. Furthermore, rigorous evaluation of explainable AI methods is paramount to ensure that AI systems are not only interpretable but also truly beneficial and trustworthy for all stakeholders involved.

The journey requires moving beyond purely technical optimization to embrace a sociotechnical perspective, where AI systems are seen as integral components of larger human and organizational systems. This involves fostering ongoing dialogue between technologists, policymakers, service providers, and the communities they serve. The emphasis on iterative development and continuous learning, inherent in the participatory modelling cycle, is crucial for navigating the evolving landscape of AI and its societal implications.

Challenges related to data governance, scalability of participatory methods, and institutional adoption remain. However, the potential to create AI-enhanced public social services that are more equitable, effective, and empowering offers a compelling motivation to address these hurdles collaboratively.

Ultimately, the pursuit of "Better AI" is an investment in a more just and supportive society. By embedding participatory principles and rigorous simulation into the core of AI development, as championed by AI FORA, we can harness the power of AI to genuinely improve public social services and enhance the well-being of all citizens. The work ahead is significant, but the path outlined offers a promising direction for looking to the future of AI with both ambition and responsibility.

References

Al-Muwawi, K., Al-Khaleefa, A., Al-Jarrah, O., & Al-Khaleefa, M. (2023). Evaluation of explainable AI techniques for interpreting machine learning models in cybersecurity firewall systems. *Journal of Information Security and Applications, 78*, 103603.

Anderson, M., & Anderson, S. L. (2015). Toward ensuring ethical behaviour from autonomous systems: A case-supported principle-based paradigm. *Industrial Robot: An International Journal, 42*(4), 324–331.

Bansal, N., & Choudhary, H. (2024). Fostering digital equity: Evaluating impact of digital literacy training on internet outcomes in rural marginalised communities in India. *International Journal of Lifelong Education, 43*(5), 473–493.

Binns, R. (2018). Fairness in machine learning: Lessons from political philosophy. *Proceedings of the 2018 Conference on Fairness, Accountability and Transparency.*

Chakrabarti, A., Tiwari, R., & Banerji, H. (2021). Migrants' narratives on urban governance: A case from Kolkata, a city of the global south. *Sustainability, 13*(2), 1009.

Coroama, L., & Groza, A. (2022a). Evaluation metrics in explainable artificial intelligence (XAI): State of the art review and challenges. *Scientific Reports.*

Coroama, L., & Groza, A. (2022b). Evaluation metrics in explainable artificial intelligence (XAI). In *International conference on advanced research in technologies, information, innovation and sustainability* (pp. 401–413). Springer.

Dignum, V. (2019). *Responsible artificial intelligence: How to develop and use AI in a responsible way.* Springer.

Epstein, J. M. (2006). Agent-based computational models and generative social science. In *Generative social science: Studies in agent-based computational Modeling* (pp. 4–46). Princeton University Press.

Epstein, J. M. (2023). Inverse generative social science: Backward to the future. *Journal of Artificial Societies and Social Simulation, 26*(2), 9.

Eubanks, V. (2018). *Automating inequality: How high-tech tools profile, police, and punish the poor.* St Martin's Press.

Ghosh, A., Saini, A., & Barad, H. (2025). Artificial intelligence in governance: Recent trends, risks, challenges, innovative frameworks and future directions. *AI & SOCIETY*, 1–23.

Inampudi, S., & Gaurav, A. K. (2024). Transforming institutions for inclusive and sustainable governance: An empirical analysis of NITI Aayog's role in India. In *Governance and sustainable development in South Asia: Bridging the gap* (pp. 177–195). Springer.

Kalasampath, K., Spoorthi, K. N., Sajeev, S., Kuppa, S. S., Ajay, K., & Angulakshmi, M. (2025). A literature review on applications of explainable artificial intelligence (XAI). *IEEE Access.*

Kathuria, V. (2021). *Data empowerment and protection architecture: Concept and assessment.* Observer Research Foundation.

Kumar, S., Raut, R. D., Queiroz, M. M., & Narkhede B. E. (2021). Mapping the barriers of AI implementations in the public distribution system: The Indian experience. *Technology in Society, 67*, 101737.

Mishra, A., Singh, S. K., Shrestha, S., Gupta, A. K., & Karki, B. (2024). Explainable AI evaluation: A top-down approach for selecting optimal explanations for black box models. *Information, 15*(1), 4.

Mittelstadt, B. D., Allo, P., Taddeo, M., Wachter, S., & Floridi, L. (2016). The ethics of algorithms: Mapping the debate. *Big Data & Society.*

Nauta, M., Trienes, J., Pathak, S., Nguyen, E., Peters, M., Schmitt, Y., Schlötterer, J., van Keulen, M., & Seifert, C. (2023). From anecdotal evidence to quantitative evaluation methods: A systematic review on evaluating explainable AI. *ACM Computing Surveys, 55*(10), 1–37.

Peters, U., & Carman, M. (2024). Cultural bias in explainable AI research: A systematic analysis. *Journal of Artificial Intelligence Research, 79*, 971–1000.

Poursabzi-Sangdeh, F., Goldstein, D. G., Hoffmann, J., Wortman Vaughan, J., & Wallach, H. (2024). Human-centered evaluation of explainable AI applications: A systematic review. *Frontiers in Artificial Intelligence, 7.*

Sasi, A., Abishek, M., Tejashree, Y., Roy, S., Suresh, D., & Sagar, S. T. (2024, September). A systematic literature review of the public distribution system in India. *International Journal of Computer Applications, 975*, 8887.

Taylor, R. R., O'Dell, B., & Murphy, J. W. (2024). Human-centric AI: Philosophical and community-centric considerations. *AI & SOCIETY, 39*(5), 2417–2424.

Veale, M., Binns, R., & Edwards, L. (2018). Fairness and accountability design needs for algorithmic support in high-stakes public sector decision-making. *Proceedings of the 2018 CHI Conference on Human Factors in Computing Systems.*

Vu, T. M., Probst, C., Epstein, J. M., Brennan, A., Strong, M., & Purshouse, R. C. (2019). Toward inverse generative social science using multi-objective genetic programming.

Whittlestone, J., Nyrup, R., Alexandrova, A., & Cave, S. (2019). The role and limits of principles in AI ethics: Towards a focus on tensions. *Proceedings of the AAAI/ACM Conference on AI, Ethics, and Society.*

Chapter 13
How Participatory Modeling Can Enable Collective Bias Mitigation when AI Is Used across Systems and Institutions

Erik W. Johnston and Reeham R. Mohammed

Abstract The rapid adoption of AI in governmental contexts is outpacing concurrent research efforts to promote responsible innovation. In the context of public institutions, the application of AI technologies has been framed as a potential means to minimize systemic bias and enhance the effectiveness of public service delivery (Mikhaylov et al., 2018). Despite extensive equity-focused research, real-world deployments still fall short of best-practice models, widening the theory–practice gap (Yigitcanlar et al., 2024). In research triangulated between empirical research of participatory modeling of systems of care in Peoria, Illinois, analyses of 311 non-emergency systems in Boston, and stakeholder interviews in institutions of public higher education, participatory methods revealed the complex interdependencies of civic infrastructures, the pathways through which bias is introduced and propagated, and the promise of biomimetic design principles—particularly those inspired by immunological analogies—to inform anticipatory, adaptive, and preventative interventions.

E. W. Johnston (✉)
School for The Future of Innovation in Society, Arizona State University, Phoenix, AZ, USA
e-mail: erik.johnston@asu.edu

R. R. Mohammed
Jimmy and Rosalynn Carter School of Public Policy, Georgia Institute of Technology, Atlanta, GA, USA
e-mail: rmohammed40@gatech.edu

P. Ahrweiler and N. Gilbert (eds.), *Participatory Modelling and Simulation to Improve AI-based Public Social Services*, Artificial Intelligence, Simulation and Society,
https://doi.org/10.1007/978-3-032-15283-1_13

An Accelerating Divide: Practice Outpacing Theory in Public AI Systems

While academic and industry research continues to generate insights into responsible AI development, the adoption and integration of these principles into public systems have lagged significantly (Davies et al. 2025). This growing divide reflects the structural challenges inherent in the public sector: under-resourced agencies, fragmented accountability, and a complex interplay of competing interests.

In a US context, the pace at which this divide is accelerating is a concern. Public higher education institutions, for example, where the widening chasm between AI's rapid development and the deliberate pace of university governance exposes a critical fault line with real consequences for teaching methods, stakeholder confidence, and institutional identity. Academic institutions—bound by shared governance structures, lengthy committee reviews, and legal or accreditation requirements—lack the flexibility and responsiveness of private-sector feedback loops, where new models can be iterated, tested, and deployed within days. Layered atop these procedural hurdles are political oversight, public accountability mandates, and liability concerns, each of which can stall even the most well-intentioned application and deepen the misalignment between technological innovation and institutional governance. To overcome this inertia, leaders across civic sectors must reimagine AI deployments not as a fixed blueprint but as a dynamic, communicative practice that evolves.

Challenges of Studying Complex Civic Infrastructures

Traditional scientific methods thrive under controlled conditions, but studying AI in the wild requires a different epistemology—one rooted in messiness, negotiation, and improvisation. Public institutions are not laboratories; they are contested arenas where power, accountability, and risk intersect. Developing rigorous, actionable knowledge in this context requires researchers to navigate these tensions with humility and flexibility (Hinrichs and Johnston 2020).

During the research studies we conducted, one of the biggest challenges we encountered was the fragility of relationships with gatekeepers. High turnover among public officials, burnout among social workers, and shifting political winds can all undermine long-term research initiatives (Davies et al. 2025). Without stable partnerships, even the most well-designed interventions risk being abandoned or misapplied, all while the use of AI continues to advance.

Another challenge, as revealed in our research on 311 non-emergency platforms, is a persistent gap between the intended design of civic infrastructure and real-world use. Low-income, ethnically diverse communities often avoid using 311 due to the lack of trust in government, data costs, and language barriers, even when the system could address their needs (Pak et al. 2017), while some government staff submit reports on residents' behalf although the system was designed for citizen use (Lee et al. 2020, 2021). Variations in reporting behavior by location and uneven service delivery across neighborhoods reveal a new form of digital divide and contribute to the emergence of information deserts (Hsu et al. 2022; Lee et al. 2020). Without anticipating these diverse behaviors and power dynamics, civic infrastructures may deepen existing inequalities.

Moreover, AI systems in public institutions are often layered atop legacy processes that were never designed with algorithmic governance in mind. This leads to situations where digital systems and analog bureaucracies clash, generating unintended consequences that are difficult to anticipate or reverse (Valle-Cruz et al. 2024). Understanding these hybrid systems demands a deep ethnographic sensitivity to how technology is interpreted, resisted, or subverted by frontline workers and citizens alike.

Compounding these relational and procedural challenges is a striking gap in evidence-based policy development. After untangling AI's clash with legacy bureaucracies, we found that many governance decisions still rest on assumptions rather than hard data about how these systems actually perform in context. This dearth of rigorous, context-sensitive research has produced a patchwork of regulations—often inconsistent or overly cautious—that leaves institutions without the nuanced strategies they need. Moving forward, it's essential to pair deep ethnographic insights with robust empirical studies so that stakeholders can design frameworks that both mitigate risks and foster innovation and equitable outcomes.

Systemic Bias as a Contagion

Bias in AI systems has been well-documented, ranging from systemic concerns with training data, facial recognition failures, to disparities in criminal justice risk assessments. Algorithmic bias manifests as systematic, unfair distortions in AI outputs—rooted in biased training data, flawed model designs, or the misalignment of societal values and algorithmic frameworks (Baker and Hawn 2022; Roselli et al. 2019). These distortions extend beyond technical glitches to reflect and reinforce historical inequalities, particularly concerning race, gender, misidentification, discrimination, and microaggressions.

In educational settings, for example, AI tools have been shown to reproduce prejudices in their datasets, resulting in unintended disadvantages for specific groups—such as racial minorities and women (Cachero et al. 2025; Li et al. 2023). From our research, we know that in some instances, AI systems used skewed lexical choices in language outputs. Additionally, AI's attempts at political correctness appear to erase the specificity of racial identity, such as avoiding the word "black" experiences and instead using "marginalized"—whereas in other instances, the persistent use of male pronouns in AI-generated responses reinforces sexist norms. Our research suggests that bias functions less like an isolated error and more like a systemic contagion. Once introduced into any part of a system, bias spreads and mutates, contaminating adjacent processes, datasets, and decision points. This phenomenon is similar to the dynamics of infectious diseases, wherein localized infections can become systemic unless identified and treated.

When the challenge of mitigating bias was viewed through a biomimetic lens, a potential response was also revealed for understanding and mitigating this threat. Drawing lessons from biology, particularly the immune system, we consider how civic infrastructures might develop an internal capacity for detecting, containing, and neutralizing bias. This perspective reframes bias not simply as a design flaw to be corrected post hoc but as a persistent and evolving threat that demands ongoing vigilance and collective, adaptive responses.

The capacity to recognize these biases often depends on the user's positionality—those from marginalized communities are more likely to perceive subtle stereotypes or exclusions that members of dominant groups may overlook (Li et al. 2024). Diverse eyes identified diverse threats: just as immune cells patrol the entire body, a network of alert, diverse stakeholders serve as frontline sentinels in our civic infrastructure. Empowered actors can continuously scan AI outputs for anomalous patterns, exclusionary language, or skewed decision rules, flagging each as an "antigen" that must be contained. Once a threat is detected, targeted "neutralizing agents" in the form of bias audits, corrective algorithmic updates, or inclusive data-augmentation protocols are deployed to quarantine and eradicate the contamination. Crucially, the system should then "remember" the encounter by updating training datasets, governance policies, and monitoring algorithms—accelerating its response to recurring or novel bias mutations. Enhancing automated detection tools with human judgment and community feedback loops allows this biomimetic framework to transform civic infrastructures into resilient, self-healing ecosystems—capable of preempting bias outbreaks and safeguarding equitable, transparent decision-making.

The Role of Participatory Modeling as an Immune Response

To test the feasibility of such an approach, we employed participatory modeling in the context of an AI-based system of care in Peoria, Illinois. This method brought together a diverse group of stakeholders, including system designers, implementers, frontline employees, community members, and researchers to collaboratively map out how the AI system functioned in practice. The objective was not only to identify points of failure or bias but also to generate a shared understanding of the system's goals, constraints, and interdependencies.

Three main threats emerged: first, non-technical barriers—transportation, documentation requirements, and internet access—kept certain people from using the service regardless of algorithm quality. Second, a lack of representation, or social mirroring, between system designers and intended users made the technology feel imposed, echoing our 311 non-emergency system findings where civic tools best served demographics most similar to their creators. Notably, this same remark was found in our research on AI in higher education where stakeholders noted that the content generated with AI tended to reflect the creators from Silicon Valley. Third, systemic research in public service environments proved exceptionally difficult. These systems exist within vast, overlapping networks of agencies, regulations, and actors, all of whom possess distinct—and often conflicting—accountabilities, goals, and incentives. Compounding this complexity is the issue of trust: gaining access to operational data and candid insights requires relationships with key stakeholders, many of whom are overburdened, transient, or both.

By inviting stakeholders to engage at any point—from problem framing through deployment—participatory modeling creates a formal and informal "permission structure" that empowers communities to shape AI throughout its lifecycle. This intervention not only surfaces potential failures and biases early on but transforms participants' relationships with the system, moving them from passive recipients to active co-designers and stewards of the system.

Governments should embed participatory governance at the heart of AI policy. Mechanisms like citizen assemblies, community advisory boards, and iterative public consultations ensure system design aligns with real-world experiences. Funding models must likewise reward and support sustained partnerships between agencies, researchers, and communities—moving beyond one-off pilots toward durable, mutually accountable relationships.

Finally, education and training need to bridge the gap between code and context. Public servants require not only digital fluency but robust ethical frameworks to guide algorithmic choices. Data scientists and engineers, in turn, should be equipped to recognize and navigate the socio-political landscapes their work inhabits—ensuring that technical expertise goes hand-in-hand with a commitment to equity. Investments in these capacities should be viewed as essential, not optional.

Toward a Duty of Care in AI Governance

A natural conclusion to these findings is the articulation of a "duty of care" framework for AI systems in the public sector. This concept borrows from medical and legal domains, where professionals are held to ethical standards that prioritize the well-being of those they serve. In the context of AI, a duty of care implies that every actor within the system—developers, policymakers, administrators, and users—shares a collective responsibility for maintaining its integrity.

Operationalizing this principle requires more than moral exhortation. It demands institutional mechanisms that embed care into every phase of the AI lifecycle: from procurement and design to deployment and evaluation. Participatory modeling offers a practical avenue for this, enabling stakeholders to surface and resolve ethical dilemmas before they become embedded in code. Legal instruments, such as algorithmic impact assessments and professional standards for AI practitioners, can further institutionalize this ethos.

Crucially, a duty of care must extend to ongoing maintenance and adaptation. Just as biological immune systems learn and evolve in response to new threats, civic AI systems must be capable of self-reflection and course correction. This requires not only technical infrastructure for monitoring and feedback but also organizational cultures that value transparency, accountability, and inclusion.

Like in matters of health, bias is not a problem to be solved once, but a condition to be managed continuously. Public institutions must evolve new capabilities, both cultural, technical, and ethical, to navigate this terrain. By embracing participatory modeling, fostering a proactive duty to care, and drawing on the adaptive strategies of biological systems, we can begin to close the gap between the practice of AI and our understanding of responsible innovation.

In the end, the promise of AI in the public sector is not merely about faster processing or more accurate predictions. It is about building systems that reflect and reinforce our highest values, including equity, inclusion, and mutual care. To achieve this, we must be willing to engage with the full complexity of the systems we seek to transform—not with pessimism, but with a disciplined and constructive optimism.

Acknowledgments Research presented in the chapter has been funded by the German VolkswagenStiftung under grant agreement number 98 560.

References

Baker, R. S., & Hawn, A. (2022). Algorithmic bias in education. *International Journal of Artificial Intelligence in Education, 32*, 1052–1092. https://doi.org/10.1007/s40593-021-00285-9.

Cachero, C., Tomás, D., & Pujol, F. A. (2025). Gender bias in self-perception of artificial intelligence knowledge, impact, and support among higher education students: An observational study. *ACM Transactions on Computing Education.* https://doi.org/10.1145/3721295.

Davies, A., Nguyen, E., Simeone, M., Johnston, E., & Gubri, M. (2025). Social science is necessary for operationalizing socially responsible foundation models. *In Proceedings of the ICLR 2025 Workshop on Human-AI Coevolution (HAIC).*

Hinrichs, M. M., & Johnston, E. W. (2020). The creation of inclusive governance infrastructures through participatory agenda-setting. *European Journal of Futures Research, 8*,(10). https://doi.org/10.1186/s40309-020-00169-6.

Hsu, J. H.-P., Wang, J., & Lee, M. (2022). Towards an expectation-oriented model of public service quality: A preliminary study of NYC 311. In: F. Hopfgartner, K. Jaidka, P. Mayr, J. Jose & J. Breitsohl (Eds.). *Social informatics* (pp. 447–458). Springer International Publishing. https://doi.org/10.1007/978-3-031-19097-1_31.

Lee, M., Harlow, J., Gordon, E., Wang, J., Johnston, E., Janzen, S., & Winter, S. (2020). *Toward understanding civic data bias in 311 systems: An information deserts perspective.* ACM CSCM 2020, ACM 978-1-4503-6819-3/20/04.

Lee, M., Wang, J., Janzen, S., Winter, S., & Harlow. J. (2021). Crowdsourcing behavior in reporting civic issues: The case of Boston's 311 systems. *Academy of Management Proceedings, 2021*(1), 16532. https://doi.org/10.5465/AMBPP.2021.16532abstract.

Li, M., Enkhtur, A., Yamamoto, B. A., Cheng, F., & Chen, L. (2023). Potential societal biases of ChatGPT in higher education: A scoping review [Preprint]. arXiv. https://arxiv.org/abs/2311.14381

Mikhaylov, S. J., Esteve, M., & Campion, A. (2018). Artificial intelligence for the public sector: Opportunities and challenges of cross-sector collaboration. *Philosophical Transactions of the Royal Society A: Mathematical, Physical and Engineering Sciences 376*, 20170357. https://doi.org/10.1098/rsta.2017.0357.

Pak, B., Chua, A., & Moere, A. V. (2017). FixMyStreet Brussels: Socio-demographic inequality in crowdsourced civic participation. *Journal of Urban Technology, 24*(2): 65–87. https://doi.org/10.1080/10630732.2016.1270047.

Roselli, D., Matthews, J., & Talagala, N. (2019). Managing bias in AI. In Proceedings of WWW'19: The Web Conference (pp. 1–6). doi:https://doi.org/10.1145/3308560.3317590.

Valle-Cruz, D., García-Contreras, R., & Gil-Garcia, J. R. (2024). Exploring the negative impacts of artificial intelligence in government: The dark side of intelligent algorithms and cognitive machines. *International Review of Administrative Sciences, 90*(2), 353–368. https://doi.org/10.1177/00208523231187051.

Yigitcanlar, T., David, A., Li, W., Fookes, C., Bibri, S. E., & Ye, X. (2024). Unlocking artificial intelligence adoption in local governments: Best practice lessons from real-world implementations. *Smart Cities* 7 (4): 1576–1625. https://doi.org/10.3390/smartcities7040064.

Chapter 14
Transferring the AI FORA Approach to another Domain: Participatory AI for Climate

Petra Ahrweiler and Blanca Luque Capellas

Abstract This chapter investigates the transferability of the AI FORA approach—an integrative methodology combining participatory design, sociological analysis, serious games, and agent-based simulation—into the domain of climate crisis response. Originally developed to examine the use of artificial intelligence (AI) in assessing eligibility for public social services, the AI FORA approach addresses core sociotechnical challenges such as algorithmic fairness, cultural perceptions of equity, and participatory system design. In its initial application, the methodology responded to the reproduction of bias in machine learning systems trained on historical data, advocating for societal negotiation of fairness and inclusiveness in technology development. The transfer of this framework into the context of natural disaster response is motivated by the growing role of AI in forecasting extreme weather events, coordinating disaster management, and informing public policy under ecological stress. However, a persistent gap remains between technological capability and societal uptake, partly due to the insufficient responsiveness of AI systems to ethical, cultural, and community-specific needs. To explore this transfer, the chapter employs a comparative matrix that structures analysis across domains using shared categories related to fairness, system design, stakeholder roles, and expected futures. In the new domain, the AI FORA methodology is adapted to support the conceptualisation of participatory AI systems aimed at climate resilience. The process involves designing serious games that enable stakeholders to engage with complex dilemmas, followed by simulation modelling that encodes stakeholder decisions and explores emergent consequences through iterative feedback loops. These simulations serve as second-order constructs of social decision-making processes, enabling participants to observe and refine the outcomes of their own design choices. The chapter demonstrates that the AI FORA approach facilitates the development of more inclusive and context-aware AI systems, even when applied in distinct societal domains.

P. Ahrweiler (✉) · B. Luque Capellas
TISSS Lab, Institute of Sociology, Johannes Gutenberg University, Mainz, Germany
e-mail: Petra.ahrweiler@uni-mainz.de

B. Luque Capellas
e-mail: bluqueca@uni-mainz.de

© The Author(s) 2026

P. Ahrweiler and N. Gilbert (eds.), *Participatory Modelling and Simulation to Improve AI-based Public Social Services*, Artificial Intelligence, Simulation and Society,
https://doi.org/10.1007/978-3-032-15283-1_14

It concludes that transferring sociologically grounded participatory methods into climate-oriented AI innovation offers a promising pathway to ethical and responsive technological futures.

Introduction

In recent years, Artificial Intelligence (AI) has become increasingly embedded in public domains, from healthcare and education to welfare and crisis management. As these technologies take on decision-making and predictive roles in areas of profound societal impact, concerns around fairness, accountability, and social legitimacy have become central. Public controversies over biased algorithms, opaque decision processes, and exclusionary system designs have underscored the limitations of conventional AI development paradigms that prioritise technical performance over sociocultural responsiveness (Diakopoulos 2016, Eubanks 2018).

These challenges are especially acute in high-stakes, complex contexts such as climate crisis response. As AI is deployed to forecast extreme weather events, coordinate emergency responses, and inform long-term climate policy (Vinuesa et al. 2020), its societal embeddedness becomes a critical factor in its effectiveness (O'Connor et al. 2024).

Yet, current approaches often fall short in engaging affected communities, reflecting local values, or addressing ethical tensions inherent in crisis governance (United Nations Climate Change, Technology Executive Committee 2025). The result is a persistent gap between technological capability and meaningful societal uptake.

This chapter explores how the AI FORA methodology—a sociotechnical framework originally developed to examine AI use in public social services—can be transferred to the climate domain. AI FORA combines participatory design, sociological analysis, serious games, and agent-based simulation to surface and negotiate issues of fairness, inclusion, and system design. Its initial application addressed the reproduction of bias in welfare eligibility algorithms, enabling stakeholders to co-construct more equitable technology through iterative engagement. By adapting AI FORA to the domain of climate resilience, the chapter investigates how participatory and reflexive methods can support the development of AI systems that are both technically robust and socially legitimate. A comparative analytical matrix is employed to structure the transfer, focusing on shared concerns across domains—such as fairness, stakeholder roles, research design, and futures thinking. The approach is operationalised through a participatory process that includes serious games to elicit stakeholder perspectives, followed by agent-based simulations that model the consequences of those design choices.

The remainder of this chapter is organised as follows. Section 2 reviews current shortcomings in the use of AI for climate and disaster management, highlighting the gap between technological capability and societal uptake. Section 3 introduces the methodological framework for transferring the AI FORA approach to the climate domain, outlining the comparative analytical matrix used for adaptation. Section 4 illustrates the transfer process through an empirical case study on smart metres for water management during droughts in Catalonia. Section 5 discusses the insights gained from this domain transfer, reflecting on the method's strengths, limitations, and wider applicability. Section 6 concludes by summarising key findings and identifying future research and policy directions.

Shortcomings of AI Use in Climate and Disaster Management

Artificial Intelligence is emerging as a powerful tool in addressing ecological crises. For example, AI-driven solutions are already enhancing resilience in disaster management such as floodings (Cowls et al. 2023; Microsoft in association with PWC 2018; Vinuesa et al. 2020). Applications range from extreme weather forecasting and flood prediction to sensor-based water management and real-time crisis response systems (Abid et al. 2021; Arfan et al. 2019; Ogie et al. 2018; Saleem and Mehrotra 2022; Schofield 2022; Tan et al. 2021). AI-driven deep learning models are improving predictive accuracy in weather forecasting, while data fusion techniques integrate satellite imagery, IoT (Internet of Things) sensors, and climate data for better decision-making. AI-powered edge-computing sensors enable real-time environmental monitoring, and automated decision-support systems are optimising water management strategies during floods.

Despite such advancements as illustrated for water management, the full potential of AI in ecological crisis management remains underutilised. A major obstacle is the disconnect between AI development and societal needs. Many AI-driven climate solutions are designed in expert silos, without adequate input from the communities most affected by climate change.

As Cowls et al. emphasise: "leveraging the opportunities offered by AI for global climate change is both feasible and desirable, but it involves a sacrifice (ethical risks and potentially an increased carbon footprint) in view of a very significant gain (a more effective response to climate change). It is, in other words, a gambit, which requires responsive and effective governance to become a winning strategy" (Cowls et al. 2023: 284). The deployment of AI in climate and disaster governance reveals structural tensions between technical rationality and social legitimacy.

One recurring issue is the technocratic orientation of many AI-based climate tools. Designed primarily by scientific and engineering experts, these systems often privilege metrics like risk probability, cost-efficiency, or damage reduction—while sidelining the social, ethical, and emotional dimensions of how communities experience and interpret environmental threats. This "model-first" approach of much climate AI tends to abstract away from local knowledge systems, cultural worldviews, and community priorities. Public trust in these systems remains limited, in part because affected populations are rarely involved in shaping their assumptions, objectives, or operational parameters. Instead, communities are positioned as recipients of predictive outputs and behavioural recommendations, rather than as co-producers of resilience strategies (Mabon et al. 2022). This reinforces a top-down logic that mirrors longstanding criticisms of climate policy-making more broadly.

Currently, Participatory AI is not widely used in developing flood warning systems, disaster prevention apps, or sensor technologies for water management. Although some initiatives involve AI in participatory modelling for water management, participatory AI for climate crisis response remains an emerging field, with only initial work currently identifiable (Gavorník et al. 2024; Khadim et al. 2023), with a few promising projects underway (e.g., PREVENIR https://sites.google.com/view/prevenir-en/home; accessed 01.04.2025). However, vulnerable communities remain largely overlooked in these innovations. Their inclusion is essential to ensure that AI systems are grounded in social need and gain broader acceptance. Vulnerable populations may include the elderly (Bischof and Jarke 2021) or marginalised indigenous communities (Lewis et al. 2012). Preliminary findings (Deni Raj 2024) highlight both ethical concerns and opportunities for Participatory AI in water management. In forecasting extreme weather and flood prediction, community-centred approaches are needed. This includes tailoring AI outputs to local contexts, using accessible language, and ensuring equitable tool deployment. In sensor networks and automated decision systems, stakeholder involvement can enhance local relevance, technological acceptance, and transparency. River basin management calls for fairness algorithms and participatory modelling to integrate local values. In leakage detection and smart metering, transparent interfaces and ethical billing practices are essential for consumer trust (Gavorník et al. 2024). It is not enough for technology to predict extreme weather—it must also assess community vulnerability and bridge the digital divide in hazard control systems. Researchers and designers increasingly recognise the importance of engaging vulnerable groups in this domain (Buchert et al. 2022; Caforio et al. 2021; Fazelpour and Danks 2021; Pérez-Escolar and Canet 2022). Ahrweiler (2025) proposes a multi-layered participatory AI approach, incorporating stakeholder engagement across the methodological, institutional, and cultural levels. Of particular importance is the integration of cultural belief systems into AI design: value systems, rituals, and shared meanings that shape how communities understand environmental risk and agency. Without attention to these cultural dimensions, AI systems are likely to remain technically impressive but socially brittle.

Methodological Framework for the Transfer of the AI FORA Approach

The AI FORA Approach: A Socio-Technical Framework for Participatory AI

The generic objective that the AI FORA approach can address is how to come from existing to more desired AI systems. However, depending on the **main challenges and problems of AI use** in each application context, this generic objective needs to be specified and concretised into **research questions** of interest.

The AI FORA research strategy that allows governments and communities to prototype socially desirable AI systems was already presented in Chap. 1. At its core, it combines agent-based simulation, serious games, and system prototyping in an iterative, participatory process. Not all methods mentioned might be applicable in all contexts: **research methods** need to be selected and adapted according to the research question identified. Townhall.

Figure 1 above annotates the participatory methods of the research strategy. Again, not all of them might be applicable in any context: **chances for interactive and participatory formats** might differ between research areas.

The process begins by analysing how AI is currently used in a specific context. This step combines policy analysis, technical investigation, and participatory system mapping workshops. The resulting conceptual model identifies **actors**, values, resources, inputs, outputs, processes, AI in use, policies in use, performance, **stakeholders**, networks, etc. This step provides the foundation for formal modelling and stakeholder engagement. An ABM is then developed to computationally simulate

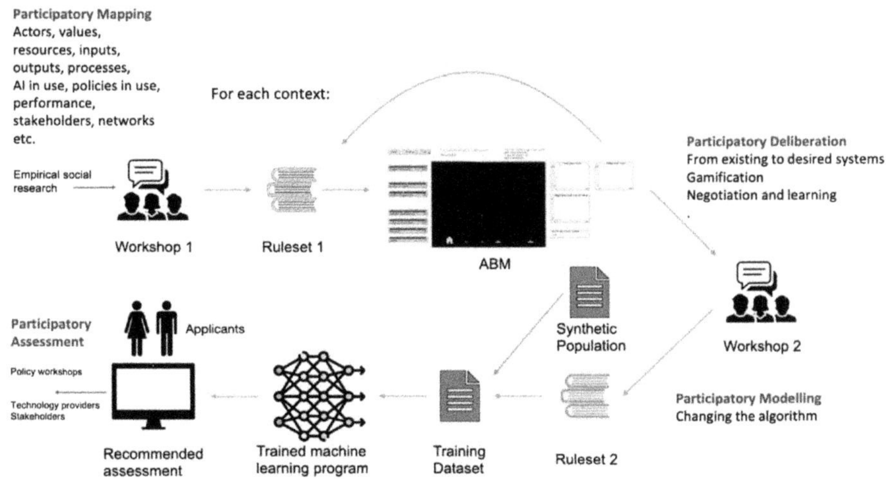

Fig. 1 The AI FORA research strategy annotated

the current system processes. Agents represent actors of the field, interacting under the existing decision rules and resource constraints.

This baseline model ("Ruleset 1") reveals systemic behaviours, bottlenecks, **ethical issues**, inequities, or unintended exclusions, and serves as a transparent artefact for stakeholder discussion.

To ensure that diverse societal perspectives inform AI design, AI FORA uses serious games. Participatory workshops immerse relevant actors and stakeholders in gamification, embedding them in simulated scenarios based on real-life applicant narratives. Participants deliberate on **fairness issues**, system criteria, and trade-offs of existing systems, collaboratively proposing improved decision rules for desired systems. This process of negotiation and learning generates a revised "better ruleset" (Ruleset 2) that captures local value judgements and practical expertise.

The ABM and serious games form a feedback loop of participatory modelling: proposed rules are tested in the model, systemic outcomes are analysed, and stakeholders review results to refine their proposals. This iterative process of "changing the algorithm" makes hidden conflicts and unintended effects visible, fostering collective learning and co-design of fairer practices.

The last steps of the process are dedicated to system prototyping in the real-world context finalised by participatory assessment of stakeholders, especially in policy workshops and interactions with technology providers.

It must be noted that this research strategy is "data hungry": Several types of data sources from different stakeholders are aimed to provide the information required to understand and to model not only the current but also the desired system. **Data availability** might differ from context to context. However, the strategy demonstrates that responsible AI design requires participatory, context-aware, and testable innovation pathways. By integrating social science, computational modelling, and stakeholder expertise, the approach bridges the gap between technological potential, societal values, and policy needs, offering a blueprint for "better AI".

At the core of AI FORA's research strategy, where we have highlighted central aspects and concepts in bold, is the recognition that values, trade-offs, and social dynamics must be surfaced and negotiated throughout system development. AI FORA does not treat AI as a finished product to be deployed, but as a contested, co-constructed system that must evolve with its social environment. It is grounded in the idea of algorithmic sovereignty—the right of publics to shape how algorithmic systems govern shared resources and institutional decisions.

Identifying Adaptation Requirements

This section proposes now to transfer and adapt the AI FORA approach from public welfare to climate resilience, testing its capacity to support inclusive, culturally responsive, and ethically grounded AI design in a radically different but similarly high-stakes domain.

For this, we use the central aspects and concepts identified above to develop a categorial transfer matrix. The matrix idea can facilitate the transfer of methodological knowledge generated during the implementation of the AI FORA project to other domains of AI application by identifying points of difference.

In doing so, the matrix encompasses both relevant research design elements (such as challenges and problems of AI use, research questions, and methodologies) and components related to research outputs (including data availability, ethical and fairness considerations, and stakeholder involvement). Together, these elements inform the transfer process, ensuring that the full scope of the developed research strategy is taken into account.

Categories identified based on research design elements are the following:

- Main challenges and problems of AI use.
- Research question.
- Research methods.
- Chance for interactive and participatory formats.

Categories identified based on research outputs are the following:

- Actors/stakeholders involved.
- Ethical issues.
- Fairness issues.
- Data availability.

The transfer matrix serves as a comparative tool for identifying differences in application context that needs special attention in adapting the research design. Table 1 shows an example for potential completion.

AI Use in Climate Crisis Response: Smart Metres for Water Management during Droughts

This section presents a concrete example of a study (Capellas 2025) that aligns with the transfer approach above.

One of the most pressing climate change-related challenges is the alteration of rainfall patterns, leading to extreme weather events such as heavy rainfall and droughts occurring across different regions (European Environment Agency 2025). In the Mediterranean Basin, droughts are becoming increasingly frequent and severe, posing significant challenges for regional governments in managing water resources. One AI-based solution being implemented to address drought periods is the use of smart metres. These devices support water management in several ways: detecting leaks, forecasting water demand, and monitoring water consumption (Centre of Innovation for Data Tech and Artificial Intelligence CIDAI 2023).

The study explores the sociological dimensions of algorithmic governance, understood as "the idea that digital technologies produce social ordering in a specific

Table 1 Example for completing the transfer matrix

Categories	AI use in public service distribution	AI use in climate crisis response
Main challenges and problems of AI use	Bias-related fairness and discrimination issues	Gap between technological capability and societal uptake
Research questions	Social justice in welfare systems; fair distribution of scarce resources; etc.	Complex dilemmas between environmental, social, economic, and other aspects of sustainability
Research methods	Qualitative methods to elicit culture-specific social justice concepts and fairness values; safe spaces concept to work with vulnerable groups for innovation	Hybrid socio-ecological methods/models; management of the commons (Elinor Ostrom) methods; integrated assessment models (IAM), etc.
Chance for interactive and participatory formats	Stakeholders of national welfare systems—esp. non-recipients of current distribution practices	Stakeholders of climate crisis–esp. communities affected by natural hazards
Actors/stakeholders involved	Well-defined, country-level welfare systems: Beneficiaries, non-beneficiaries, workers in social service agencies, service providers, etc.	Stakeholders in affected territories, helpers, crisis response managers, district officials, NGO supporting affected social groups etc.
Ethical issues	Researching marginalised groups not receiving social services	Working with traumatised people having been subject to climate crisis; privacy regarding data collection and processing by AI systems
Fairness issues	Socio-economic justice issues	Environmental justice issues
Data availability	Access might be restricted by public institutions	Complexity and heterogeneity of data sources

way" (Katzenbach and Ulbricht 2019), in the context of water management during climate change-related droughts. The project specifically examines the challenges of deploying smart metres to enable municipal governments to monitor household water use. The urgency of drought situations often leads to measures that would not be implemented under normal conditions, such as surveillance of households and the imposition of fines for unauthorised water usage. These decisions often transcend the influence of local actors and involve a complex web of governance and account-ability. This situation shows a gap between technological capability and societal uptake and becomes a **challenge regarding AI use**.

In Catalonia, where a drought has been ongoing since 2021 (Agència Catalana de l'Aigua 2025), several municipalities have started implementing smart metres to monitor household water usage. This marks the first time such technology is used in this way, since in previous droughts this technology was not developed in such a way. This deployment raises several challenges: citizens are surveilled in their private homes, and non-compliance with drought regulations can result in fines. Additionally, the data collected through smart metres are often managed by water distribution companies, which may be privately owned rather than state-run. This situation raises not only **ethical questions** but also **concerns about fairness**, particularly regarding whether water use restrictions are imposed equitably across the population.

The study addressing this use of AI deals with the following **research question**: *How does algorithmic governance for water management during droughts shape social reality interacting or conflicting with participatory and communitarian governance (models) in water management?* This research question highlights the dilemmas arising between providing an urgent response to climate change challenges and considering other aspects of sustainability, such as fairness in resource distribution or locally based solutions.

To answer this question, **research methods** include empirical research and the development of an agent-based model, both using **participatory formats**. Key **actors and stakeholders** identified in the research include the national water agency, municipal governments, water distribution companies, households, and AI systems. However, the decisions made by these actors often extend beyond local concerns and intersect with state-level and international regulations, as well as climate-related events. **Data availability** must be addressed in relation to the diversity of stakeholders and data types, ranging from water consumption data to discourse or information captured in interviews, media content, and relevant documents.

Discussion

Reflections on Transferability

The AI FORA approach transfers effectively because both the original welfare eligibility context and the climate crisis domain share structural challenges: a gap between technological capability and societal uptake (Sect. 2) and a lack of early-stage involvement of those most affected. In both cases, AI FORA's participatory design cycle combining serious games with agent-based modelling creates a platform where fairness criteria can be debated, tested, and refined.

In the climate case, this is visible in the smart metre for drought management example (Sect. 4), where municipal governments, private water companies, and households have divergent priorities. The participatory process helps reconcile these perspectives. However, adaptation is needed: Climate governance involves more heterogeneous and geographically dispersed stakeholders than welfare systems and often demands rapid decision-making under crisis conditions (e.g., prolonged drought in Catalonia). Likewise, the Safe Spaces approach used for vulnerable welfare recipients requires modification to work with traumatised or crisis-affected communities, where engagement must consider emotional strain and loss.

Strengths of the AI FORA Method

AI FORA's transparency comes from exposing the "decision rules" of AI systems through simulations. In the welfare context, this clarified how eligibility criteria excluded certain groups; in the climate case, it could reveal how drought-related fines or usage restrictions are applied and whether they disproportionately affect some communities (Sect. 4).Its inclusiveness is achieved by giving all stakeholder types, from state agencies to households, an equal opportunity to influence design. This contrasts sharply with the technocratic orientation of many existing climate AI tools noted in Sect. 2, which often sideline local knowledge systems. The scenario-building process, which merges real-life narratives with game-based deliberation, is particularly valuable in climate adaptation. For example, stakeholders in the Catalonia drought case can experiment with alternative water allocation rules, see modelled outcomes, and refine their proposals before they are implemented.

Limitations and Challenges

Three main limitations emerge when transferring the approach:

1. Scalability: As with the welfare pilot, running participatory simulations with large and diverse climate stakeholder groups is resource-intensive and may be logistically complex.
2. Institutional uptake: In both domains, agencies may be reluctant to integrate participatory outputs into policy. In the smart metre case, for instance, water distribution companies control much of the data and decision-making, limiting opportunities for public input.
3. Methodological complexity: Integrating sociological fieldwork, participatory gaming, and simulation modelling requires broad expertise and high-quality data. In climate contexts, the diversity of data types—from sensor readings to interview transcripts—adds another layer of complexity (Sect. 3).

Implications for Responsible AI in Other Critical Infrastructure Domains

The climate case reinforces AI FORA's potential as a blueprint for Responsible AI in other infrastructures where societal trust is as crucial as technical accuracy. The combination of participatory engagement, transparent modelling, and iterative rule-testing could be applied to areas like energy grids, public health, or transportation planning.

As seen in both the welfare and climate applications, the key is to treat AI as a living sociotechnical system that evolves with its governance environment, rather than a one-off technical product. This orientation ensures that predictive and decision-support capabilities are continuously aligned with changing social needs, and that communities retain agency in shaping the systems that govern their resources.

Conclusion

The transfer of the AI FORA approach from public welfare to climate crisis response has yielded several important insights. First, the core strengths of the method—transparency in decision processes, inclusiveness of diverse perspectives, and the ability to explore complex trade-offs through scenario-building—proved robust across domains. At the same time, the transfer revealed the need for context-specific adaptations. Climate-related applications require broader stakeholder engagement, integration of socio-ecological modelling, and ethical safeguards for working with crisis-affected communities. The Catalonia drought case, in particular, highlighted how participatory processes can help bridge the persistent gap between technological capability and societal uptake.

This work contributes to both participatory AI and socio-environmental resilience. It shows that participatory modelling can surface hidden value conflicts, make algorithmic decision-making intelligible to non-experts, and co-produce rulesets that are more socially legitimate. In the climate domain, such approaches can strengthen resilience by embedding local knowledge and cultural values into AI systems that govern critical resources. More broadly, the findings affirm that AI governance benefits from being treated as an ongoing negotiation between technical systems and their social environments.

Looking forward, three avenues merit particular attention. First, applying AI FORA to additional critical infrastructure domains such as energy, health, and transportation can test its flexibility and uncover domain-specific adaptations. Second, longitudinal studies are needed to observe how Participatory AI systems evolve over time and under shifting socio-political conditions. Third, policy integration is essential: Embedding Participatory AI processes into formal governance frameworks can ensure that co-created solutions influence real-world decision-making, rather than remaining experimental artefacts.

By following these pathways, AI FORA can continue to bridge the gap between technological innovation and societal resilience, contributing to the development of AI systems that are not only effective but also fair, trusted, and responsive to the communities they serve.

Acknowledgements Research presented in the chapter has been funded by the German VolkswagenStiftung under grant agreement number 98 560.

References

Abid, S. K., Sulaiman, N. S. W., Chan, U., Nazir, M., Abid, H., Han, A., Ariza-Montes, A., & Vega-Muñoz, A. (2021). Toward an integrated disaster management approach: How artificial intelligence can boost disaster management. *Sustainability, 13*, 12560. https://doi.org/10.3390/su132212560.

Agència Catalana de l'Aigua (2025). Catalunya, epicentre del canvi climàtic. Analitzem la sequera de 2021–2024. Retrieved 11 Aug 2025, from https://aigua.blog.gencat.cat/2025/07/31/analit zem-la-sequera-de-2021-2024/.

Ahrweiler, P. (2025). Cultural beliefs and participatory AI: Unlocking untapped catalysts for climate action. *Sustainability 17*(9), 4172. https://doi.org/10.3390/su17094172.

Arfan, M., Khan, Z., Qadri, N., Hameed, M. H., & Amir, A. R. (2019). Role of artificial intelligence (AI) in combined disaster management. *Organization Theory Review* 3 (2): 97–121. https://doi.org/10.32350/OTR.0302.05.

Bischof, A., & Jarke. J. (2021). Configuring the older adult. In: *Socio-gerontechnology: Interdisciplinary critical studies of ageing and technology*, Peine, A. Marshall, B. Martin, W. & Neven, L. (Eds.). (pp. 197–212). Routledge. https://doi.org/10.4324/9780429278266-18.

Buchert, U., Kemppainen, L., Olakivi, A., Wrede, S., & Kouvonen, A. (2022). Is digitalisation of public health and social welfare services reinforcing social exclusion? The case of Russian-speaking older migrants in Finland. *Critical Social 43*(3), https://doi.org/10.1177/026101832 21105035.

Caforio, A., Pollini, A., Filograna, A. S., & Passani, A. (2021). Design issues in Human-centered AI for Marginalized People. *ITAIS 2021 Proceedings,* 5. https://aisel.aisnet.org/itais2021/5.

Centre of Innovation for Data tech and Artificial Intelligence (CIDAI) (2023). Llibre blanc sobre la Intel·ligència Artificial aplicada a l'Aigua. Retrieved August 11, 2025, from https://storage.cdn.eurecat.org/CIDAI/WhitePapers/WP-IA-Aigua.pdf.

Cowls, J., Tsamados, A., Taddeo, M., & Floridi, L. (2023). The AI gambit: Leveraging artificial intelligence to combat climate change—Opportunities, challenges, and recommendations. *AI & SOCIETY* 38:283–307. https://doi.org/10.1007/s00146-021-01294-x.

Deni Raj, E. (2024). *Review participatory AI in flood management (working paper).* Indian Institute of Information Technology Kottayam.

Diakopoulos, N. (2016). Accountability in algorithmic decision making. *Communications of the ACM 59*(2), 56–62. https://doi.org/10.1145/2844110.

Eubanks, V. (2018). Automating inequality: How high-tech tools profile, police, and punish the poor. St. Martin's Press.

European Environment Agency (2025). Extreme weather: Floods, droughts and heatwaves. Retrieved August 11, 2025, from https://www.eea.europa.eu/en/topics/in-depth/extreme-wea ther-floods-droughts-and-heatwaves?activeTab=07e50b68-8bf2-4641-ba6b-eda1afd544be.

Fazelpour, S., & Danks. D. (2021). Algorithmic bias: Senses, sources, solutions. *Philosophy Compass, 16*(8): e12760. https://doi.org/10.1111/phc3.12760.

Gavorník, A., Podroužek, J., Oreško, Š., Slosiarová, N., & Grmanová, G. (2024). Beyond privacy and security: Exploring ethical issues of smart metering and non-intrusive load monitoring. *Telematics and Informatics 90*, 102132. https://doi.org/10.1016/j.tele.2024.102132.

Katzenbach, C., & Ulbricht, L. (2019). Algorithmic governance. *Internet Policy Review, 8*(4), https://doi.org/10.14763/2019.4.1424.

Khadim, F. K., Bagtzoglou, A. C., Dokou, Z., & Anagnostou, E. (2023). A socio-hydrological investigation with groundwater models to assess farmer's perception on water management fairness. *Journal of Hydrology, 620,* 129481.

Lewis, V. A., Larson, B. K.,McClurg, A. B., Boswell, R. G., & Fisher, E. S. (2012). The promise and peril of accountable care for vulnerable populations: A framework for overcoming obstacles. *Health affairs (Project Hope) 31*(8), 1777–1785. https://doi.org/10.1377/hlthaff.2012.0490.

Capellas, B. L. (2025). Algorithmic governance for water management during climate change-related droughts: A working paper [working paper]. SSRN. Retrieved 14 Oct 2025, from https://papers.ssrn.com/sol3/papers.cfm?abstract_id=5587250.

Mabon, L., Barkved, L., de Bruin, K., & Shih, W.-Y. (2022). Whose knowledge counts in nature-based solutions? Understanding epistemic justice for nature-based solutions through a multi-city comparison across Europe and Asia. *Environmental Science & Policy, 136,* 652–664. https://doi.org/10.1016/j.envsci.2022.07.025.

Microsoft in association with PWC (2018). *How AI can enable a sustainable future.* Report in the wake of the world economic forum. Retrieved 1 Apr 2025, from https://www.pwc.co.uk/sustainability-climate-change/assets/pdf/how-ai-can-enable-a-sustainable-future.pdf.

O'Connor, R., Bolton, M., Saeri, A. K., Chan, T., & Pearso, R. (2024). Artificial intelligence and complex sustainability policy problems: Translating promise into practice. *Policy Design and Practice, 7*(3), 308–323. https://doi.org/10.1080/25741292.2024.2348834.

Ogie, R. I., Rho, J. C., & Clarke, R. J. (2018). Artificial intelligence in disaster risk communication: A systematic literature review. In *5th international conference on information and communication Technologies for Disaster Management (ICT-DM),* (pp. 1–8). IEEE. https://doi.org/10.1109/ICT-DM.2018.8636380.

Pérez-Escolar, M., & Canet, F. (2022). Research on vulnerable people and digital inclusion: Toward a consolidated taxonomical framework. *Universal Access in the Information Society, 22,* 1059–1072. https://doi.org/10.1007/s10209-022-00867-x.

Saleem, S., & Mehrotra, M. (2022). Emergent use of artificial intelligence and social Media for Disaster Management. In M. Saraswat, S. Roy, C. Chowdhury, & A. H. Gandomi (Eds.). *Proceedings of international conference on data science and applications (lecture notes in networks and systems, Vol. 287, pp. 195–210).* Springer. https://doi.org/10.1007/978-981-16-5348-3_15.

Schofield, M. (2022). An artificial intelligence (AI) approach to controlling disaster scenarios. In: M. Ali (Eds). *Future role of sustainable innovative Technologies in Crisis Management,* (pp. 28–46). IGI Global. https://doi.org/10.4018/978-1-7998-9815-3.ch003.

Tan, L., Guo, J., Mohanarajah, S., & Zhou, K. (2021). Can we detect trends in natural disaster management with artificial intelligence? A review of modeling practices. *Natural Hazards 107,* 2389–2417. https://doi.org/10.1007/s11069-020-04429-3.

United Nations Climate Change, Technology Executive Committee. (2025). *Artificial intelligence for climate action: Advancing mitigation and adaptation in developing countries.* United Nations Framework Convention on Climate Change. Retrieved 15 Sep 2025, from https://unfccc.int/ttclear/misc_/StaticFiles/gnwoerk_static/AI4climateaction/f2922b97c4cf431996c468e622127eb5/112f8be560ea447dab5ff2e53ab3f6e4.pdf.

Vinuesa, R., Azizpour, H., Leite, I., Balaam, M., Dignum, V., Domisch, S., Fellaender, A., Langhans, S. D., Tegmark, M., & Fuso Nerini, F. (2020). The role of artificial intelligence in achieving the sustainable development goals. *Nature Communications 11,* 233. https://doi.org/10.1038/s41467-019-14108-y.

Chapter 15
Collaborative Creativity in Extended Realities: Findings from Co-creative Design Sessions in Augmented and Virtual Reality

Ruben Schlagowski and Elisabeth André

Abstract This chapter presents a study exploring XR technologies' potential in group and co-creativity. During the study, we let participants use HMD-based AR and VR applications for collaborative creativity after participating in a co-creative design workshop featuring analog materials like pen and paper. After the creative XR sessions, we interviewed participants to investigate the requirements for collaborative creative work in XR. The results of our qualitative analysis reveal various opportunities and challenges for XR applications that may be helpful in group creativity. Furthermore, we highlight XR's creative potential by showing various creative works that were created during the co-creative XR sessions.

Introduction

Co-creativity and group creativity can be both challenging and fulfilling. Even though empirical evidence exists for groups being less productive in brainstorming tasks than individuals, group members often have the subjective sensation of it being fun and productive (see, for instance, Homma et al. (1995)). Creativity in groups can also be helpful for application designers and HCI researchers who want to understand user needs and develop solutions that meet them. For instance, Weitz et al. (2024) conducted a collaborative design workshop to prototype design solutions for explainable artificial intelligence (XAI) systems directly with end-users. In this workshop, participating workers created prototypes for specific XAI software tools, including verbal explanations. During such co-creative design workshops, materials such as pen and paper, flip charts, and Post-its are used to model personas, user stories, and

R. Schlagowski (✉) · E. André
Chair for Human-centered Artificial Intelligence, University of Augsburg, Augsburg, Germany
e-mail: ruben.schlagowski@informatik.uni-augsburg.de

E. André
e-mail: andre@informatik.uni-augsburg.de

© The Author(s) 2026

P. Ahrweiler and N. Gilbert (eds.), *Participatory Modelling and Simulation to Improve AI-based Public Social Services*, Artificial Intelligence, Simulation and Society,
https://doi.org/10.1007/978-3-032-15283-1_15

finally develop paper prototypes that fulfill user needs. Figures 1 and 2 show pictures of the workshop conducted by Weitz and colleagues in Estonia.

However, in recent years, new technologies and devices in the Extended Reality (XR) and Mixed Reality (MR) have gained momentum that may enable new ways to conduct such collaborative creative work. This includes Head-Mounted Displays (HMDs) that can provide Augmented Reality (AR) and Virtual Reality (VR) experiences. These devices provide unique opportunities for creativity in groups, as interactive *virtual* tools and materials can be used for creative tasks such as music making or brainstorming. These tools and materials do not obey certain physical rules. For instance, a holographic whiteboard may be scaled infinitely, and drawing may not be limited to two dimensions, as creative collaborators can draw in three dimensions. Furthermore, participants in XR may contribute to creative sessions from a distance, while having the experience or sensation of *being there* or experiencing co-presence with other group members (Schlagowski et al. 2023).

Fig. 1 An instructor of a co-creative design workshop at work

Fig. 2 Participants of a co-creative design workshop using analog materials

To understand how users are and want to be creative in XR, we let participants of a co-creative design workshop use both AR and VR headsets directly after a traditional paper prototyping session (see Fig. 3).

They would collaboratively conduct creative work in shared XR environments, such as 3D drawing mental models and modelling user stories using virtual sticky notes. After the creative XR sessions, we conducted a semi-structured group interview to understand the participants' requirements for XR applications that could be helpful for collaborative creative work, such as the co-creative design workshop they had previously experienced. In this paper, we report on the findings of the qualitative analysis of these interviews while also showcasing some creative works of the participants.

Fig. 3 Two participants are conducting the AR drawing tasks on the left while three seated participants are conducting the VR task in Vive Sync on the right

Fig. 4 A virtual whiteboard in the HTC Sync VR app

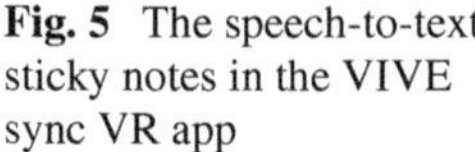

Fig. 5 The speech-to-text sticky notes in the VIVE sync VR app

Related Work

Extended reality (XR), including both virtual and augmented reality, offers new possibilities for supporting collaborative creativity in design contexts such as prototyping and co-creative workshops. Recent work in HCI demonstrates how immersive technologies can facilitate real-time collaboration, embodied ideation, and stakeholder engagement.

For instance, CollaboVR by He et al. (2020) introduced a flexible VR whiteboard that supports freehand sketching and animation in multiuser environments, showing that configurable layouts and embodied interaction can significantly enhance co-creative collaboration. In a related direction, Paraschivoiu et al. (2025) developed CityCraft, an augmented reality platform for collaborative urban design. Deployed in public spaces, it enabled groups to prototype and revise 3D city elements on-site, helping even non experts engage in accessible, meaningful co-creation. Another approach, Performative Prototyping by Weijdom (2022), combined performance and social VR to allow de signers to "act out" interactions, offering a powerful method for embodied ideation and participatory exploration of design concepts.

Psychological research has further clarified XR's impact on the creative process. A literature review by Lyu et al. (2023) concluded that immersive environments support creativity by enhancing presence, perspective-taking, and engagement. They also highlighted that users benefit from the motivational and cognitive affordances of VR, such as lower abstraction thresholds and embodied feedback. Complementing this, Wang et al. (2024) analyzed 254 student design projects and found that group collaboration in VR resulted in more spatially distributed and conceptually divergent designs than individual work, emphasizing how group dynamics and tool use in XR can shape creative output.

Finally, XR has shown promise for eliciting user requirements, especially from non-designers. Dane et al. (2024) presented CoHeSIVE, a VR system that lets citizens co-design public spaces through immersive future scenarios. Participants reported increased confidence in their decisions and a stronger sense of agency, underscoring VR's value in participatory design processes. Similarly, Nguyen et al. (2023) developed a VR based Collaborative Scenario Builder that enabled emergency responders to co-create training simulations. The study showed that immersive prototyping helped these domain experts articulate their needs and ideas, despite having no prior design experience.

Together, these studies demonstrate that XR technologies can not only foster group creativity but also serve as effective tools for engaging diverse stakeholders in the design process through immersive, intuitive, and collaborative environments. However, to the authors' knowledge, no prior study had directly compared AR and VR applications in the context of co-creative design workshops that seek to include end-users in the design of digital applications.

Study Procedure

In 2023, we held a co-creative design workshop ($N = 5$) in Estonia with workers from the Estonian Unemployment Insurance Fund (EUIF).[1] The primary objective of this workshop was to develop XAI prototypes for the AI-driven software "OTT," which assists workers at EUIF in identifying reasons and key features contributing to a client's unemployment status using AI systems. Utilizing a user-centered design strategy along with a question-focused XAI design process, the workshop encouraged the collaborative creation of XAI interfaces tailored for OTT by using creative materials, such as pens, paper, cardboard, and Post-its. More on this workshop is discussed in detail in the study by Weitz et al. (2024).

After the workshop, we let participants use two types of XR devices running multiuser XR applications that support creative processes, either in VR or AR:

- We brought three HTC Vive Focus 3 standalone VR headsets running VIVE sync,[2] a virtual meeting software that enables co-located and remote collaboration in virtual workspaces. It has features like virtual whiteboards and speech-to-text sticky notes that can be used to work on ideas collaboratively.
- The participants could use three Microsoft HoloLens 2 devices running Graffiti 3D,[3] an app that lets participants draw in three dimensions in a shared XR environment.

Two technical supervisors (one visible on the right of Fig. 3) instructed the participants on how to use the applications and devices before proceeding to the co-creative session. Two other supervisors observed the participants and took notes (visible on the back in Fig. 3).

---

[1] Estonian name: Eesti Töötukassa (homepage: https://www.tootukassa.ee/en)

[2] https://sync.vive.com

[3] https://apps.microsoft.com/detail/9npqpk9ngtzr?hl=en-US&gl=SG

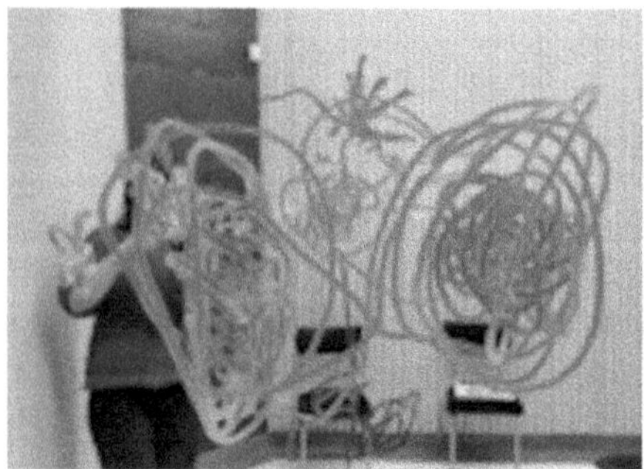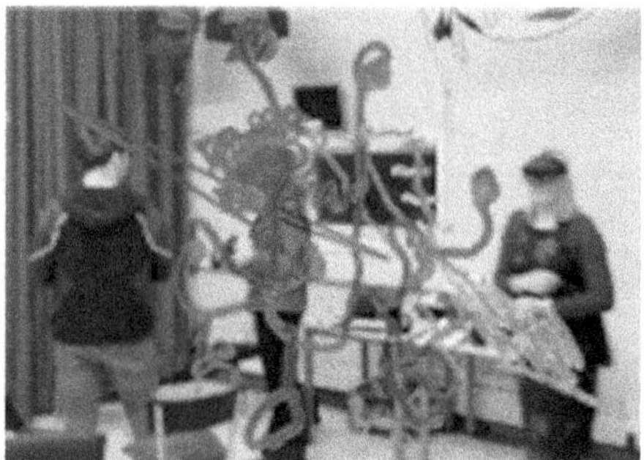

Fig. 6 Two example 3D drawings of participants' imaginations of the OTT AI model, painted collaboratively using Microsoft HoloLens 2 AR HMDs

As soon as the participants felt comfortable using the devices and applications, we gave them two tasks, one for AR and one for VR, each lasting for 30 minutes before switching to the next (other) task.

- *Task in VR:* In VIVE sync, use the sticky notes and virtual whiteboard features (see Screenshots in Figs. 4 and 5) to model an improved process of consulting an unemployed person in chronological steps.
- *Task in AR:* In Graffiti 3D, make a 3D drawing collaboratively that illustrates how you imagine the AI of OTT to look from the inside. Some results are displayed in Fig. 6.

As soon as the creative sessions were completed, we conducted a semi-structured group interview posing open questions, during which we recorded audio. Question 1 aimed to recall memories of the earlier co-creative design workshop, and questions 2–5 addressed the XR experiences:

1. Reflect on the co-creative sessions of the workshop: What went well, what was challenging?
2. Please share your thoughts on the AR and VR demos you just witnessed!
3. Can you imagine using the AR/VR hardware you just tried in a co-creative workshop we just did? Why?
4. Do you think AR or VR is more promising? Why?
5. How do you think an AR or VR application should look to be useful in co-creative design sessions?

Fig. 7 Aspects and features of the VR app that participants praised

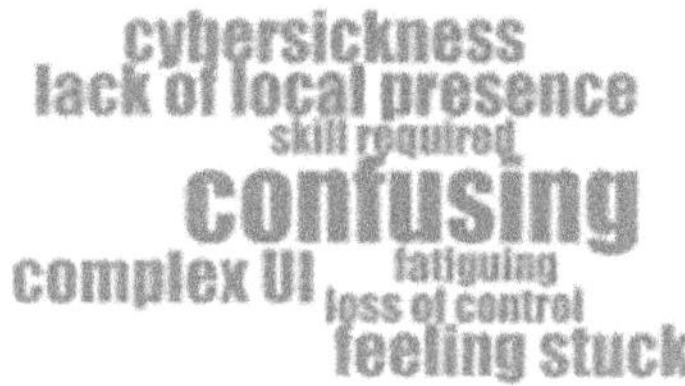

Fig. 8 Aspects and features of the VR app that participants criticized

Fig. 9 Feature requests for the VR applications

Fig. 10 Aspects and features of the AR app that participants praised

Interview Results

We transcribed the audio recordings and conducted a summative content analysis using MaxQDA.[4] Below, we report on our findings and show the results of the qualitative analysis using code or word clouds (Figs. 7-12), which show themes or codes that were mentioned more frequently in a proportionally larger font.

Fig. 11 Feature requests for the AR application

---

[4] https://www.maxqda.com/

Fig. 12 XR feature requests that were uttered independent of the used XR technology

Feedback on VR Experience

Figures 7 and 8 show aspects that participants explicitly praised and criticized about the co-creative VR experiences. In the VIVE sync VR app, they liked the sticky notes (2 mentions) and the ability to cluster them spatially (2 mentions) to summarize content semantically. One participant stated: "If you can use it to summarize things, it could be easy to look at all that you have and get a full picture." One participant thought it was entertaining, stating: "I think it excites you enough to be focused enough on the subjects that are coming there." Also, one participant thought being in VR is "fun." Virtual whiteboards and the speech-to-text input for sticky notes were positively mentioned once.

However, in contrast to the AR app, the VR app was also heavily criticized by participants (see Fig. 8). Four times it was stated that the App was too complex and "confusing." Explicitly, the UI was reported to be too complex (2 mentions) and that there was skill required to use the application efficiently (1 mention). Two participants reported experiencing cybersickness. Two times it was mentioned that the participants felt "stuck" and were not sufficiently aware of their surroundings (lack of local presence, two mentions). Other utterances included the experience of fatigue and the subjective sensation of the loss of control (two mentions).

Participants noted that the true potential of the VR app was hard to grasp in the study's co-located setting. For instance, one participant stated, "We would need to have a real [remote] meeting there to grasp what is missing." And that a key challenge would then be representing participants: "I need a human face-to-face." This is congruent with three requests for better character customization and one for face tracking (see feature requests in Fig. 9). Three times the feature of remote meetings was requested, which is a feature that the VIVE sync app already supports. However, as the participants used the VR app in a co-located situation, they were not aware of that feature specifically. Other requests for VR specifically were an Internet Browser, voice chat, and better graphics (one mention each).

Feedback on the AR Experience

Participants universally praised the AR 3D drawing experience using the HoloLens 2 devices and rarely criticized it. When asked directly (question 4), four participants said they preferred AR for co-creativity. Participants heavily praised the ability to move freely in their surroundings (2 mentions, see Fig. 10) while experiencing their surroundings unaltered (local presence, one mention). The 3D drawing was mentioned positively as a feature (one mention) and one participant stated the app as "fun." These positive utterances were confirmed by the rest of the group, which understates their significance.

Both used virtual tools in the VR application, the speech-to-text sticky notes and virtual whiteboards, were requested as features within the AR application (four mentions each, see Fig. 11. One participant wished for more brush stroke options, and another wanted geometric forms to place in 3D space. Also, the ability to have "big screens" was requested once.

General Feature Requests for Co-creative Sessions

When asked about the applicability of XR technologies within co-creative design work shops, participants uttered various features independent of the employed technology (AR or VR). However, as most participants heavily preferred AR, they were mostly thought of in an AR context. Figure 12 shows the code cloud for these features. Two participants wished to have PowerPoint support to show presentations during co-creative sessions. Also, two times, data visualization features were requested. One participant stated: "We could very quickly pull statistics from our database and throw them in the air, e.g., client backgrounds." Another requested feature was that sticky notes scaled automatically according to the number of text characters they should display (two mentions). Other feature requests (one mention each) were the support of physical and virtual keyboards, the ability to share screens, and the ability to have lines to interconnect sticky notes.

Discussion

The significance of co-presence and local presence in AR: A theme that was frequently mentioned during the interview was the importance of the users' ability to move freely and of being aware of their surroundings while immersed in XR. This might stem from projecting the co-creative workshop experience they previously participated in onto a possible XR solution. Additionally, features and virtual content perceived as *an addition* to the familiar world may be simpler for participants to absorb and adapt to compared to VR technologies and environments, which can initially feel overwhelming. The participants described this sensation as "feeling stuck," "fatiguing," and "con fusing" (see codecloud in Fig. 8). Additionally, experiencing the other creative collaborators unobstructed and not as virtual avatars was perceived as a clear advantage and requirement, with participants stating they need to experience their collaborators "face-to-face."

XR can be inspiring: Participants mentioned that they were merely creative in their day jobs as unemployment consultants. However, the creations that were created in the XR sessions, especially the modeling of mental models of AIs, were regarded as highly creative by test supervisors. Example models are depicted in Figs. 6 and 13. This left the impression that the artistic feature of collaborative 3D drawing in XR inspired the workshop participants and unexpectedly revealed their significant creative potential. Hence, the authors encourage further research in creative domains such as fine arts and sculpting featuring XR technologies. To our beliefs, vast potential may lie here, not only for creative professionals, but also for hobbyists who may even experience XR technologies.

VR's potential for remote creativity: Most participants heavily preferred the AR experiences for their collaborative creative work. However, participants also agreed that VR has vast potential in creative remote collaboration. However, remote collaboration, including features such as voice chat, was neither demonstrated nor tested during the workshop. One participant stated: "We would need to have a real meeting there [in VR] to grasp what is missing," and another said: "If from afar, then VR." A key challenge here, however, is the design of virtual avatars, as one of the most requested features for the VR app was further avatar customization options. We note, however, that those were already included in the app we used (HTC VIVE sync) but not demonstrated, as participants used pre-configured neutral characters in the VR sessions.

The XR feature ambivalence: Participants often stated that they felt over-whelmed by the user interfaces they had to deal with while being creative in VR.

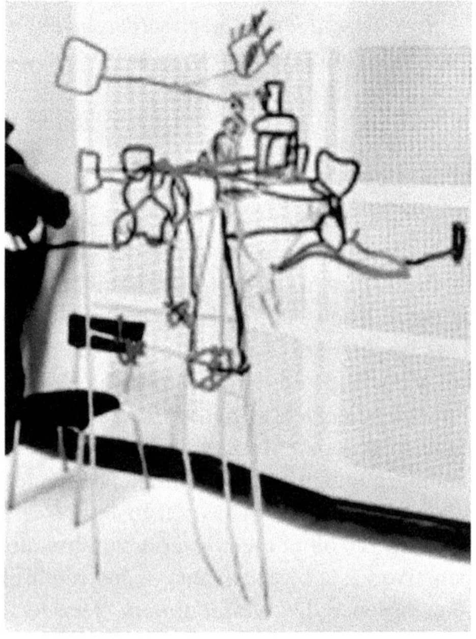

Fig. 13 An example 3D painting illustrating the mental model of the OTTAI model that was drawn during the workshop. It was created in a few minutes while drawing collaboratively using Graffiti 3D on multiple HoloLens2 devices

In addition to having to adapt to new input and output modalities, this was also attributed to the general complexity of the UI systems. However, participants also requested more complex features to be productive in XR, including screen sharing, data visualization, and PowerPoint support (see Fig. 12). Designing a successful XR collaboration app is challenging as its creators need to find an intricate balance of feature variety and complexity. Providing comprehensive tutorials and introductions that successfully explain and introduce features may provide a good entry point for users.

The potential of XR in co-creativity: Aside from having some concrete concerns and issues, not a single participant questioned the applicability or the general idea of introducing XR technologies into collaborative creativity. Instead, participants were generally positive and constructive in their feedback for the applications and experiences they witnessed. This left the authors with the general impression that, if the applications and use cases match, XR could benefit the participants and even provide value. Participants explicitly liked the idea of having virtual large screens and the ability to cluster information spatially in three dimensions with virtual sticky notes. The idea of drawing interconnections between content arranged in 3D space was also brought up. A common theme here was a wish for features that were exclusive to the VR application, such as virtual whiteboards and 3D speech-to-text sticky notes (see Figs. 4 and 5) in an optical-see-through AR application like they had experienced on the HoloLens 2 devices.

Conclusion

This chapter reports on a study that let participants conduct collaborative creative work in AR and VR after they had experienced a co-creative design workshop. Our qualitative analysis of the described post-hoc interview revealed various potentials and pitfalls of employing XR technologies in collaborative design sessions and workshops that usually employ heavy use of analogue materials such as pen and paper, sticky notes, white boards, and paper prototypes. 3D drawing in AR was especially praised, and VR's potential for remote collaborative work was mentioned. Furthermore, the importance of experiencing local and social presence in co-located sessions was emphasized, and we report participants' ambivalent needs and opinions on feature complexity and diversity within XR applications for collaborative creativity.

Acknowledgements Research presented in the chapter has been funded by the German VolkswagenStiftung under grant agreement number 98 560.

References

Dane, G., Evers, S., van den Berg, P., Klippel, A., Verduijn, T., Wallgrün, J. O., & Arentze, T. (2024). Experiencing the future: Evaluating a new framework for the participatory co-design of healthy public spaces using immersive virtual reality. *Computers, Environment and Urban Systems, 114*, 102194. https://doi.org/10.1016/j.compenvurbsys.2024.102194.

He, Z., Du, R., & Perlin, K. (2020). CollaboVR: A reconfigurable framework for creative collaboration in virtual reality. In *In 2020 IEEE international symposium on mixed and augmented reality (ISMAR)*, 542–554. IEEE. https://doi.org/10.1109/ISMAR50242.2020.00074.

Homma, M., Tajima, K., & Hayashi, M. (1995). The effects of misperception of performance in brainstorming groups. *The Japanese Journal of Experimental Social Psychology, 34*(3), 221–231.

Lyu, Q., Watanabe, K., Umemura, H., & Murai, A. (2023). Design-thinking skill enhancement in virtual reality: A literature study. *Frontiers in Virtual Reality, 4*, 1137293. https://doi.org/10.3389/frvir.2023.1137293.

Nguyen, Q., Pretolesi, D., & Gallhuber, K. (2023). Collaborative scenario builder: A VR co-design tool for medical first responders. In *Proceedings of the 2023 ACM Conference on Information Technology for Social Good (GoodIT '23)*, (pp. 342–350). Association for Computing Machinery. doi:https://doi.org/10.1145/3582515.3609553.

Paraschivoiu, I., Steiner, R., Wieser, J., & Meschtscherjakov, A. (2025). Crafting cities together: Co-located collaboration with augmented reality for urban design. In *Computer supported cooperative work (CSCW)*, 1–43. Springer.

Schlagowski, R., Nazarenko, D., Can, Y., Gupta, K., Mertes, S., Billinghurst, M., & André, E. (2023). Wish you were here: Mental and physiological effects of remote music collaboration in mixed reality. In: *Proceedings of the 2023 CHI Conference on Human Factors in Computing Systems* (pp. 1–16). Association for Computing Machinery. doi:https://doi.org/10.1145/3544548.3581162.

Wang, P., Miller, M. R., Han, E., DeVeaux, C., & Bailenson. J. N. (2024). Understanding virtual design behaviors: A large-scale analysis of the design process in virtual reality. *Design Studies, 90*, 101237. https://doi.org/10.1016/j.destud.2023.101237.

Weijdom, J. (2022). Performative prototyping in collaborative mixed reality environments: An embodied design method for ideation and development in virtual reality. In *Proceedings of the Sixteenth International Conference on Tangible, Embedded, and Embodied Interaction (TEI'22)* (pp. 1–13). Association for Computing Machinery. doi:https://doi.org/10.1145/3490149.3501316.

Weitz, K., Schlagowski, R., André, E., Männiste, M., & George, C. (2024). Explaining it your way: Findings from a co-creative design workshop on designing XAI applications with AI end-users from the public sector. In: *Proceedings of the CHI Conference on Human Factors in Computing Systems*, (pp. 1–14). Association for Computing Machinery.

Chapter 16
Participatory Modelling for 'Better AI'

Petra Ahrweiler

Abstract This chapter synthesises findings from the AI FORA project, which explored how participatory modelling can support the design of 'Better AI' in welfare systems. Across five of its case studies, the project used agent-based modelling (ABM), serious games, and policy dissemination to investigate fairness, transparency, and legitimacy in algorithmic governance. The results show that participatory approaches, where practitioners, policymakers, and citizens co-design and deliberate on models, enhance the transparency of decision processes, surface hidden biases, and align AI systems more closely with ethical and social values. Cases demonstrated both the potential of AI to improve efficiency and fairness, and the risks of reinforcing structural inequities when stakeholder involvement and data quality are lacking. Dissemination activities in Europe, Asia, and the United States further underscored that policy impact depends less on technological fixes than on institutional reforms, capacity building, and inclusive governance. The chapter concludes that participatory modelling is both a methodological innovation and a democratic imperative, providing Safe Spaces to negotiate fairness and embedding the principles of the European AI Act into practice.

Introduction

The increasing use of AI in welfare systems raises pressing questions about fairness, transparency, and accountability in public service delivery. While AI promises efficiency and scalability, its reliance on administrative data and opaque algorithms risks reinforcing structural inequities and eroding public trust. The AI FORA project responded to these challenges by advancing participatory modelling as a means of

---

P. Ahrweiler (✉)
TISSS Lab, Institute of Sociology, Johannes Gutenberg University, Mainz, Germany
e-mail: Petra.ahrweiler@uni-mainz.de

© The Author(s) 2026

P. Ahrweiler and N. Gilbert (eds.), *Participatory Modelling and Simulation to Improve AI-based Public Social Services*, Artificial Intelligence, Simulation and Society,
https://doi.org/10.1007/978-3-032-15283-1_16

185

designing 'Better AI', i.e. AI that is context-sensitive, ethically aligned, and democratically legitimate. At the project's core lay the hypothesis that stakeholder involvement enhances both the transparency and the ethical alignment of AI-supported decision-making.

This chapter synthesises AI FORA's findings from modelling and simulation as well as from interaction with policymakers. Cases span diverse domains—social service assessments in Spain, unemployment counselling in Estonia, asylum procedures in Germany, targeted subsidies in Iran, and food distribution in India—yet they shared a commitment to involving practitioners, policymakers, and citizens in the process of testing, refining, and governing AI systems. Together, these cases demonstrated how participatory modelling can reveal hidden biases, negotiate interpretations of fairness, and generate actionable insights for policy reform.

The chapter is organised as follows: The next section evaluates and compares the design and outcomes of the simulation models, reviews the participatory processes that were used, and identifies the insights gained about fairness and accountability. The third section reflects on dissemination to policy audiences, examining how modelling results can inform debates on algorithmic governance (Danaher et al. 2017; Yeung 2018) and connect with emerging regulatory frameworks such as the European AI Act (European Union 2024). The chapter concludes by drawing broader lessons about the role of participatory modelling in shaping AI systems that serve equity and democratic accountability.

Evaluating the Findings of Modelling and Simulation

The key hypothesis of AI FORA is that stakeholder involvement improves both the transparency and the ethical alignment of AI-supported decision-making. Current algorithmic tools and administrative data used in welfare assessments often reflect and reinforce existing structural inequalities; without careful co-design and continuous evaluation, AI risks institutionalising bias rather than correcting it. This key hypothesis was translated for a modelling environment where ABM can effectively capture the complexity of welfare systems, reveal hidden decision-making dynamics, and serve as a testbed for evaluating alternative policies and AI rule sets. Participatory modelling approaches, particularly when combining ABM and gamification, can lead to more legitimate, context-sensitive, and equitable AI systems for public social services. Models can allow stakeholders to experiment safely with new rules and explore their systemic consequences before real-world deployment. Gamification and serious games can externalise tacit knowledge and facilitate stakeholder deliberation around fairness, trade-offs, and algorithmic design; this combination enhances stakeholder understanding of algorithmic systems and encourages collective reflection. Core research questions are about the characteristics and dynamics of existing systems, about requirements of desired system futures, and about the impacts of 'changing the algorithm' on system performance.

The research presented in this volume offered an opportunity for evaluating the findings of modelling and simulation against the key hypothesis and these core research questions, especially concerning challenges for existing or future AI use in social assessment for public service distribution. Most of the case studies brought data from empirical research to models[1] and used participatory anticipation, projection, and realisation along a modelling strategy that was designed to support the transition from existing to desired systems for 'Better AI'.

The Spanish ABM

The Spanish ABM was originally planned as a kind of theorem-checking device for the assessment algorithm in place in the empirical system under investigation, in this case social assessment in Catalonia. The ABM's purpose was not only to ensure that the ruleset was coherent and complete, but to offer an informed starting point for devising a better algorithm by stakeholder involvement. The ABM simulations (Sabater et al. in this volume) revealed substantial variation in how social workers applied the SSM-Cat, even when evaluating identical applicant profiles. This inconsistency underscored the absence of a shared interpretive culture across agencies. Through repeated rounds and gamification workshops, participants recognised the importance of developing common decision-making protocols and structured training to align fairness standards. The ABM also demonstrated that certain assessment criteria used informally by practitioners were missing from the official matrix, raising questions about whether tools should adapt to practice or vice versa. Importantly, the simulations showed that deliberation within a participatory modelling environment can foster greater consistency, transparency, and awareness of bias in welfare allocation. The model and the accompanying gamification workshops were employed not only as an analytical tool but as a participatory forum where practitioners, policymakers, and community stakeholders co-create interpretive frameworks and deliberate on equity. This hybrid approach, further strengthened by cluster analysis, represented a significant step forward in developing context-sensitive, transparent AI systems for public services.

The German ABM

The case study in Germany planned for an ABM on the tipping points for investigating the agency of refugees (for more and quicker integration into society and the job market) and legitimacy of administrative decisions (for accountability and correctness of bureaucratic procedures in granting asylum) and the trade-offs between

---

[1] The modelling activities originally envisaged for Ukraine, China, the United States, and Nigeria could not take place due to resource constraints.

these two policy objectives under conditions of potential AI integration. The model (Spaeth et al. in this volume) simulated key stages of the asylum process—registration, hearing, decision, and appeals—capturing how administrative workload, documentation, interpreter quality, and support networks influence outcomes. The **sensitivity analysis** showed that high staff workloads significantly increase erroneous decisions, reflected in high appeal rates and a greater share of successful appeals. Conversely, when bureaucracy is well-resourced, fewer errors occur, boosting legitimacy but also revealing systemic shortcomings such as slow integration of refugees into the job market due to overly cumbersome procedures and red tape. By combining quantitative simulations with qualitative narratives drawn from refugee experiences, the ABM demonstrated how structural features—such as interpreter assignment or federal state practices—critically shape refugee trajectories. Narratives underscored the 'Kafkaesque' experience of asylum seekers, marked by helplessness and opaque decision-making, while also illustrating tipping points where supportive networks or legal aid could alter outcomes. Importantly, the model revealed that legitimacy is not only tied to efficiency but also to fairness and transparency across multiple decision points.

From an evaluative perspective, the German ABM's contribution lies in **making visible the systemic trade-offs between bureaucratic efficiency and refugee agency**. It provides policymakers with a diagnostic tool to test how institutional design, rather than purely technical fixes, influences perceived legitimacy. The study cautions that AI integration must not merely optimise administrative throughput but should be embedded in frameworks that strengthen accountability, transparency, and trust. Overall, the ABM adds value by bridging micro-level experiences with macro-level dynamics, offering both explanatory insight and a reflective space for considering reforms.

The German ABM directly contributes to AI FORA's core hypothesis by demonstrating that *stakeholder involvement—particularly refugees, supporters, and practitioners—makes otherwise opaque bureaucratic processes visible and debatable.* Through participatory modelling and narrative integration, the ABM translated refugees' experiential knowledge into the simulation design, thereby surfacing how interpreter quality, document practices, or administrative workload shape fairness and legitimacy. This process not only enhanced the *transparency* of asylum decision-making by showing how different inputs affect outcomes but also facilitated *ethical alignment*, as *stakeholders identified points where systemic biases or organisational cultures disadvantage vulnerable groups.* In doing so, the German ABM illustrated that *co-creation does not simply refine technical accuracy but also embeds values of fairness, accountability, and trust into potential pathways for AI integration.*

The Estonian ABM

The ABM in Estonia was planned to shift the focus more explicitly to citizens and their requirements concerning AI systems in the context of (un)employment services.

Particular attention was to be directed towards potentially vulnerable groups for gaining a deeper understanding of their interactions with and needs related to AI systems. The Estonian ABM and serious game (Männiste et al. in this volume) revealed that just adding variables does not automatically equate to more fairness: Introducing new factors to consider (health, caregiving responsibilities, etc.) helped capture individual vulnerabilities but also shifted attention from collective fairness to individual cases. H.

This revealed a trade-off: More nuanced data may improve individual assessments but risks undermining broader systemic equity. The model showed that consultants' discretion remained essential. Even with structured algorithms, subjective interpretation (e.g., assessing health conditions) introduced variability in outcomes. While algorithmic transparency was valued, participants raised concerns about potential system gaming by more digitally literate clients. This highlighted a delicate balance: explainability had to be pursued without undermining system integrity.

The model highlighted that *fairness* in algorithmic decision-making is not fixed but contextual and negotiated. It *emerged as a negotiated process* shaped by how stakeholders (here: students playing consultants and clients) interacted with the ruleset and adapted it over time. This *underlined the importance of participatory approaches in AI-supported welfare systems.*

Participants saw algorithms as support tools, not replacements for human decision-making. They proposed decision-tree or adaptive models that evolve based on client responses, rather than rigid scoring systems. This reflects the *need for flexible, context-sensitive AI* that can better capture real-life complexities. Finally, the exercise underscored that *fair assessments often require cross-sector collaboration*, since criteria like health or caregiving responsibilities demand expertise beyond a single institution.

The Iranian ABM

The Iran case study constructed an ABM informed by insights gained from the analysis of the Iranian Targeted Subsidies Plan (TSP) to explore future scenarios involving the implementation of various policy options. The ABM captured household-level heterogeneity and dynamic behaviours such as income generation, consumption, savings, sudden income jumps, and bankruptcies while simulating the long-term effects of subsidy policies (Bashiri in this volume). This allowed for a more realistic analysis than static economic models, especially in contexts where household diversity and economic volatility are significant. Key findings of the model highlight both the strengths and limitations of the TSP. On the positive side, subsidies targeted at the lowest four income deciles provided short-term welfare improvements, economic stabilisation, and increased transparency and trust. Policymakers could also dynamically test alternative subsidy scenarios based on the systematic use of the Iranian Welfare Database, thereby improving targeting accuracy and accountability. However, the simulation revealed that the plan's overall effectiveness is severely constrained by macroeconomic factors outside the subsidy system, most notably inflation, sanctions, and currency devaluation. These external shocks erode the real value of subsidies, limiting their capacity to reduce poverty and income inequality in the long term.

While the Iranian case study focused primarily on technical aspects of agent-based modelling and data-driven household classification, *the experience of the TSP also illustrated the potential value of a participatory approach*, as emphasised in the AI FORA project. Engaging low-income households, social workers, NGO, and community representatives in deliberative workshops could have helped refine the eligibility criteria used for subsidy allocation, ensuring that classifications align more closely with lived realities and perceptions of fairness. Participatory simulation sessions or serious games, in which stakeholders explored different allocation scenarios under conditions of inflation or sanctions, would have allowed policymakers to anticipate social impacts and adjust policies accordingly. Such participatory methods not only improve the transparency of complex subsidy systems but also strengthen their ethical alignment, turning beneficiaries into co-designers of welfare policy rather than passive recipients.[2]

The Indian ABM

The case study in India highlights how the Public Distribution System (PDS), while critical to ensuring food security for over 800 million citizens, suffers from systemic inefficiencies—corruption, leakage, inequities, and weak accountability (Jo et al. in this volume). By simulating the micro-level interactions of key actors such as beneficiaries, fair price shop operators, suppliers, trucks, and inspectors, the ABM demonstrates how localised behaviours and logistical constraints aggregate into system-wide outcomes. The case study's model successfully illustrates how targeted inspections reduce corruption, how improved logistics boost fairness, and how real-time oversight enhances trust in welfare delivery. Overall, the Indian modelling approach demonstrates how ABM can uncover structural weaknesses in welfare governance and offer pathways for ethical AI integration. A core strength of the model lies in its *integration of Responsible AI principles*—fairness, transparency, and accountability—directly into the simulation as performance metrics. This methodological innovation not only enabled ethical evaluation of system dynamics but also showcased *how AI FORA's central hypothesis—that participatory and transparent approaches improve AI-supported decision-making—could be operationalised in large-scale welfare contexts.*

---

[2] Iran was added to the project post-award as a self-funded case study: available resources did not allow for participatory methods.

Comparative Evaluation of ABM in AI FORA

All models were assessed against AI FORA's central hypothesis: *Stakeholder involvement improves transparency and ethical alignment of AI-supported decision-making.* Across cases, ABM proved useful to surface hidden dynamics, test rule changes, and provide safe environments for exploring fairness and legitimacy. Gamification and participatory elements particularly strengthened these outcomes. To complement the narrative synthesis, Table 1 provides a comparative overview of the five ABM case studies. It distils each case into its purpose, key findings, contribution to AI FORA's central hypothesis, and main limitations.

This tabular perspective highlights both the diversity of contexts—ranging from welfare allocation in Spain to food distribution in India—and the common challenges of balancing fairness, transparency, and legitimacy in AI-supported decision-making. Taken together, the five cases contain important lessons for the role of ABM in public welfare governance.

First, participatory approaches clearly strengthen both transparency and ethical alignment. The Spanish, Estonian, and German models directly engaged stakeholders—social workers, students, or refugees—surfacing interpretive practices, fairness concerns, and legitimacy challenges. By contrast, the Iranian and Indian cases remained primarily technical exercises, offering analytical insights but lacking the stakeholder deliberation needed to align with AI FORA's participatory vision. Second, ABM proved especially effective at revealing trade-offs: between individualised and systemic fairness (Estonia), between efficiency and legitimacy (Germany), or between technical accuracy and lived realities (Iran). In Spain and India, ABM helped operationalise fairness, transparency, and accountability either through shared interpretive frameworks or explicit performance metrics. Across all cases, however, limitations in data quality, model simplification, and representativeness persisted, cautioning against over-interpretation. The comparative evaluation of ABM in AI FORA underscores its dual value: as a technical tool to simulate complex welfare systems and as a participatory arena to deliberate on fairness, legitimacy, and accountability. Where participatory elements were integrated, models not only illuminated system dynamics but also fostered collective reflection, aligning with AI FORA's central hypothesis. Future research should combine the technical robustness of models like Iran and India with the participatory depth of Spain, Estonia, and Germany, moving towards AI-supported welfare systems that are both analytically rigorous and democratically legitimate.

However, these five case studies had several common limitations, which must be borne in mind when considering their implications. First, the quality and representativeness of data posed persistent challenges. Administrative datasets often suffered from inconsistencies, coverage gaps, and embedded biases, undermining the reliability of simulations and decision-support models. For example, in Spain and Estonia, classification errors and subjective assessments weakened the robustness of household-level modelling, while in Iran, indicators such as foreign travel or bank transactions risked excluding households with irregular or informal incomes. These

Table 1: Comparative Grid

Case	Purpose/Focus	Key findings	Contribution to AI FORA hypothesis	Limitations
Spain (Catalonia, SSM-cat)	Test consistency of social assessment tool (SSM-cat) and explore fairness in allocation	Large variation in interpretation of identical profiles; missing criteria sparked debate on tool vs. practice	Participatory workshops fostered shared interpretive culture; deliberation for transparency and fairness	Biased administrative data; limited to Catalonia stakeholders
Estonia (unemployment services)	Explore fairness perceptions in algorithmic career counselling through serious games	Adding variables captured individual needs but reduced systemic equity; discretion and subjectivity remained crucial	Showed fairness as contextual and negotiated; highlighted role of adaptive, flexible models and cross-sector collaboration	Workshops involved students, not real clients; model simplified real system; only short-term perceptions
Germany (asylum system)	Examine trade-offs between bureaucratic legitimacy and refugee agency under possible AI integration	High workloads → more errors and appeals; narratives revealed difficult experiences; support networks crucial	Participatory modelling made opaque processes visible; integrated refugee perspectives into simulation; bridged micro- and macro-dynamics	Simplified asylum stages; excluded political/legal dynamics; limited representativeness of narratives
Iran (targeted subsidies plan)	Simulate household heterogeneity, subsidy allocation, and long-term economic impacts	Short-term welfare gains eroded by inflation, sanctions, devaluation; annual reclassification improved transparency and trust	Demonstrated potential of data-driven targeting; participatory approaches could refine eligibility and align with lived realities	Heavy reliance on administrative data; no participatory element; macroeconomic shocks external to model
India (public distribution system)	Model corruption, logistics, and accountability in ration distribution	Inspections reduced corruption; logistics improved fairness; oversight boosted trust	Embedded responsible AI metrics directly in simulation; operationalised hypothesis at scale	Lacked participatory validation; abstracted from real-world practices; no direct stakeholder engagement

issues highlight how reliance on administrative records may distort rather than clarify the lived realities of target populations.

Second, the scope and ecological validity of participatory elements were constrained. In some contexts, such as Estonia, workshops drew on students rather than real clients, limiting the applicability of results to policy practice. In Spain, engagement was restricted to a small group of social workers and policymakers from a single region, which cannot capture the diversity of institutional arrangements across the country. The Indian case study, by contrast, omitted participatory processes altogether, reducing the model's ability to incorporate contextual sensitivities or stakeholder perspectives.

Third, all models necessarily simplified complex institutional and social processes. The German ABM, for instance, reduced the asylum process to a handful of stations and attributes, omitting geopolitical dynamics, evolving legal frameworks, or subtle forms of discrimination. While such abstraction is essential for tractability, it constrains explanatory power and limits the capacity to capture rapidly changing organisational cultures or political pressures.

Finally, the time horizons of analysis were often short-term. Case studies generally focused on immediate perceptions or systemic thresholds rather than long-term impacts on fairness, trust, or social outcomes. As a result, while the models provided valuable diagnostic and reflective insights, their prescriptive power for policy design remains limited.

Assessing Policy Dissemination Activities

Including the full variety of multi-stakeholder perspectives had been crucial for the legitimacy of 'Better AI' design. Modelling activities presented in this volume tried to provide a quality space for participation and negotiation, where the diverse voices of all stakeholding communities could impact the shape of future AI systems in social welfare.

However, Birhane et al. (2022) had warned against 'participation washing' (see discussion in Ahrweiler et al. 2025), which meant avoiding that participation of stakeholders had no consequences for decision-making: stakeholders need to see that their agency is increased by participation and that their input makes a difference. How could modelling results co-produced by heterogeneous stakeholders reach decision makers, the main target audience (Waibel et al. 2021) for the research presented in this volume? Governmental decisions on AI use in public administrations of national welfare systems provide one important access point for 'Better AI'. Research results need to be made known to this audience and lead to policy learning and impact for change.

Dissemination of Research to Policy in Spain

Spanish policy modelling addressed public administrators as the main client group. It concluded that the inclusion of multiple stakeholders would be necessary for periodic policy evaluation and to update ethical standards in emerging ethical challenges and responsibilities in AI-based social services. The research recommended rigorous oversight to mitigate unforeseen impacts and ensure alignment with societal norms and ethical standards through responsive governance structures (Sabater et al. in this volume).

The Spanish policy dissemination chapter demonstrated how participatory approaches can bridge the gap between technical design and lived realities in AI-driven social services. By foregrounding compositional, contextual, and collective dimensions, and by embedding continuous oversight and grassroots participation, it provided a model for policy change that advanced AI FORA's mission of fair, open, and responsible automation. At the same time, it suggested that participatory processes must be scaled, diversified, and sustained to ensure AI remains responsive to the complex and evolving realities of social service provision. Spanish policy clients, particularly those involved in social service delivery and digital innovation agendas, reacted to the AI FORA results with a mix of recognition and cautious interest. On the one hand, the modelling activities—especially the ABM demonstrations of inconsistency in welfare assessments—resonated strongly with policy-makers, as they mirrored long-standing concerns about regional variation and the lack of coherent protocols across agencies. The simulations were seen as a *diagnostic mirror* that validated anecdotal experiences with empirical evidence, strengthening the case for structured training and common interpretive frameworks. On the other hand, the uptake of modelling insights into policy practise remained gradual.

While there was enthusiasm for using simulation as a safe testbed for assessing fairness criteria and potential AI rulesets, institutional inertia, resource constraints, and limited technical expertise within administrations posed barriers to direct adoption. Still, the participatory nature of the AI FORA process increased legitimacy in the eyes of policymakers, who acknowledged that models and workshops could support the European AI Act's national implementation strategy. The Spanish case shows how research impact is less about immediate policy change and more about cultivating readiness: policymakers left with both a clearer understanding of algorithmic governance risks and a toolkit for embedding participatory methods into future AI initiatives.

The Spanish dissemination activities also carried wider implications for the concept of *algorithmic governance* and the practical rollout of the European AI Act. The workshops showed that algorithmic tools in social services do not merely automate existing procedures but actively reconfigure how decisions are made, monitored, and legitimised. In this sense, AI systems become part of governance itself—shaping power relations between administrations, frontline workers, and citizens. By highlighting compositional, contextual, and collective dimensions, the Spanish case demonstrated that algorithmic governance must be grounded in participatory and place-sensitive frameworks if it is to avoid reinforcing structural inequalities.

This insight directly resonates with the AI Act's requirements for *risk classification, human oversight, and transparency obligations*: Spain's experience suggests that these obligations cannot remain box-ticking exercises, but need to be operationalised through continuous community involvement, auditing, and contextual adaptation. Thus, the Spanish policy lessons provide a practical pathway for embedding the AI Act's abstract principles into everyday governance, ensuring that regulation translates into equitable outcomes on the ground.

Dissemination of Research to Policy in Germany

In Germany, policy dissemination activities targeted current AI policies to integrate refugees into German society and job market. Policymakers from regional and federal levels, NGO representatives, and experts on migration and asylum procedures participated in the dissemination activities (Spaeth et al. in this volume), where a simplified asylum system model was used as a discussion tool, based on the AI FORA ABM still under development.

Policy clients' reactions centred on several points: participants stressed that refugees often lack clear guidance. They welcomed the idea of AI-based tools to provide transparent information packages, including counselling and links to support organisations, which could improve refugees' agency during the asylum process. Policymakers confirmed that inefficiency and lengthy asylum procedures are major problems, largely linked to fragmented and low-quality data. They saw potential in AI to streamline bureaucracy, speed up recognition of documents and qualifications, and improve translation services. However, they also stressed that poor data quality risks introducing unfairness at every stage. Clients acknowledged persistent inequalities in asylum outcomes depending on, for example, variations between federal states or individual administrators' discretion. They valued the AI FORA modelling results for making such biases and 'margins of discretion' visible, but they also warned that AI should not reinforce these inequalities. AI was seen as potentially useful in reducing unfairness only if embedded in broader institutional reforms. The workshop highlighted that AI could be helpful in areas like career counselling and early labour market integration, but only if processes are redesigned to include refugees and supporting organisations in public administration workflows. The dissemination event therefore reinforced the view that technology cannot be a quick fix, but must be combined with participatory, systemic reforms. There were several key lessons for policymakers that emerged from this work on legitimacy in asylum governance and the role of AI. Agent-based modelling showed that overstretched administrations produce more errors, generating high appeal rates and undermining trust. Ensuring adequate staffing and resources is thus essential not only for efficiency but also for fairness. Refugee narratives further revealed that opaque procedures, poor interpretation, and inconsistent decisions foster helplessness, emphasising the need for transparency in both processes and outcomes. AI cannot substitute for sound institutional design: while it may improve information access and streamline procedures, legitimacy challenges arise primarily from structural and political factors such as organisational bias and federal variation. Embedding AI in governance frameworks that safeguard fairness, accountability, and human rights is therefore imperative.

Participatory approaches, incorporating refugee and supporter perspectives, proved vital for exposing hidden biases and designing systems responsive to lived realities. Stakeholder engagement should be treated as a prerequisite, not an add-on, to AI adoption. The German dissemination findings reinforced these insights, showing both opportunities and risks of algorithmic governance in asylum. They aligned with the EU AI Act's principles, stressing that algorithmic tools must be coupled with institutional reform, democratic safeguards, and mechanisms to protect refugee agency.

Dissemination of Research to Policy in Estonia

In Estonia, policy modelling examined fairness in unemployment services. The ABM simulated the OTT, the decision-support system of the Estonian Unemployment Insurance Fund (EUIF), modelling jobseekers and consultants within a structured allocation process. The serious game, conducted with social science master's students, allowed participants to take on the roles of clients and consultants, testing and adapting algorithmic rules over multiple iterations. The outcomes had already been shared with the management of the EUIF, the main client group of the research, enabling it to enhance its implementation processes. Further clients of policy dissemination were key public institutions and policy support bodies, including the Estonian Statistical Board, Social Insurance Board, Health Board, the Foresight Centre of the Parliament, and the Tartu City Government (see Vihalemm et al. in this volume).

Their reception of the AI FORA modelling results was generally positive. They valued how the ABM and serious game findings made fairness dilemmas and algorithmic trade-offs concrete, especially the insight that adding more variables does not automatically produce fairer results. Participatory modelling was seen as an important awareness-raising and reflection tool that could inform future policy design. At the same time, participants stressed that for such models to have practical policy impact, Estonia needs stronger data infrastructures, improved interoperability, and clear ethical safeguards. They underlined that while the AI FORA simulations offered valuable conceptual and diagnostic tools, their uptake requires institutional reforms and sustained capacity building. In short, dissemination clients welcomed the project's contribution as a stimulus for debate and as an educational resource but emphasised that policy implementation must go hand in hand with systemic reforms.

Data governance was identified as the most pressing issue. Barriers such as limited interoperability between institutions, inconsistent classifications, and outdated or inaccessible datasets hamper the development of reliable AI tools. Participants stressed the need for a *national data strategy* that aligns infrastructure with societal goals and ensures high-quality, ethically governed data. Furthermore, participants discussed an unresolved *tension between privacy and personalisation* of services. Estonia has developed strong privacy instruments (e.g., consent services, data trackers), but these can limit personalisation and adaptability of welfare provision. The discussion highlighted that the debate cannot be reduced to 'more privacy versus more efficiency', but must move towards *balanced solutions* that respect rights while enabling innovation. The simulation game further demonstrated that citizens were more willing to share data if benefits are tangible—a valuable insight for policymakers designing future welfare systems.

A key result of dissemination was a reinforced understanding that AI in welfare must be *human-centred*. Algorithms should not only be transparent and explainable but also *co-created with stakeholders*. Inclusion of practitioners, policymakers, and citizens in the design phase fosters both *trust* and *practical relevance*. The Estonian policy dissemination activities thus validated the AI FORA approach of participatory governance. Finally, they underlined the urgent need for *capacity building*. With 30% of data-related posts in the Estonian public sector unfilled, the shortage of interdisciplinary expertise limits the effective governance of AI. Dissemination thus framed AI FORA findings as a call for *training, cross-sector collaboration, and digital literacy*, for both professionals and the public.

The Estonian dissemination chapter showed clear policy impact by moving the debate away from technical optimisation towards systemic, participatory, and ethical considerations. It validated AI FORA's hypothesis that *stakeholder involvement improves transparency and ethical alignment*. Limitations included the relatively small workshop sample of eight experts and the absence of direct citizen voices beyond student simulations. Still, the dissemination managed to bridge technical findings from ABM and serious games into *practical, policy-relevant lessons* for Estonia's welfare governance.

The Estonian findings highlight two specific lessons for the EU AI Act's framework:

- First, ensuring compliance with the AI Act requires *robust national data ecosystems* and interoperable standards, without which even the most advanced legal safeguards risk remaining ineffective.
- Second, participatory modelling approaches like those piloted in AI FORA provide a *practical methodology for implementing the Act's provisions on stakeholder involvement, bias detection, and continuous monitoring.*

Thus, the Estonian dissemination shows that the European AI Act will only achieve its aims if supported by *institutional reforms, cross-sector expertise, and participatory governance mechanisms* at national level. Estonia's experience illustrates that algorithmic governance cannot be reduced to legal compliance alone but must be grounded in *inclusive and context-sensitive practices* that build trust in AI-enabled welfare systems.

Implications of Policy Modelling for Iran

Although no direct policy dissemination activities such as policy workshops were conducted in Iran, from a methodological standpoint, the ABM bridged technical analysis and policy needs by offering a testbed for experimenting with different policy designs in a transparent, data-driven way (Bashiri in this volume). Its strength consisted in linking household-level simulation to systemic outcomes, thereby showing both the micro- and macro-level effects of subsidy interventions by policy. Overall, the Iranian modelling provided valuable insights into the potential of ABM for policy evaluation in highly volatile economic contexts. It underlined that while data-driven targeting and transparency can strengthen public trust and improve subsidy allocation, these measures alone cannot overcome structural economic pressures.

For policy, the key lesson was that targeted welfare reforms have to be embedded within broader macroeconomic stabilisation strategies to achieve sustainable poverty reduction and equity goals. Some direct policy recommendations can be deduced from the Iranian case study:

- Improve targeting through data-driven methods.

  - Enhance the accuracy of identifying eligible households by refining and cleaning the Iranian Welfare Database (IWDB).
  - Ensure regular updates of household data and use AI/ML tools to predict income behaviour, bankruptcy risk, or hidden vulnerabilities.

- Strengthen resistance to external economic shocks.

  - Complement cash subsidies with broader macroeconomic stabilisation policies, especially those addressing inflation, sanctions, and currency devaluation.
  - Recognise that subsidies alone cannot counter structural economic inequalities without supportive economic reforms.

- Maintain transparency and public trust.

  - Continue the practice of annual reviews and public disclosure of household groupings.
  - Use these transparency measures to strengthen citizen trust in subsidy allocation and reduce perceptions of arbitrariness.

- Integrate complementary support measures.

  - Consider extending the model to test alternative policies, such as non-cash subsidies (e.g., food vouchers) or investments in education and training.
  - Explore policy mixes that combine direct cash transfers with broader social welfare interventions.

- Leverage ABM as a policy-support tool.

- Use agent-based modelling as a dynamic simulation environment for testing alternative scenarios before implementation.
- Apply ABM in participatory settings (e.g., with policymakers and citizen representatives) to evaluate trade-offs in subsidy design.

Implications of Policy Modelling for India

Similar implications can be drawn from the India case study, in which the ABM bridged technical analysis and policy demand: there needs to be continuous improvement of the Public Distribution System (PDS) to address the diverse needs of its beneficiaries and enhance its role as a critical safety net in India's social welfare landscape. By embedding *fairness, transparency, and accountability* as measurable indicators within the simulation, the Indian model demonstrated how targeted interventions—such as increasing inspection frequency, improving stock logistics, and introducing adaptive oversight—can significantly improve service delivery. Policymakers can use such models as *policy sandboxes*, testing the systemic impact of different regulatory or operational strategies before large-scale deployment.

The simulations also underscored that corruption and leakage are not merely technical flaws but structural risks requiring *continuous monitoring and responsive governance frameworks*, aligning with India's broader push towards digital public infrastructure. Furthermore, the findings suggest that scaling such ABM to district or state levels could help identify regional vulnerabilities, tailor inspection strategies, and improve trust in welfare systems. In short, the Indian ABM showed that *computational models can serve as diagnostic and anticipatory tools*, guiding reforms that make large-scale welfare systems not only more efficient but also more ethically robust.

AI FORA Policy Modelling in the United States

In the United States, a dedicated workshop 'Policy Modelling meets Policy Practice' was held in Washington D.C. at the side of the Annual Modeling and Simulation Conference 'ANNSIM 2024' to inform policy representatives of the White House and others about the results of the American case study. The workshop exposed US policymakers and modellers, many with backgrounds in public health, defence operations, border security, and environmental policy, to the AI FORA agenda of fairness and participatory modelling. The workshop deliberately invited US policymakers experienced in federal science and technology policy, security, and public administration, alongside academic modellers. This reflected American institutional priorities, where AI and modelling are often framed in terms of national security, resilience, and large-scale system management rather than welfare administration. It was designed as a 'Trojan horse' intervention (see Johnston et al. in this volume), embedding AI FORA's insights on participatory modelling within an established US modelling community that typically values technical sophistication and predictive power over ethical deliberation.

By bringing policymakers and practitioners into co-modelling exercises, the event sought to make US decisionmakers active discoverers of insights rather than passive recipients of European case results. Discussions reflected US-specific preoccupations: pandemic response modelling, climate adaptation, urban zoning and displacement, and AI FORA-specific: welfare eligibility simulations.

These examples aligned with current *US federal and state policy debates* about preparedness, equity, and risk management. The workshop highlighted structural challenges distinctive to the American science–policy interface: a strong academic incentive system focused on novelty and publication and a *fragmented governance landscape* where data access and authority are dispersed across agencies. Participants pointed to the need for *translational research centres and boundary-spanner roles* in the US to connect computational modelling with policymaking more effectively. Ethical debates during the workshop resonated with American policy concerns about the *representation of marginalised groups, power asymmetries, and transparency in defence and border modelling*. Indigenous land-use modelling and vaccine equity simulations were cited as examples of US-based participatory projects that could inspire future AI FORA-like work.

The US policy dissemination activities *situated AI FORA principles within American institutional and cultural contexts*—especially the modelling and simulation community that shapes defence, security, and public health policy.

Comparing Policy Dissemination across AI FORA Case Studies

The AI FORA project sought to ensure that modelling results did not remain confined to academic discourse but were disseminated to policy audiences across participating countries. Dissemination was conceived not as a peripheral add-on, but as a core element of the project's methodology: By engaging policymakers, administrators, and practitioners with participatory models, simulations, and workshops, the project aimed to generate not only awareness but also policy learning and readiness for change. A comparative look across the national dissemination activities reveals both striking commonalities and context-specific differences in how modelling results were received, interpreted, and translated into policy debates.

Shared Patterns of Reception

Across all case studies, the dissemination activities confirmed AI FORA's key hypothesis: *Stakeholder involvement enhances transparency and ethical alignment of AI-supported decision-making.* Whether through gamification workshops in Spain and Estonia, policy dialogues in Germany, or simulation-based policy sandboxes in India and Iran, the participatory approach was consistently recognised by policy clients as adding legitimacy to both the research process and its policy relevance. In practice, this meant that AI was rarely seen as a replacement for human judgement, but rather as a support tool that could augment administrative processes, improve transparency, and provide diagnostic insights into systemic weaknesses. Another common thread was the centrality of *data quality and governance.* In Spain, Germany, and Estonia, policymakers identified fragmented, inconsistent, or biased datasets as a core barrier to fair and effective AI integration in welfare provision. Similarly, in Iran and India, while large administrative datasets were available and provided a strong basis for technical modelling, the challenge lay in ensuring that data-driven classifications did not misrepresent lived realities or reinforce structural inequalities.

Across contexts, dissemination activities highlighted the need to couple technical AI design with institutional reforms in data infrastructures, governance frameworks, and accountability mechanisms. They reinforced the perception that *AI alone cannot 'fix' structural problems.* Policy clients valued simulations and workshops as Safe Spaces for experimentation and reflection, yet they cautioned against technological quick fixes. Instead, the models were seen as tools for diagnosis, awareness-raising, and policy preparation—contributing to long-term readiness rather than immediate reform. This insight resonates strongly with ongoing European debates on algorithmic governance and the implementation of the EU AI Act: Regulation must be accompanied by participatory practices and institutional reforms to ensure that principles such as fairness, transparency, and accountability translate into practice.

National Differences

Despite these shared patterns, the dissemination experiences varied considerably in focus, reception, and impact pathways. *Spain* centred on social services and welfare assessments. Here, policy administrators welcomed the ABM demonstrations as a *diagnostic mirror* that empirically confirmed long-standing concerns about regional variation and inconsistent assessment protocols. The modelling results resonated strongly with anecdotal evidence, and policymakers expressed cautious interest in embedding participatory evaluation into welfare governance. Yet, uptake into practice was gradual, constrained by limited technical expertise and institutional inertia.

Germany focused dissemination on asylum and refugee integration policies, with policymakers and NGOs as key clients. The simplified asylum system model and accompanying discussions made biases in interpreter quality, federal state practices, and administrative discretion visible. Policy clients valued these insights for exposing 'margins of discretion' and legitimising calls for systemic reform. At the same time, they underlined that AI could only play a supportive role, for example in providing digital counselling or translation tools, and that legitimacy problems were rooted in deeper institutional and political structures. Dissemination thus reinforced the need for participatory design and systemic reforms as preconditions for any meaningful AI integration.

Estonia, with its reputation as a digital pioneer, offered a different perspective. Here, dissemination reached a broad set of public institutions, including the Unemployment Insurance Fund, the Statistical Board, and the Foresight Centre of Parliament. Clients appreciated how serious games and ABM simulations made fairness dilemmas tangible, particularly the insight that adding more variables does not automatically produce fairer outcomes. However, participants stressed that systemic reforms, in particular improved data infrastructures, interoperability, and capacity building, were indispensable for turning such conceptual insights into practice. The Estonian case thereby shifted the debate from technical optimisation towards systemic, participatory, and ethical considerations.

Iran presented a case where dissemination in the form of participatory workshops did not take place, but where the ABM of the Targeted Subsidies Plan itself offered important lessons for policy. The model showed that targeted subsidies can provide short-term welfare improvements and build trust through transparency, yet its effectiveness is severely constrained by macroeconomic shocks such as inflation and sanctions. Dissemination here was primarily technical, and the case revealed the need for participatory approaches that could complement data-driven classification with lived perspectives of low-income households. Such methods could have strengthened both fairness and legitimacy in subsidy allocation.

India also used ABM as a diagnostic and anticipatory tool, focusing on the Public Distribution System. Dissemination underscored how embedding fairness, transparency, and accountability as measurable indicators in the model created a shared vocabulary with policymakers. Clients valued the ABM as a policy sandbox that could test interventions such as targeted inspections or improved logistics.

However, they also recognised that corruption and leakage were structural risks that required continuous monitoring and responsive governance frameworks, beyond what modelling alone could solve.

The *United States* offered a markedly different context. Here, dissemination was embedded in a national policy modelling workshop in Washington D.C., framed less around welfare administration and more around national security, resilience, and large-scale system management. The 'Trojan horse' approach of participatory co-modelling succeeded in engaging policy representatives by allowing them to discover insights through active participation. While the framing differed from European welfare debates, the US case illustrated that participatory modelling can be flexibly adapted to diverse institutional cultures, provided it aligns with policy priorities and institutional logics.

Implications for Algorithmic Governance

Taken together, the dissemination experiences across countries illuminate the opportunities and limits of participatory policy modelling as a pathway towards 'Better AI'. Spain, Germany, and Estonia demonstrate how participatory approaches can bring policy clients closer to the principles enshrined in the EU AI Act—such as transparency, human oversight, and risk-based governance—by embedding them in practical deliberative settings. Iran and India, while less participatory in dissemination, highlight how modelling can serve as a diagnostic and anticipatory tool but also underline that without participatory engagement and systemic reforms, data-driven AI risks falling short of ethical alignment. The US case, finally, shows how dissemination strategies must adapt to national policy cultures, with participatory modelling offering a versatile 'Trojan horse' for bridging the gap between technical research and policy practice. Across contexts, the lesson is clear: Participatory modelling and serious games provide powerful methods for exposing biases, surfacing tacit knowledge, and building shared frameworks for fairness. Yet, their policy impact depends on more than technical insight: It requires institutional willingness, systemic reforms, and sustained engagement with the very communities whose lives are shaped by algorithmic governance.

Policy Lessons of AI FORA

Taken together, the AI FORA dissemination activities across Spain, Germany, Estonia, Iran, India, and the United States underscore a shared reality: *algorithmic governance in welfare contexts is as much about institutions and culture as it is about technology.* Models and serious games provided valuable policy sandboxes, enabling stakeholders to test rules, explore systemic effects, and confront ethical dilemmas in a safe environment. Yet, across all cases, uptake into practice depended on whether institutions were willing and able to translate these insights into reforms of data governance, participatory processes, and administrative design.

Several *takeaway lessons for policymakers* emerged. First, governments must *invest in translation capacity*—dedicated roles or 'knowledge brokers' that bridge technical research on bias and predictive modelling with the policy world.

Here, the AI FORA project played that translational role as knowledge broker by organising policy workshops. However, it would be preferable if this role would be institutionalised from the side of the clients, creating a further actor outside the knowledge-generating research project. Second, *participatory governance needs to be institutionalised*: citizen panels, co-design workshops, and community scorecards should become standard features of AI in welfare systems, moving beyond ad hoc consultation. Third, as especially the Spanish case study emphasised, AI systems must be treated as *dynamic and evolving*, requiring continuous auditing, recalibration, and stakeholder feedback to prevent unintended harms. A central thread is the need to address data bias systematically. Without robust standards for quality, comparability, and ethical safeguards, AI will simply reproduce existing inequities. Similarly, the dissemination effort highlighted the value of *fostering interpretive cultures*: training, simulations, and collaborative exercises help frontline staff and administrators develop shared understandings of fairness and consistency in applying algorithmic tools. Policymakers should also adopt *hybrid evaluation approaches*— using ABM and gamification not only to refine algorithms but also to anticipate systemic effects, identify hidden assumptions, and explore alternative governance scenarios.

Finally, dissemination shifted the narrative: *AI should be seen neither as a panacea nor a threat, but as a complex tool requiring inclusive, place-sensitive governance*. Routine and binary decisions may be automated, but complex and ethically sensitive cases demand hybrid approaches where algorithms support, but do not replace, human judgement. Continuous cross-sectoral collaboration is vital to counteract both algorithmic and human bias. As the AI FORA cases demonstrate, simulation and participatory modelling are powerful instruments for building such reflective, accountable governance frameworks—turning the abstract obligations of the EU AI Act and broader algorithmic governance debates into practical, actionable strategies.

Conclusion

Across the diverse case studies presented in this volume, participatory modelling emerges as both a methodological innovation and a democratic imperative for the governance of AI in welfare systems. Whether through agent-based modelling, serious games, or hybrid participatory workshops, the AI FORA project demonstrates that technical optimisation alone cannot ensure fairness, transparency, or legitimacy. Instead, meaningful stakeholder involvement—of social workers, policymakers, refugees, beneficiaries, and citizens—proved essential for surfacing hidden biases, contextualising algorithmic rules, and negotiating what fairness means in practice.

A central lesson is that algorithmic governance must be understood not as a purely technical domain but as an arena where power, trust, and accountability are constantly renegotiated. The Spanish and Estonian cases highlighted how participatory approaches can build interpretive cultures around fairness, while the German study illuminated systemic trade-offs between bureaucratic legitimacy and refugee agency. The Iranian and Indian cases underscored that even well-designed technical systems remain vulnerable to structural inequities and macroeconomic pressures unless accompanied by participatory oversight and institutional reform.

Taken together, these findings confirm AI FORA's central hypothesis: Stakeholder engagement enhances the ethical alignment and transparency of AI-supported decision-making. Yet, they also caution against 'participation washing': participatory methods only build legitimacy when they demonstrably shape outcomes and inform policy practice. For this reason, participatory modelling should not be treated as a one-off experiment but institutionalised as part of an ongoing cycle of evaluation, recalibration, and co-design.

Looking forward, the challenge for policymakers is to embed such approaches into broader governance frameworks, aligning them with the requirements of the European AI Act and similar regulatory initiatives worldwide. Doing so means investing in translation capacity, robust data infrastructures, and sustained participatory mechanisms that allow affected communities to shape AI systems as co-designers rather than passive subjects. Only then can AI in welfare provision evolve from a source of risk and exclusion into an instrument of equity, trust, and democratic accountability.

Acknowledgement Research presented in this chapter has been funded by the German VolkswagenStiftung under grant agreement number 98 560.

References

Ahrweiler, P., Späth, E., Siqueiros García, J. M., Capellas, B. L., & Wurster, D. (2025). Inclusive technology co-Design for Participatory AI. In: P. Ahrweiler (Ed.). *Participatory artificial intelligence in public social services. Artificial intelligence, simulation and society*, (pp. 35–62). Cham: Springer. https://doi.org/10.1007/978-3-031-71678-2_2.

Birhane, A., Isaac, W., Prabhakaran, V., Díaz, M., Elish, M. C., Gabriel, I., & Mohamed, S. (2022). Power to the people? Opportunities and challenges for participatory AI. In: *Proceedings of the 2nd ACM Conference on Equity and Access in Algorithms, Mechanisms, and Optimization (EAAMO'22)*, 1–8. doi:https://doi.org/10.1145/3551624.3555290.

European Union (2024). Regulation (EU) 2024/1689 of the European Parliament and of the Council of 13 June 2024 on laying down harmonised rules on artificial intelligence and amending Regulations (EC) No 300/2008, (EU) No 167/2013, (EU) No 168/2013, (EU) 2018/858, (EU) 2018/1139 and (EU) 2019/2144 and Directives 2014/90/EU, (EU) 2016/797 and (EU) 2020/1828 (Artificial Intelligence Act). *Official Journal of the European Union, L 2024/1689, 12 July 2024*. https://eur-lex.europa.eu/legal-content/EN/TXT/?uri=CELEX%3A32024R1689

Danaher, J., Hogan, M. J., Noone, C., Kennedy, R., Behan, A., de Paor, A., & Galway, L. P. (2017). Algorithmic governance: Developing a research agenda through the power of collective intelligence. *Big Data & Society, 4*(2), 1–21. https://doi.org/10.1177/2053951717726554.

Waibel, D., Peetz, T., & Meier, F. (2021). Valuation Constellations. In: *Valuation Studies, 8*(1): 33–66.

Yeung, K. (2018). Algorithmic regulation: A critical interrogation. *Regulation & Governance, 12*(4), 505–523. https://doi.org/10.1111/rego.12158.

GPSR Compliance
The European Union's (EU) General Product Safety Regulation (GPSR) is a set
of rules that requires consumer products to be safe and our obligations to
ensure this.

If you have any concerns about our products, you can contact us on

ProductSafety@springernature.com

In case Publisher is established outside the EU, the EU authorized
representative is:

Springer Nature Customer Service Center GmbH
Europaplatz 3
69115 Heidelberg, Germany